Power and Legitimacy in Technical Communication

Volume II: Strategies for Professional Status

Edited by

Teresa Kynell-Hunt
Northern Michigan University

Gerald J. Savage
Illinois State University

Baywood's Technical Communications Series
Series Editor: CHARLES H. SIDES

Baywood Publishing Company, Inc.
AMITYVILLE, NEW YORK

Baywood Publishing Company, Inc.
26 Austin Avenue
Amityville, NY 11701
(800) 638-7819
E-mail: baywood@baywood.com
Web site: baywood.com

Library of Congress Catalog Number: 2002042671
ISBN: 0-89503-246-5 (cloth)

VOLUME II: Strategies for Professional Status
ISBN: 0-89503-247-3 (cloth)

Library of Congress Cataloging-in-Publication Data

Power and legitimacy in technical communication / edited by Teresa Kynell-Hunt, Gerald J. Savage.
    p. cm. - - (Baywood's technical communications series)
    Includes bibliographical references and index.
    Contents: v. 1. The historical and contemporary struggle for professional status.
    ISBN 0-89503-246-5
    1. Communication of technical information. I. Kynell-Hunt, Teresa. II. Savage, Gerald J. III. Series.

T10.5.P67 2003
808'.0666- -dc21

2002042671

Table of Contents

PART I.
HISTORICAL PERSPECTIVES FOR PRESENT
AND FUTURE STRATEGIES

PART II.
STRATEGIES FOR CONTEMPORARY PRACTICE

PART III.
STRATEGIES FOR ALTERNATIVE FUTURES

Dedication

To Crust and Squirrel,
Outrageous Nephews

and

To Sue Flotte,
Wise and tenacious woman

Acknowledgments

This collection of essays grew out of our first collaboration dealing with issues of power, status, and legitimacy in technical communication. We must first of all thank the contributors themselves who have remained not only patient but enthusiastic about the project as it has developed and ultimately expanded to this second volume. Equally vital to the success of the project has been the Baywood Technical Communications Series Editor, Charles Sides, whose advice, advocacy, and belief in the project have kept us going. Editing a collection is a somewhat difficult process logistically; editing two collections is nothing short of daunting. Our work was made infinitely more manageable because we worked with wonderful, committed individuals. Many thanks to all of you.

We would like to thank, again, J. Harrison Carpenter, Angela Eaton, Margaret FalerSweany, Kathy Moran, and Bill Williamson, chapter reviewers for this volume as well as the previous one. Their prompt and thoughtful reviews and their encouragement for the project were inspiring to contributors and editors alike.

Sue Savage helped with formatting this book as well as the previous one during much of what was supposed to be a vacation, a sacrifice we humbly appreciate — and regret that we needed so much. Our debt to her is not yet fully paid.

Thanks to the journals *Technical Communication* and *Technical Communication Quarterly* for permission to reprint the award winning essays by Marj Davis, Jimmie Killingsworth, and Teresa Kynell-Hunt included in this volume.

Teresa wishes to thank, first of all, her dear friend and colleague Jerry Savage. His insight, wisdom, attention to detail, and generosity of spirit made the process a pleasure. She wishes to thank, as well, her dear friends Kristi Carter, Fiona Gibbons, and Shelley Russell. Her sister, Marsha Bays, and her brother, Joe Hunt, have been a remarkable source of good humor and support, and her crazy nephews, Crust and Squirrel, are a constant inspiration. Finally, she wishes to thank her fiancé, Harry Whitaker—linguist, writer, biting satirist, sailor, and best friend. Eres tu, Hal.

Jerry thanks Teresa Kynell-Hunt, who first proposed this collaboration. Always a professional, she nevertheless always put the most important things first—friendship, patience, understanding. Jerry acknowledges and thanks friends and family too numerous to list for their interest and encouragement. And, as always, his own personal thanks to Sue, Sarah, and Jennifer.

Creating Strategies for Status in Technical Communication

Gerald J. Savage and Teresa Kynell-Hunt

The notion of strategy suggests action on a grand scale. It has military and political overtones and implies large commitments of resources — human, intellectual, economic, and temporal. It is often perceived as business-as-usual for the established and powerful but as hubris for the unestablished and powerless.

As the technical communication field has gained self-awareness — an uneven process of at least the past century — the struggles for recognition and acceptance, which for a long time no doubt seemed merely interpersonal or the inevitable rites of passage that every newcomer must endure, have moved toward the political and ideological. Yet apparently only very recently has the question of professional stature begun to be defined in terms of strategies that must be orchestrated across the field. Increasingly, certain themes are repeated — the necessity for change, the need for a body of knowledge of our own, the problem of how to establish our legitimacy, and the importance of being able to determine certain conditions of practice. We are hardly at a point where we are hearing anything like consensus about what it would mean to realize these themes, but the fact that we are more and more often having the conversation across the entire field — at conferences, meetings, special issues of journals, and in the editorial pages of our journals — seems to signify that we may be very close to articulating coherent strategies in which significant numbers of people in the field will join.

1

As George Hayhoe observes, "There will probably always be a tension between academics and practitioners in technical communication, just as there is in most disciplines" [1]. This tension between industry and academia in our field has defined a line of division on the issue of strategic thinking. But, perhaps because of the frequency with which people from each of these realms move back and forth; perhaps because we are, after all, professional communicators in the business of resolving misunderstandings; perhaps because of persistent efforts at the level of our professional organizations — this skirmish line no longer seems nearly as impervious as it did even a few years ago. Hayhoe has been a consultant for decades and editor since 1996 of the flagship journal for the Society for Technical Communication, the leading professional organization for practitioners. But he recently became director of the M.S. technical communication program at Mercer University. Louise Rehling, a contributor to this collection, has worked on both sides of the field and recently returned to industry while on leave from San Francisco State University. Another notable case in point is a recent book edited by Barbara Mirel and Rachel Spilka, in which most of the contributors have extensive industry or consulting experience as well as academic experience [2].

In the present volume of essays on the struggle for status, power, and legitimacy in technical communication, we focus particularly upon historical, practical, and theoretical aspects of what might be called revisionary strategies for our field. The authors in this collection acknowledge certain historical realities about technical communication and they address issues that have troubled and preoccupied us for years. At the same time, however, the strategies proposed are largely aimed at changing agendas across the entire field, not at individual measures to be undertaken incrementally, day by day and task by task, in particular workplaces. It will be clear that, although each of the authors in the collection are deeply concerned about the advancement of the field and generally are focused on common professionalization themes, they would not all agree on strategies for advancement. We hope, however, that by bringing together these contending perspectives we may help both expand participation and focus the dialogue on professionalization strategies.

PART I: HISTORICAL PERSPECTIVES FOR PRESENT AND FUTURE STRATEGIES

In the first section of this book, essays by Teresa Kynell-Hunt, Elizabeth Tebeaux, and Elizabeth Overman Smith address historical dimensions of the field that set the stage for strategies we might apply in the struggle for professional status. Although none of these authors suggests that the past determines the future, each of their studies reveals historical realities of professionalization that we must contend with as we think about the future of technical communication.

Teresa Kynell-Hunt traces the emergence of technical communication, beginning from low status engineering writing courses at the turn of the century when the engineering field was itself striving for professional recognition. She recounts the efforts of pioneering technical communication scholars such as Samuel Earle and Sada Harbarger who began to theorize our field's vital relationship to the design and use of technologies. Finally, she traces the field's development to World War II when engineering and technical communication took on far more social importance than ever before.

In an argument similar in some ways to Kynell-Hunt's, Elizabeth Tebeaux calls for the field of technical communication to give up its longing for legitimacy in the terms of liberal humanism and to define itself in relation to the needs of its audiences, its task domains, and its modes of practice in industry. Despite the political necessity for technical communication scholars to establish themselves as bona fide scholars within the field of English studies, Tebeaux argues that we need to consider how we might "return to our roots" in the days when the primary focus of technical writing instruction was to help students write effectively in the workplace. Tebeaux reviews the struggles of technical communication teachers to earn promotion and tenure in traditional English departments and their strategies of turning to research that focused more on theory and "non-ephemeral" issues than on the needs of industry and on the tools of communication that industry writers need to command. These strategies, she argues, have allowed us to establish ourselves in the academy, but at an unacceptable cost both to ourselves as a discipline and to our students.

The consequence, she says, is that technical communicators graduating from our programs are typically unprepared for the realities of their jobs and in fact simply are not competent writers. Such failures assure the continuing lack of recognition of professional status and authority for practitioners by their employers and colleagues in other professions. The solution, she argues, is to abandon liberal humanist research agendas and focus on socially useful teaching and research.

Elizabeth Smith examines the evolution of technical communication during a nine-year period, 1989-98 as evidenced in citations in five professional journals in the field. The "transmit" — those concepts that represent a historically evolving discipline — frames Smith's discussion on how our collective writings, thirty years of "conversations," as she puts it, helps to establish our power and status as a discipline. Her findings may support Samuel Earle's vision that status, power, and legitimacy are best defined within a discipline [3], for she notes a shift away from citing the scholarship of related fields to the emergence of topics and sources more specific to technical communication. Included in these emerging topics are the rhetoric of technology, visual design, computer documentation, and ethics of technical communication. Smith argues that much of our power and authority comes not only from understanding the ways rhetoric operates in the specialized media and contexts in which we work, but from recognizing as well that our tendency to cite sources within—and not without—the field of technical communication points to our growing maturity as a field.

PART II: STRATEGIES FOR CONTEMPORARY PRACTICE

In this section, essays by Marjorie Davis, Louise Rehling, and Robert Johnson discuss current dimensions and problems of the practice of technical communication, as well as the relationships and disjunctions of practitioners with academics, of theory with practice. All three essays dovetail and overlap in terms of defining problems but differ in terms of the strategies the authors propose.

Marjorie Davis compares professionalization factors in medicine and engineering to the emergence of technical communication. She describes what she calls "the new professionals" in technical communication, practitioners with broad technical and theoretical knowledge who think of themselves as members of a distinct profession and not as people who "drifted into the field" from some other field. Davis argues that, while the new professionals themselves represent new, higher standards of professionalism for technical communication, we need to continue to work toward even greater stature. She identifies several major steps our field must take toward continued professionalization. Key issues, according to Davis, are research in current areas of practice, accreditation for technical communication programs, and licensing for practitioners. Unless we pursue such broad strategies, Davis warns, our professional future is at risk.

Louise Rehling is a former technical communicator who became an academic, teaching in the technical communication program at San Francisco State University. Again working in industry while on leave from SFSU, Rehling seems to navigate the boundaries of academe and industry easily. Her chapter, an extension of an article she published in 1998, addresses the problem of mutual disregard between professors and practitioners. The academy, she asserts, looks to the workplace for obvious curricular support; the result, however, can mean that acquiescing to practitioner goals ultimately defines the momentum of the classroom experience. This can, as Rehling point outs, result in a disservice to students, a denigration of faculty expertise, and an elevation of technology beyond other important considerations. She argues that we need to see our differences as opportunities for learning from each other and from each other's contexts of practice. Rehling argues that learning to value the perspectives and work of our colleagues in industry and academia is essential to our being recognized and valued by those outside of our field, our clients, employers, and the people who use the work of technical communicators. As long as we lack respect or recognition for each other within our field, she suggests, we can hardly hope to be respected or recognized by those beyond the field.

Robert Johnson looks at the phenomenal growth of our field and suggests that growth alone should not be our goal. Instead, using metaphors from environmental philosophy, he argues for "deeply sustainable" growth, which he says we should approach in terms of our relationship with technology, our academic programs, and our individual roles as professionals within the communities we are part of. Johnson takes up two central concerns in professionalization processes: a concern for controlling and limiting growth for the sake of the sustained effectiveness of the field, and a concern for orienting the field as a whole to ethical conduct, stewardship of technology, and social responsibility. Johnson concludes by reminding us that the goal for academic programs is not necessarily to grow larger, but to grow more concerned, more culturally sensitive. We must, he argues, redefine growth as it applies to the discipline with our goal being "sustainability" — more focused and recognizable programs. Johnson reminds us also that we should become stewards of the technologies that are naturally a part of technical communication, the stewardship model representing a more realistic, consensual perspective than the implied antagonisms of "camps" — workplace vs. academic ways of perceiving communication.

PART III: STRATEGIES FOR ALTERNATIVE FUTURES

In the last section of the collection, Carolyn Rude, Nancy Roundy Blyler, Gerald Savage, and Jimmie Killingsworth look to the future of our field and offer ways of reconceptualizing and repositioning it.

Carolyn Rude extends the discussion of the social role of technical communication, exploring the prospects for our field to have a role beyond industry to influence public policy. Rude examines "best practices" by evaluating computer documentation, using the model as a potential guide for the next phase of technical communication in policy discourse. She points out that our field has "roots in rhetoric and civic discourse" and that "these roots impel a continuing consideration of how the field might use its knowledge for the public good." So far, she argues, we have used our critical competence primarily to expose problems in communication practices in a few areas of public concern. What remains to be done is to expand our scope of inquiry to a wider range of social issues, to move beyond critique, and to develop positive alternatives to harmful practices. Thus, Rude ties research to our responsibility to society. She calls for research and pedagogical emphases that will help us to define best practices more precisely and also over a wider range of contexts, particularly beyond industry. She concludes by examining strategies for developing knowledge on communication in the social sphere.

Nancy Blyler proposes alternative approaches to research that could lead to notions of knowledge better suited to practices beyond the conventional industrial contexts in which our field has traditionally operated. Blyler suggests, contrary to Tebeaux and Davis, that technical communication research is already focused too exclusively on corporate concerns and practices. She argues that such research leaves out possibilities for the field which could lead to other, perhaps more socially beneficial outcomes. Blyler looks at recent efforts in the fields of anthropology and sociology to democratize ethnographic research, proposing that we might make use of the radical methodologies included within the general category of critical interpretive research, approaches which put the responsibility and purpose for the research in the domain of the research subjects. Such "grass roots" work does not primarily result in scholarly knowledge nor in what Tebeaux calls "non-ephemeral" knowledge, nor does it produce knowledge that serves the interests of industry. Instead, it helps people improve their circumstances, meet their own community needs and goals, and empowers people who might otherwise be silenced and ignored by institutional research agendas.

Gerald Savage envisions technical communicators as practical rhetoricians in the spirit of the ancient sophists. Savage regards much of our field's current practice and our desire for professional status to reflect modernist values with roots in the industrial revolution. He argues that we should even more emphatically embrace the inherently rhetorical nature of technical communication. "Rhetoric" has multiple meanings and associations, but Savage clearly identifies practitioners of technical communication as rhetoricians in the sophistic sense, as engaged social and political communicators. In a departure from the now recognizable instrumental vs. rhetorical discourse debate, Savage advocates three roles for postmodern practice: the "trickster" as a metaphor for social change, the "fool" as an individual able to cross boundaries, and the "sophist" as a politically ambivalent nomad who does not seek the rights of institutional or disciplinary citizenship.

Finally, M. Jimmie Killingsworth reflects upon our urge to predict the future of our field, our various imagined utopias and dystopias, and reminds us that we cannot know the future. He examines what he describes as our fantasies and points out that as fantasies become part of our culture they assume the status of myths that we believe. Killingsworth focuses upon one prevalent myth in technical communication, the myth of "immediate communication." He chooses to discuss this notion because he thinks that "Of all the possible myths that touch upon the business of technical communication . . . it will be foremost in the near future and because it stands to do great damage to the spirit of our profession."

We believe Killingsworth's essay is a good one to end this book because in looking at the future, Killingsworth also reminds us not to take futuristic solutions to today's problems too seriously. He cautions against the idea that technologies somehow will solve communication problems that are as old as language — problems we attempt to address by invoking such notions as "clarity" and by seeking communication technologies that somehow are supposed to bring about the communion of our separate souls. Killingsworth reminds us that we are irrevocably involved in a practice of signs, of media, of mediation, and that no technology can eradicate these practices and bring about a perfect correspondence of intention and understanding. He argues that however much we need technology, we also need to approach all technologies, or rather our uses and expectations of them, in a critical spirit, remembering, as he puts it, "In every new communication initiative, something is lost along with what is gained."

REFERENCES

1. G. F. Hayhoe, Back in the Classroom, *Technical Communication, 49*:3, pp. 273-274, 2002.
2. B. Mirel and R. Spilka, *Reshaping Technical Communication: New Directions and Challenges for the 21st Century,* Lawrence Erlbaum Associates, Mahwah, New Jersey, 2002.
3. T. Kynell-Hunt, Status and the Technical Communicator: Utilitarianism, Prestige and the Role of Academia in Creating Our Professional Persona, in *Power and Legitimacy in Technical Communication, Volume I: The Historical and Contemporary Struggle for Professional Status,* T. Kynell-Hunt and G. J. Savage (eds.), Baywood, Amityville, New York, 2003.

PART I

Historical Perspectives for Present and Future Strategies

CHAPTER 1

Technical Communication from 1850–1950: Where Have We Been?[1]

Teresa Kynell-Hunt

Recently, a number of articles on both pedagogical and theoretical applications in Technical Communications have argued that teachers should be at least as concerned with teaching the ethical, social, and political ramifications of the discipline as they are with teaching the forms and models associated with the discipline. In fact, Gerald Savage, in his 1996 "Redefining the Responsibilities of Teachers and the Social Position of the Technical Communicator," argues that in addition to teaching ethical concerns, we should as well help students "to reconceive the profession as one that can be practiced in alternative ways that would permit them greater autonomy and professional integrity" [1, p. 310]. Current trends in our journals and in our professional conferences reflect concerns for autonomy and status for technical communicators. These trends are not surprising, particularly given the growth and maturity of the discipline. Before we can consider, however, where we are headed as a discipline and before we can contribute to the shaping of future theoretical and pedagogical trends, we might pause to consider where we have been as a discipline since that history forms the foundation upon which the future will be built. This brief study, therefore, of the curricular shifts that led to

[1] This essay was originally published under the same title in *Technical Communication Quarterly, 8*:2, pp. 143-151, 1999.

the formation of a recognizable technical communication pedagogy hopes to provide some evidence of that foundation.

In this chapter, I plan to evaluate curricular shifts in the discipline, particularly as technical communication pedagogy grew out of writing requirements for engineers at roughly the turn of the century. Thus, this study will focus on shifts in an engineering curriculum, shifts which made possible a milieu conducive to the changes necessary for English experiments that resulted in a recognizable technical communication pedagogy. Thus, this condensed study focuses on the history of the discipline of technical communication *pedagogy*; the *practice* of technical communication is, of course, far more ancient (see, for example, [2]). Though not all-inclusive (for more detail, see [3]), this study identifies curricular patterns, evaluates key shifts, and isolates an engineering environment out of which technical writing may have ultimately emerged.

EARLY ENGINEERING CURRICULAR PATTERNS AND STATUS CONCERNS

First, some background on the discipline of engineering from roughly 1850 to the 1862 Morrill Acts. Most engineers, during this roughly 12-year period, were not taught in college environments—they were trained either in apprenticeships or they picked up a random engineering or science course within a standard baccalaureate curriculum (see [4]). Certainly there were exceptions, namely West Point, "the earliest college-level institution to offer engineering training," and Rensselaer, founded in 1824 as "Rensselaer School," the first private institution to offer engineering training in America [4, p. 463]. However, virtually anyone working as an engineer during or prior to this period was usually perceived by members of the "professional" class as "vocational." By 1862 and the Morrill Act, which established a permanent endowment of acreage and funding to promote both liberal and practical education, land-grant colleges like Purdue and the polytechnics emerged as places where engineering would become a curriculuar alternative. One can imagine the cultural split brewing in this environment as traditional liberal arts schools perceived their mission as higher education, whereas the land grant colleges appealed to the middle class desirous of a professional trade. The result of these two types of education? Status concerns.

By 1870, engineers were concerned that they continued to be perceived as vocational workers. One engineering faculty member at Ohio State University was so concerned about the lingering stigma of vocationalism that he dismissed the term *shop* for *mechanical laboratory*. "Why not call a chemical laboratory a medicine shop?" he asked [5, p. 63].

The perception that engineering education was vocational created difficulties for two reasons. First, other classes of professionals who were educated in academic programs still tended to perceive engineers as workers trained to do something specific but not educated per se. Second, the "tag" of vocationalism, once established, took hold and was difficult to excise. Early impressions often linger, and the perception of "training for a trade" was slow to disappear. In order to counter the often negative perceptions of the profession of engineering, educators embarked on curricular revision as one means to elevate the social status of engineers.

CURRICULAR REVISION AND THE ROLE OF ENGLISH

This curricular revision led, in part, to the formation of the Society for the Promotion of Engineering Education (the SPEE) in 1893. Interestingly, at SPEE's first meeting in August in Chicago, engineering educators discussed, among other things, the role of English in the curriculum. The concern over English instruction was related to the near illiteracy of many graduating engineers, further complicating lingering status concerns. Though no English faculty spoke at that first meeting, a civil engineer, Mansfield Merriman, presented a paper on the "Training of Students in Technical Literary Work." He concluded his presentation with these words: "The only way to learn to write is to write" [6, p. 264].

Writing, as a result, became part of the necessary means to solve both the illiteracy problem and remaining status concerns. Unfortunately, engineering students took the required composition course—a current-traditional melange of drills, practices, and rhetorical exercises—and little more. Composition on its own, though, couldn't solve the culture or status concerns as literature could. So, for a period, engineering students took a second English course in literature. By this time, near the end of the nineteenth century, the students themselves were beginning to rebel against extra coursework in an already crowded curriculum. They could find no purpose in either composition (on lofty topics like courage, honor, or patriotism) or literature. One faculty member, in fact, noted that engineering students often perceived their English teachers "as not masculine." "One cannot," he continued, "simply glide into a classroom and greet a class of engineers with a sweet schoolgirl smile and my is not this a beautiful spring morning" [7, p. 301]. English, in either form, simply wasn't working well either to educate engineers or to ennoble them.

Compounding the problem was the lack of English faculty involved in the discussion at the national level. From roughly 1893-1910, the dialogue on English courses was virtually limited to engineering faculty members. Another factor, the training of teachers of English in literature, meant that the few English faculty teaching in an engineering environment were pioneers, charting a course very different than the one they were prepared to face. If composition already held the relatively low status of "service" course, imagine the status accorded *engineering English* or *engineering composition* as it was sometimes called.

An important shift in perceptions occurred, however, toward the end of the first decade of the twentieth century. As engineering faculty called for better writing skills and looked for ways to accord greater status to engineers, some began to look at the culture associated with engineering itself. In a paper entitled "A Combined Cultural and Technical Engineering Course," a mechanics professor, George Chatburn, argued that technical engineering courses included in them the cultural value necessary and sufficient for any engineer. In effect, he wondered how engineers could function in society if they had no connection to the history of that society. He saw the vital role of the engineer in a civilized society and in so suggesting it, hinted at the missing element in English instruction as well. How could engineers embrace writing or literature if the discipline had no direct relevance to their future professional lives [8, p. 225]?

ENGINEERING ENGLISH:
A CONTEXT FOR WRITING

By the end of the decade, educators realized that English instruction had to be tied to students' interests. The way to make that connection, some suggested, was first to tie English to engineering through engineering topics themselves, providing, then, a real-world context for writing. Second, English instruction should be less focused on literature and the compositional modes and more focused on the actual writing engineers might face in their professional lives. Samuel Chandler Earle, a professor of English at Tufts, offered one foundational model of change in his 1911 paper "English in the Engineering School at Tufts College." Earle's role in the formulation of an early technical writing course cannot be overemphasized. Earle, in fact, described his English course as *radical*, noting that English was perceived as the "last bit of salvage from the arts course remaining in the engineering school and as the only means of true culture in a curriculum otherwise hopelessly practical" [9, p. 34]. Earle proposed a course as broad and varied as that given students in arts because, he believed, "true culture comes not from turning aside to other interests as higher, but from so conceiving their special work that it will be worthy of life's devotion" [9, p. 35].

Earle proposed a technical writing prototype course because "no lawyer, minister, dramatist, novelist, or poet would assume that because he had had general training in composition he could become a master of his peculiar form without special study" [9, p. 37]. Composition and/or literature, Earle argued, was simply not enough. And importantly, the course he proposed, though somewhat reflective of requirements in composition, was not a composition course.

Although Earle referred to his course under a variety of titles—*technial exposition, engineering writing, or engineering English*—the differences from traditional composition courses were apparent. Earle proposed four separate "abilities" that he believed would make English more relevant to engineers:

1) the ability to put into words an abstract thought;
2) the ability to describe, in writing, an object not present;
3) the ability to write for different audiences;
4) the ability to give a concept full treatment by demonstrating understanding in writing [9, p. 37].

Borrowing from the rhetorical modes, specifically description, Earle reconceived the standard description paper into a mechanism or product description. He added to that, however, two considerations still important today: translating the conceptual into writing and understanding the audience for whom a document is intended.

Who, though, would teach the course that Earle envisioned? Engineers? English faculty? Earle called for cooperation between the two departments, suggesting, in fact, that English faculty be in actual contact with engineering work. However, roughly five years after Earle's paper, the SPEE's Committee on English noted that "the attitude reported between instructors in English and instructors in other departments extends all the way from open hostility to sympathetic cooperation. Between the two extremes is a sort of mild tolerance of one another's existence" [10, p. 180]. Clearly, even with Earle's fundamental call for English that mattered and greater cooperation among faculty, technical communication was slow to flourish. In fact, the chair of the committee on English reported that faculty did not aspire "to become teachers of engineering English, but to get a disagreeable job off their hands as quickly as possible in order that they may bask in the sunshine of pure culture in some other more congenial department" [10, p. 182].

One faculty member who embraced the concept of an engineering English course, Sada Harbarger from Ohio State University, presented in 1920 a paper on the "Qualifications of the Teacher of English." Harbarger taught engineering English and passionately embraced the discipline. She believed that the instructor "associates English with reality and finds an objective for his students' thoughts—he makes the connection of English with engineering apparent" [11, p. 302]. She also argued that engineering and English faculty had to cooperate in order for the discipline of engineering to advance.

TEACHING THE TECHNICAL WRITING COURSE

While no one involved in higher education could fashion an engineering English that would be attractive to all English faculty (the deplorable "service" tag lingered), in the 1920s the call to cooperate culminated in a technical writing course that in all likelihood was the syngergistic result of 1) experiments in composition courses, 2) the role of English in an engineering curriculum, 3) the increased valuation of engineering itself, and 4) the valiant efforts of a few who fashioned and shaped the course into a prototype course recognizable to us today. Indeed, English instructor J. Raleigh Nelson noted that

> I teach the course in engineering reports to seniors. I do not believe anybody was ever born to begin more poorly adapted to do this work than I, because I had no technical training, or no particular taste for engineering. It was a very big cross to me. I took it up as a consecrated cross and I bore it bravely. I made myself think it was necessary [12, p. 264].

By the mid-1920s, more and different kinds of engineering English texts emerged, including the second edition of T.A. Rickard's *A Guide to Technical Writing* [13], Sada Harbarger's *English for Engineers* [14], and Sam Trelease and Emma Yule's *Preparation of Scientific and Technical Papers* [15]. As important as the textbooks were, the important question by the end of the decade, though, involved the qualifications of the teachers using those books. English faculty still usually obtained degrees in literature and many of them still perceived the service course engineering English as little more than drudgery.

By the mid 1930s, some were attempting to answer that question. In a 1938 address to the SPEE on "Improving the Status of English Instructors in Technical Colleges," an Iowa State College professor, J. Raymond Derby, suggested that teachers of technical writing or technical exposition should be trained at "land grant colleges that stress science and technology but already possess strong departments of English competent to offer majors and the Master's degree" [16, p. 253]. This, of course, was the logical place for experiments in training technical communication faculty. It was at the land-grant schools that engineers first wrestled with issues of status, professionalism, and academic recognition. How appropriate, then, that the English course that emerged during the struggle for academic recognition would find the land-grant schools the proper place for training teachers to further develop and carry the course. As Robert Connors has pointed out, the discipline was becoming a "thriving industry by 1938, having produced its own authors, experts, and directors" [17, p. 338].

By the end of the 1930s, though, America braced for the inevitable changes that first one and then two world wars would bring. Advances in weaponry and technology meant more jobs in manufacturing, so the need for technical communication had never been greater. Defense-related production influenced the development of technical writing for two reasons. First, as the sophistication of weaponry increased, manufacturers needed writers to explain that technology to workers who lacked a technical background. Second, engineers, who had previously been largely responsible for writing user documentation to accompany their creations, had only a few English courses to draw upon for the challenge of explaining technology to the sometimes technologically ignorant. Technical writing, then, was realizing full status as a discipline because people were being hired to do it.

From 1940 to roughly 1950, though, old issues, like the place of a "humanistic stem" in an engineering curriculum resurfaced. The Hammond Reports, one in 1940 [18] and one in 1944, expressed concern over too much practicality in the curriculum. Should the engineer pursue a purely professionial curriculum? Should English education serve to humanize the engineer? Should engineering students stay in school longer, if necessary, in order to take more "culture" courses? As ironic as it might seem, by 1950 engineering questions began to resemble engineering education questions postulated in the nineteenth century.

The desire for a humanistic stem for engineers, was, in part, a means to prepare them for service and productivity to self and society. But as they debated more literature courses for engineers, what educators didn't consider was the humanistic stem implicit in technical communication. To write about technology for users presupposed a human link; technical writing, functional writing, acknowledged society by its very existence. Interestingly, this discipline that bridged technology and humanism was neither purely scientific nor purely humanistic; the discipline bridged both and yet was claimed by neither.

The roughly 45 years that would follow this period are rich for examination. While technical communication's place might seem secure by roughly 1950, this is only partially true. Connors found that nearly every college was offering the course by the mid-1950s; nevertheless, in 1976 the Society for Technical Communication (STC) listed only 19 academic degree programs in technical communication [19, p. 2].

So where have we been? From the turn of the century to the mid-1920s, we have been part of an engineering curriculum, but only insofar as experimentation allowed. English faculty, most with degrees in literature, inherited the difficult, shifting curriculum of the engineer and sought ways to make English real and valuable to the engineer. From the 1920s to the 1950s, we solidified our place as a distinct discipline, distinct from composition and literature courses and, yes, distinct, too, from enginering courses. But where did we end up? Was Carolyn Miller right that we are still relegated to the category of "skills" course [20]? With the further advent of computer technology, where are we headed as programs in the field proliferate? Those questions, and questions regarding our future, are more difficult to answer. We occupy a place in both business and English departments. We are still a feature of both scientific and engineering curricula. We are clearly here to stay; examining our history as a discipline in this country sheds some light on how we have endured and flourished in the academy.

REFERENCES

1. G. J. Savage, Redefining the Responsibilities of Teachers and the Social Position of the Technical Communicator, *Technical Communication Quarterly*, 5:3, pp. 309-327, 1996.
2. E. Tebeaux, *The Emergence of a Tradition*, Baywood, Amityville, New York, 1997.
3. T. C. Kynell, *Writing in a Milieu of Utility: The Move to Technical Communication in American Engineering Programs 1850-1950*, Ablex, Norwood, New Jersey, 1996.
4. T. S. Reynolds, The Education of Engineers in America before the Morrill Act of 1862, *History of Education Quarterly*, 32, pp. 459-482, 1992.
5. M. A. Calvert, *The Mechanical Engineer in America*, The Johns Hopkins Press, Baltimore, 1967.
6. M. Merriman, Training of Students in Technical Literary Work, *Proceedings of the Society for the Promotion of Engineering Education*, 1, pp. 259-264, 1893.
7. H. L. Creek, Teachers of English in Engineering Colleges: Selection and Training, *Proceedings of the Society for the Promotion of Engineering Education*, 47, pp. 300-313, 1939.
8. G. R. Chatburn, A Combined Cultural and Technical Engineering Course, *Proceedings of the Society for the Promotion of Engineering Education*, 15, pp. 222-229, 1907.
9. S. C. Earle, English in the Engineering School at Tufts College, *Proceedings of the Society for the Promotion of Engineering Education*, 19, pp. L33-L47, 1911.
10. C. W. Parks, Report of the Committee on English, *Proceedings of the Society for the Promotion of Engineering Education*, 24, pp. 177-182, 1916.

11. S. A. Harbarger, The Qualifications of the Teacher of English for Engineering Students, *Proceedings of the Society for the Promotion of Engineering Education, 28*, pp. 299-306, 1920.
12. J. R. Nelson, Conference of Teachers of English, *Proceedings of the Society for the Promotion of Engineering Education, 30,* pp. 255-282, 1922.
13. T. A. Rickard, *A Guide to Technical Writing* (2nd Edition), John Wiley and Sons, New York, 1923
14. S. A. Harbarger, *English for Engineers* (2nd Edition), McGraw-Hill, New York, 1923.
15. S. F. Trelease and E. S. Yule, *Preparation of Scientific and Technical Papers* (3rd Edition), The Williams and Wilkins Co., Baltimore, 1937.
16. J. R. Derby, Improving the Status of English Instructors in Technical Colleges, in *English Notes. Proceedings of the Society for the Promotion of Engineering Education, 43,* pp. 252-256, 1938.
17. R. J. Connors, The Rise of Technical Writing Instruction in America, *Journal of Technical Writing and Communication, 12:4,* pp. 329-352, 1982.
18. H. P. Hammond, Report of Committee on Aims and Scope of Engineering Curricula, *Journal of Engineering Education, 30,* March 1940.
19. J. W. Souther, Teaching Technical Writing: A Retrospective Appraisal, in *Technical Writing: Theory and Practice,* B. E. Fearing and W. K. Sparrow (eds.), Modern Language Association of America, New York, pp. 2-13, 1989.
20. C. R. Miller, A Humanistic Rationale for Technical Writing, *College English, 40:6,* pp. 610-617, 1979.

CHAPTER 2

Returning to Our Roots: Gaining Power through the Culture of Engagement

Elizabeth Tebeaux

If technical communication will have an important place in academe and industry in this new century, if our field will have power, academic technical communicators need to understand that the direction we are currently taking our discipline could ensure its lack of relevance and thus power. I'm assuming, of course, that by "relevant" we mean that our efforts in technical communication research and teaching *should* result in better communication processes and documents produced in non-academic settings, that business and industry should recognize and respect us as contributing to productivity, and that this recognition produces industry financial support for technical communication programs. However, lack of consensus on that goal—improved workplace writing—may not be possible or even desired by many academics. My thesis is simple: Either we work to improve the quality of both the technical communicators we provide the workplace and the faculty responsible for that effort, or technical communication will become nothing more than another form of academic discourse studied by academics but ignored by those who generate and use this form of discourse.

The major problem facing the field of technical communication may be a lack of a clear mission: What are we trying to accomplish in the academy's technical communication teaching, research, and service? Are our current objectives concerned with relevance from the perspective of the workplace? Do the technical communicators we prepare perceive their preparation as effective? Do students who study technical communication in our service courses enter the workplace prepared to communicate effectively? A cursory glance at many articles currently published in our journals often suggests that we are more concerned with talking to each other about theoretical and often highly political or philosophical issues than in attempting to improve communication in non-academic settings.

CURRENT STATUS OF ACADEMIC TECHNICAL COMMUNICATION

Those of us who have been teaching technical communication for 20 or more years recognize that technical communication has moved from a focus on the pragmatic and the applied to the arcane and the academic. Much of what we do as research or scholarship often has little application to the contexts in which technical writing occurs. Many of those who produce these pieces have never worked outside the academy and express distaste for the culture of business. If you survey *Journal of Technical Writing and Communication, The Technical Writing Teacher/Technical Communication Quarterly*, and *Journal of Business Communication*, all launched in the late 1960s or 1970s, you will see the shift in emphasis. For example, from 1970-1991 a plethora of published studies focused on communication needs of the workplace and the effectiveness of business and technical writing courses by graduates [1, 2]. Since 1991, however, this type of research has all but disappeared, and those studies that do focus on communication practices clearly state that appropriate academic preparation for workplace communications is lacking [3-6]. Despite occasional articles on legal writing, procedures and instructions, proposal development, and analyses of failed communications, the shift in research has definitely been away from the practical to the theoretical, political, and the philosophical.

A cameo summary of this situation is evident in the winter 1998 special issue of *Technical Communication Quarterly* edited by Patricia Goubil-Gambrell, who states the following in her introduction:

> It is clear that the discipline has a concern for research methods, yet it is telling where these calls are coming from and what they are asking for. . . . Notably, what these calls and what this issue of *TCQ* problematize is the nature of the relationship between the discipline of technical communication, the part of the field that pursues theory and knowledge through research, and the profession of technical communication, the part of the field that applies theory and knowledge. Technical communicators in the corporate world

recognize the need for research, but don't seem to find much of what the academy produces very valuable. Because the methods researchers use determine the product, the fact that many practitioners do not find value in academic research constitutes, in some way, an indictment of the methods of the academy, as well as the questions that the academy thinks should be asked. Academics, on the other hand, find some of the kinds of questions that practitioners want answered too limited in scope and not concerned with more abstract issues involved in workplace technical communication activities. This gap between researchers and practitioners exists in part because the goals and the reward systems for those in the academy and those in the profession differ [7, p. 6].

Gambrell's observation could also apply to the most recent discussion of research, the July 2001 special issue of *Journal of Business and Technical Communication*. The opening article, "Itext: Future Directions for Research on the Relationship between Information Technology and Writing," co-authored by 11 academics, focuses on what academic technical communication faculty think should be the focus of research [8]. All contributors, as well as those whose work is cited, are academics. No indication surfaces that any of these topics have been influenced by non-academic organizations that generate technical communication in various forms, that anyone outside academe is interested in or has endorsed or suggested this research. Davida Charney, the guest editor for this collection, states that the ideas presented are based on "decades of important studies of texts, of readers and writers, and of social interactions" [9, p. 267]. But important from whose perspective? The academy or the workplace? Given the speed at which technology is changing, many of these issues will be irrelevant or dated by the time academic articles dealing with the various topics are published, challenged, defended/refuted. A larger question, how will these issues and the resulting research influence practice and even preparation of technical communication practitioners, is not addressed. Again, how much of what is recommended will be relevant to future technical communicators?

Charney's statement of key research areas to be discussed in later issues, in addition to those targeted in the opening article, include "investigating and improving communication between professionals and between professionals and the public" and "how rhetorical appeals in scholarly journal articles influence scientific readers. . . . Other areas, such as pedagogy, also deserve attention" [9, p. 268]. These approaches similarly avoid utilitarian applications and the recognition that outcome based learning and reconsideration of what constitutes higher education — not teaching — is the current and continuing focus in higher education.

What these recommended research agendas suggest — and the essays in the two special issues of *JBTC* reflect this conclusion — is that faculty are less interested in solving real problems in the workplace and preparing technical writers than in generating theories of workplace writing that have purely intellectual interest [10, 11]. Many faculty, particularly humanities faculty, oppose U.S. corporations which hire the bulk of technical communication graduates because they consider the corporate financial culture morally and socially corrupt. This perspective also adds another complicating problem into the mix of issues. What has happened and why?

PHILOSOPHICAL ROOTS OF
THIS SHIFT

This shift, in a large sense, stems from the nature of the university culture in general. As Mark C. Taylor, Cluett Professor of Humanities at Williams College, recently observed, today's university springs from Kant's 1798 blueprint of the university, which was divided into the higher faculties of law, medicine, and theology (professional) schools, and the lower faculties, which Kant defined as the arts and sciences. From Kant's perspective, the higher faculties, "are charged with providing practical education, whereas the responsibility of the lower faculty is disinterested inquiry and critical reflection. The value of the education provided by the higher faculties is its social, political, and economic utility. The lower faculty, by contrast, is resolutely nonutilitarian and devoted to reason as such" [12, p. 41]. To fulfill this function, the lower faculty must be grounded in the principle of autonomy, which has three basic tenets:

1. Reason must be governed only by reason and not by any external interests or goals.
2. Scholars cannot be evaluated by outsiders but can be judged only by other scholars (i.e., peer review).
3. The critical judgments that members of the lower faculty are charged with making require freedom from outside influence and disregard for the practical consequences of their assessments (i.e., academic freedom).

The structure of Kant's university embodies his central philosophical ideas. The distinction between the critical and the professional (or vocational) faculties mirrors the difference between rhetorical and practical reason . . . these polarities can in turn be translated into the distinction between nonutilitarian and utilitarian education [12, p. 42].

As Taylor states, this university plan has produced a series of polar oppositions: Low faculties revere what is useless, unprofitable, and scholarly. High faculties revere what is useful, profitable, and vocational. These dichotomies of knowledge and understanding pervade Platonic thought as well as the modern university—and the issues that swirl around any form of pragmatic education, such as technical communication, business, or engineering. In short, humanities faculty perceive the practical as the work of the devil because the work of the humanities is not supposed to be utilitarian.

The gist of this conflict, as it affects technical communication, forms the basis of Teresa Kynell's book, *Writing in a Milieu of Utility*. As Kynell states, both engineering and engineering writing struggled from their inception because they were deemed to sully the traditional bachelor of arts curriculum [13, p. 9]. Pragmatism was viewed as the enemy of real education. Although John Henry Newman saw liberal education as leading to better professional people [13, p. 7], the dichotomy between the utilitarian and scholarly aims of education has never disappeared. The fact that the German university concept of research was combined with the undergraduate teaching model of Oxford and Cambridge has produced an uneasy combination, even though this hybrid model, to quote Nannerl Keohane, former President of Duke University, should produce "a company of scholars engaged in discovering and sharing knowledge, with a responsibility to see that such knowledge is used to improve the human condition" [14, p. 103].

This hybrid university allowed the expansion of disciplines, including engineering, which has struggled with curriculum issues from 1850 onward. As both Kynell [13] and Connors [15] stated, technical writing emerged and persisted because composition and literature courses were not effective in preparing engineers for the kind of writing the practicing engineer would need [13, p. 12]. Thus, technical writing was born, but the tension between the utilitarian and the purely educational has persisted. Humanities faculty reject pragmatic instruction, while professional faculties, which have expanded into business, engineering, as well as the original professions, find that traditional humanistic education does not prepare their graduates for careers, the focus of their education. [16]

Basically, the conflict between technology and humanism as the focus of the college experience defines the root of the conflict, which has existed since the mid-nineteenth century and intensified with the rise of industrialism and now high technology. Or, as Kenneth Prewitt, Senior Vice President at the Rockefeller Foundation in 1993, stated, "the precursor of today's research universities was being shaped during the sharply contested shift from religious learning to scientific knowledge as the core purpose of higher education" [17, p. 85]. Humanities faculty view the utilitarian nature of technical communication, and all vocational programs, as antithetical to the goal of the university. Kynell cites Charles William Eliot, President of Harvard, who wrote in an 1869 article for the *Atlantic Monthly*, that "The practical spirit and the literary or scholastic spirit are both good, but they are incompatible. If commingled, they are both spoiled" [13, p. 6].

I would like to suggest that the animosity between technical communication and the humanities departments that house many technical communication programs continues because technical communication has more affinities with Kant's "higher" faculties and the inherent pragmatism of the subject. In contrast, traditional English and humanities studies continue as the most traditional of the "lower" faculties with their commitment to non-ephemeral subject matter, "arts for art's sake," if you will. Thus, technical or engineering writing teachers have historically struggled for respect both within English departments and engineering departments. Conner's description of the situation in the early 1930s is often the case in 2001:

> Despite the demand for technical writing, most English teachers who made a specialty of it were still underpaid and little recognized in their own departments. Interest in composition teaching caused teachers to "lose caste" among their departmental peers and was seen as "professional suicide" by younger teachers. Engineering teachers still did not give English teachers the cooperation they felt was necessary, and engineering students often seemed to have little respect for the sorts of teachers being turned out by graduate schools in English. It was said in the thirties that many English teachers "appear to their critics as not of a sufficiently masculine type or of enough experience in the world outside their books to command the respect of engineering students" and they were called "effeminate" by some students. (One student was quoted in 1938 as calling his teacher "a budding pinko") [15, p. 337].

From a current perspective, the issues facing technical communication are no different from issues facing other disciplines charged with providing needed skills and knowledge to undergraduates. Many faculty throughout universities, particularly research universities, believe that providing these skills shouldn't be their responsibility. But, as

Keohane [14] and an imposing group of respected academics have argued since Allen Bloom's *The Closing of the American Mind* [18],[1] lack of attention to providing students basic skills is at the root of the public's suspicion about the value of the research university. More recently, universities are faced with increasing demands for accountability and outcome-based assessment by accrediting groups. Parents, governing boards, and state legislatures all want to know that higher education is producing students who have the skills to thrive in an increasingly complex world where students need knowledge not covered by the traditional university curriculum. As Nannerl Keohane states, universities sell the value of the college degree by boasting about the earning power of those with degrees to justify the increasingly higher prices charged [14, pp. 110-111]. Thus, parents and legislatures want education that will live up to these claims and increase the economic stability of their children. They care very little about faculty "research" that has no value to the production of an effective citizenry or workforce. As Jorge Klor de Alva, President of the University of Phoenix, stated in a recent *Educause* (2000) article:

> The contemporary disconnect between what traditional higher education provides, especially in research institutions and four-year colleges, and what society wants can be gleaned in part through a 1998 poll of the fifty state governors. The aptly titled inquest, "Transforming Post-Secondary Education for the Twenty-First Century," revealed that the top four items perceived to be most important were (1) encouraging lifelong learning (97%), (2) allowing students to obtain education anytime and anyplace via technology (83%), (3) requiring postsecondary institutions to collaborate with business and industry in curriculum and program development (77%), and (4) integrating applied or on-the-job experience into academic programs (66%). In contrast—and most tellingly—the four items judged to be of least importance were (1) maintaining faculty authority for curriculum content, quality, and degree requirements (44%); (2) preserving the present balance of faculty research, teaching load, and community service (32%); (3) ensuring a campus-based experience for the majority of students (21%); and (4) in last place—enjoying the support of only one of the governors responding—maintaining traditional faculty roles and tenure (3%) [19, p. 34].

---

[1] Jaroslav Pelikan, *The Idea of the University*. New Haven, Connecticut: Yale University Press, 1992; Martin Anderson, *Imposters in the Temple*. Englewood Cliffs, New Jersey: Simon & Schuster, 1992; Derek Bok, *Universities and the Future of America*. Durham, North Carolina: Duke University Press, 1990; Bartlett Giamatti, *A Free and Ordered Space: The Real World of the University*, New York: W.W. Norton, 1988; Henry Rosovsky, *The University: An Owner's Manual*, New York: W. W. Norton, 1990; John Searle, "The Storm Over the University," *The New York Review of Books*, pp. 34-42, December 6, 1990. Charles J. Sykes, *ProfScam: Professors and the Demise of Higher Education*, Washington, D.C.: Regnery Gateway, 1988.

What is intriguing is that technical communication can so easily respond to the needs outlined in this survey, yet we seem to have become a traditional humanities discipline that places academic research above the needs of society. What are the causes of the shift that has taken technical communication into an increasingly ethereal world of academic research, one in which scholarship on ideology is valued by faculty more than research in effective proposal development?

RECENT HISTORY OF TECHNICAL WRITING IN THE ACADEMY

Both Kynell [13] and Connors [15] have provided discussion of the history of technical writing in the nineteenth and early twentieth centuries, but I want to begin where both end — recent history of technical communication — based on my own observations of what has happened, particularly since 1970. A bit of back-tracking is, however, necessary.

As both Kynell and Connors stated, technical communication began as engineering English or technical writing. A number of colleges, such as Texas A&M University where I have taught since 1974, had technical writing courses as early as 1913. These courses, particularly those at technical and engineering schools, recognized that students needed preparation for the kind of writing they would do outside the academy. The content often focused on business letters, principles of correct usage and sentence structure, public speaking skills, instructions, proposals, specifications, and contracts. Many students took composition, technical writing, public speaking, and perhaps one or two literature courses.

Technical writing developed rapidly in the 1970s, probably even more rapidly than it had after World War II. Enrollments in the basic course grew quickly (and ominously if you were a traditional literature teacher viewing the growth). The college degree was becoming the ticket for riding the Train of Success and meaningful employment. By 1980, the traditional technical writing course had expanded into multiple courses — basic and advanced technical writing, technical editing, courses in standards and specifications, technical style, graphics, and perhaps technical manual preparation. By 1985, however, many faculty teaching technical writing were newly-minted literature Ph.D.s, who were worried about getting tenure. The early technical communication doctorates found the non-academic market too lucrative, so that the bulk of technical writing faculty were either retooled literary Ph.D.s or graduates of emerging rhetoric programs. In many universities, these programs struggled against entrenched literary studies which were launching increasing numbers of courses in literary theory. Rhetoric, too, began to assume a theoretical direction for self-protection, if for no other reason.

The job market was grim, and many devoted literature lovers moved, albeit with clenched teeth, into the world of technical writing. Jobs existed for new Ph.D.s who could and would teach technical writing. Many of these new graduates hoped that they could eventually move to their literary specialty. Their dreams of teaching "real English," along with their thinly-disguised distaste for technical writing, were buoyed by senior faculty who told them that "technical writing" was just a "service" course that was not part of the mission of English departments, where the bulk of technical writing was taught. "Doing time" in technical writing or composition was part of the new assistant professor's experience.

Within this group of new hires, however, were a few dedicated teachers who believed in the value of technical writing. We learned of the millions of dollars lost in the work place because of poor writing; the number of people who died because of faulty instructions, specifications, and procedures; and the general loss of productivity from the explosion of paperwork that nobody read because many reports were poorly written — obtuse, diffuse, and writer- rather than reader-centered. Statements by representatives in business and industry were adamant about the need for employees who could write well. Studies of qualifications needed by new college graduates rated communication skills at or near the top [2, pp. 419, 422].

Technical communication programs began to emerge in land-grant, technical, or engineering schools where the liberal arts view was dominated by the more pragmatic disciplines. The fact that technical writing was admired by business and industry and requested by disciplines outside of the liberal arts didn't help those of us trying to build academic careers in English departments, even those in land-grant universities. Amid the condescension many of us took from those who did "real" scholarship in English literature, technical communication faculty had to figure out how to survive to tenure, and survival meant fitting into the existing liberal arts culture. To get tenure, technical communication faculty had to learn how to play the prestige game, because technical writing clearly lacked prestige. With literary theory becoming the "in" topic in many English departments, the direction was set for how technical writing would have to go to survive and shed the ugly mantle composed of threads of the ephemeral and the pragmatic.

Enter humanism, circa 1981, which quickly became the lifeline to legitimize technical writing. The result: dozens upon dozens of articles about the humanistic aspects of technical writing, an intense focus on the rhetorical aspects of technical writing, a dramatic decrease in pedagogical scholarship and applied research (unless it could be tied to one of the trendy theoretical, humanistic topics). Rhetoric programs gained acceptance when rhetoric began to merge with literary theory and showed that it, too, was unquestionably humanistic. Together, both technical writing and rhetoric developed theories that drew from other disciplines, such as art, sociology, anthropology, psychology, and history. Plain English in technical writing publications was replaced by the jargon of theories drawn from the social sciences. As Elizabeth Garber, Professor of English at Harvard, notes, discipline envy has become the rage:

> Over the past century alone my own discipline of literary studies has yearned to be, or to model itself on: linguistics, anthropology and ethnography, social science, natural science, psychoanalysis, sociology, history, and various strands of philosophy, from aesthetics to ethics. . . . New disciplines develop; others fade away. Envy, or desire, or emulation, the fantasy of becoming that more complete other thing, is what repeats.
>
> I think we need to take cognizance of this tendency in academic and intellectual life to imagine that the truth, or the most revealing methods, or the paradigm with the answer, is just over the road a piece [20 p. B8].

Thus, by the late 1980s, articles in theory, philosophy, politics, and rhetoric of technical communication appeared in abundance, along with (thankfully) really useful research in document design, readability and style, and graphics. Articles on pedagogy were derided as ephemeral or nonintellectual, and any article that smacked of "how to" classified the author as nonintellectual. Panels began to appear at MLA on the application of literary theory to technical writing, although much of the discussion did not seem to be useful or applicable. Technical communication faculty breathed a sigh of relief when technical writing panels became an annual event at the MLA meeting. Clearly, if one could "talk the literary talk," one could get tenure.

Many faculty, perceiving the coming transformation of computing, started working on computer-aided instruction and online documentation. Studies in the history of technical writing emerged to help legitimize our field of study, which by now had adopted a less pragmatic moniker — technical communication. Tenure for technical communication faculty was less of a problem, IF candidates produced work that was clearly scholarly — historical, theoretical, rhetorical, or philosophical but not pedagogical.[2] Applied research had to be justified through association

[2] For different approaches and revealing discussions on tenure, see *Issues in Promotion and Tenure for Faculty in Technical Communication: Guidelines and Perspectives,* Elizabeth Tebeaux (ed.), Association of Teachers of Technical Writing, 1995; Richard C. Gebhardt and Barbara Gebhardt, *Academic Advancement in Composition Studies: Scholarship, Publication, Promotion, Tenure,* Mahwah, New Jersey: Lawrence Erlbaum, 1997.

with work in recognized fields such as literary theory, cognitive theory, or ergonomics. New journals appeared, such as *Computers and Composition, Management Communications Quarterly, Journal of Advanced Composition,* and *Written Communication.* Our new moniker, technical communication, sounded more elevated than technical writing and showed that our field was embracing all types of communication activities — speech, graphics, media, literature, communication — in various fields such as marketing, engineering, and health. Science writing was deemed a separate field by some, as was business communication, even though the distinction wasn't at all clear. Interesting polemic surfaced about the definition of "technical" communication. The publications were interesting, but fewer and fewer exemplified useful analysis and solutions to problems of workplace communication. Articles were also becoming increasingly jargonistic as writers studied technical communication against theories excerpted from literature to sociology, anthropology, and psychology. Most importantly, technical communication *had* to be "rhetorical," and that meant that a continuing list of articles appeared on how technical communication responded to not only Aristotle and Cicero, but also Bacon, Toulmin, Bakhtin, Foucault, Derrida, Eco, postmodernism — whatever rhetorical theory was/is currently in vogue.

By the late 1980s and early 1990s, degree programs in technical communication were developing — master's programs, then doctoral programs, and finally bachelor's programs — all designed to either 1) prepare technical communicators for jobs in business, government, or research organizations and/or 2) prepare faculty to stock the growing number of technical communication degree programs which needed Ph.D. faculty to teach theory, philosophy, and other specialized courses.

From the beginning of this period of program development, graduate programs were the preferred areas for program development. As in other disciplines throughout the university, undergraduate instruction was becoming the ugly sister: she had to be politely acknowledged in public, but behind closed doors she was ignored as much as possible [14, pp. 108-110]. In arguing for degree programs, proposals described the need for technical writers, not the need for well-prepared faculty to teach undergraduate and graduate students in engineering, business, government, and science who needed top-notch writing and speaking skills.

In English departments, teacher education was as much a casualty as technical communication. Devotion to developing competent public school English teachers was simply not prestigious or intellectual enough to deserve resources, quality faculty, or the "serious research" label, particularly about the kind of writing instruction secondary students really needed. Many English faculty blithely assumed that English majors could write, and if they couldn't they would learn from reading good literature.[3] In short, there was no point in providing either writing or writing pedagogy courses for those planning on teaching in the public schools. Despite decline in literacy, even among college-bound students, those who wanted to focus on writing often had a difficult time in English departments.

By the early-mid-1990s, the basic "service" courses in technical communication were becoming as tainted as freshman composition, even though demand steadily increased in two-year as well as four-year colleges. Many tenure track faculty, even those with technical communication degrees or fields, were no longer interested in service courses. Tenure-track faculty opted instead to teach courses in gender, ethnicity, politics of language, ethnography, Marxism and language, environmental rhetoric, philosophy of language, and theory borrowed from various disciplines as these could be applied to technical communication. Despite the emergence of technology and the maturation of word processing, instruction in the use of software lagged in many programs because of the suspicion that instruction in software was too vocational and utilitarian and not humanistic. Graduate students, many poorly trained, were given the responsibility of teaching the services courses—freshman English as well as technical writing. The focus in graduate technical communication programs began to shift from the applied to the theoretical and the philosophical.

That attitude, I suggest, has become pervasive in many academic departments housing technical communication courses and programs. Following the Kantian university model, research with practical applications is still seen as "nonintellectual," while theory is intellectual. Plain English is non-intellectual, while the same content presented in obfuscatory diction is intellectual. The faculty focus has become the production of clones, a persistent characteristic of the German university [14, pp. 101-113]. Graduate students began to teach a larger and larger percentage of "service" courses. The problem was (and is) that many graduate students have not had significant non-academic job experience and do not understand issues that surround workplace writing. (Many, for example, spend large amounts of time teaching style sheets, rather than document design or content selection in terms of perceived audiences and purposes.) Most were otherwise excellent teachers who realized that a career teaching English was not their only option. In addition, jobs were available for people who had knowledge of technical and business communication.

---

[3] Elizabeth Tebeaux, Technical Writing for English Majors: Discourse Education for the Information Age, *Teaching English in the Two-Year College,* 17, pp. 201-212, 1990.

The problem for departments trying to hire people in technical communication was finding the committed technical communication faculty member and weeding out the imposters who planned to use technical communication as a stepping stone to "real" English courses like Chaucer, Shakespeare, and literary theory. The colleges of engineering, science, agriculture, and business wanted more and more sections of technical writing service courses. Not enough faculty were available, even at the two-year college level. Despite the demand, faculty were reserved to teach the courses in theory and philosophy, while lecturers and graduate students handled the bulk of the "service" courses. Technical writing courses that were designed about workplace research—what skills and competencies new colleges graduates and technical writers actually needed on the job—began to diminish. Graduate students and lecturers, many of whom had no concept of the world of work, taught academic topics like correct footnote style, academic style, genre, and technical reports that looked like research papers and focused on topics that had little relevance to non-academic settings.

THE CURRENT SITUATION AND ITS BROADER IMPLICATIONS

We have indeed come a long way in terms of becoming a real discipline. We have a number of established journals, several book series devoted to different facets of technical communication, professional associations, extensive theories and philosophies drawn from a wide range of social science disciplines, and a documented history. But in attempting to become an accepted member of the "lower faculties" and reshaping technical communication into a liberal art, we are also in the process of weakening the programs for producing practitioners. Technical communication now means academic degree programs in technical communication, where the continued focus is on developing clones to stock new and existing degree programs in technical communication which are becoming less focused on applications and more on the study of various social and rhetorical theories, gender issues, genre, literacy, multiculturalism/internationalism, and ethics. Even fewer faculty than before want to teach "service" courses like technical writing or technical editing. The rationale: Academic technical communication faculty should be involved in the serious business of producing clones, books, and theoretical articles. Focusing on bachelor's programs is less desirable than focusing on graduate programs because teaching graduate students is more prestigious than teaching undergraduates, and one can teach more theory in graduate courses. Ironically, many technical communication faculty are unemployable in the disciplines whose discourse they analyze.

For example, how many people who teach scientific discourse ever took more than two science courses as part of core undergraduate curriculum?

A SHIFT IN PRIORITIES

The result has been a shift in priorities as technical communication faculty have sought to fit the humanistic model. Pragmatic goals, such as preparing public school teachers to teach writing, preparing technical communicators for career ladders in non-academic jobs, and teaching the undergraduate engineering, science, or technology major to write for the world of work, have been sacrificed to goals that are more in keeping with appropriately humanistic faculty research, much of which was/is becoming more arcane and less useful. Many faculty who objected to the emphasis on theory were afraid to fight back, while others, wanting to be accepted by their departmental colleagues, fled willingly from pragmatic work that was deemed ephemeral by liberal arts standards. Dissertations in technical communication as well as curricula have shown the effects of this shift. How can theoretically-based graduate programs producing faculty who are not equipped to understand the needs of the workplace prepare technical communication specialists for the workplace? Therein lies the problem, which has been discussed from various perspectives.

For over two decades, the Society for Technical Communication has voiced concern about technical communication programs. As Hayhoe, Stohrer, Kunz, and Southard wrote in 1994,

> At a joint academic-industry workshop hosted by the STC Board of Directors in its January 1993 meeting, the industry panelists questioned whether graduates of our academic programs are as well prepared for careers in technical communication as their peers who have been trained in other disciplines. The problem, the panelists agreed, is that our graduates' backgrounds are too theoretical, and many lack expertise in such practical areas as time management, critical thinking, and interviewing techniques. Most significantly, some of them are not as proficient writers as some graduates in other fields. Theory must not be studied in isolation from practical application [21, p. 15].

Patrick Moore [22, 23] as well as Southard and Reaves [24] and Barchilon and Kelley [25] have advocated the educational needs for technical communicators that can only be described as liberal arts of the twenty-first century: practice with software technologies—graphics, desktop publishing, online help, HTML programs—information design, project management, usability testing, negotiation, personnel administration, organization theory, communication law, critical thinking, and, I would add, change management communications. Technical communicators must understand the cultures of the disciplines that foster technical communication as well as the needs of international users in these disciplines. Fundamentally, however, technical communicators must be excellent writers and editors who can organize and present material.

Faculty with roots in both the academy and the workplace — Rebecca Barclay, Thomas Pinelli, Michael Keene, John Kennedy, and Myrer Glassem — argued that "academic programs must improve their understanding of workplace culture, organization, and communication." "Teaching the textbook does not prepare students for the cultural and organizational constraints that influence communication habits and practices" [26, p. 325]. Similarly, Feinberg and Goldman provide a detailed list of competencies for technical communication majors [27, pp. 21-25], a list that parallels that recommended by Barchilon and Kelley [25, p. 595], who also suggest ways that these competencies can be implemented in a technical communication program.

Scanlon and Coon encouraged more emphasis on computer technology, more emphasis on writing, more practical, marketable skills; less theory; more emphasis on business-related courses, including TQM, ethics, and entrepreneurship; audience analysis, sentence structure, grammar, spelling, and punctuation. Faculty need to develop "strong, focused writers, who have a practical appreciation of how technology shapes and facilitates technical communication and who will be prepared to grow with the technological change that will inevitably occur during their career" [28, p. 445]. The solution: Programs that develop technical communicators need to focus research on workplace issues. As Moore stated, "technical communication professors need to discover what practicing communication professionals and users need. Technical communication professors do not need to go shopping in other academic specialties such as philosophy, sociology, and history for their theories. We should talk to users, managers, technicians, decision-makers, and other users and developers of technology, and create theories based on that research" [23, p. 218]. As Smeltzer and Suchan wrote in 1991:

> The need for academics to provide research relevant to practitioners is particularly compelling given the finding of one study that less than 15 percent of the managers surveyed read academically produced research. . . . [Research] should not be derived from questions unanswered in academic literature or from the belief that one's research interests are automatically relevant. . . . Rather it is important to look at current trends and predict future ones [29, p. 184].

Does all the polemic about the "right" theory of technical communication really matter? Yes, if as Patrick Moore suggests, theory illuminates what is taught in technical communication classes. But in an era of change, preparing technical communicators to succeed requires not just a liberal arts curriculum with a few technical courses thrown into the mix, but a reformulated, highly interdisciplinary program that is heavy on pragmatics and breadth of exposure, perhaps a heavily interdisciplinary technical communication degree combined with an MBA, or a technical communication degree program combined with one of the new MS programs in biotechnology. Such a combination, producing a 5–6 year degree program, would give technical communicators more credibility within the organization at large. A major way of assessing what is needed in the communication part of the curriculum is to examine what is happening in the workplace and deriving curriculum from what such an assessment yields [30-32]. This recommendation means that curriculum should reflect the actual needs of the workplace, not just research on other academic disciplines and how they may be useful to technical communication.

Given the focus of current research in technical communication, concerns are valid that an increasing quantity of what technical communication students need isn't covered in rhetoric or the standard bachelor's program steeped in a traditional liberal arts curriculum. As Moore has argued, for example, students need help understanding and dealing with the internal political struggles that shape the communication context [33]. Canadian researchers Aviva Freedman and Christine Adams concluded that "when students leave the university to enter the workplace, they not only need to learn new genres of discourse but they also need to learn new ways to learn such genres. The two kinds of processes, although sharing certain fundamental features, are different enough that the transition from one setting to the other poses particular problems for students, eliciting feelings of disjuncture, anxiety, or displacement" [5, p. 424]. Similarly, Pomerenke [3], in studying writers at a major insurance corporation, and Huettmann [6], who examined audience concerns in a hospitality consulting firm, both see major dislocations in academic preparation of technical writers and the needs of actual writers.

Richardson and Liggett sharply phrased this point in establishing research questions that in themselves suggest that academic technical communication is off target:

> Unlike workplace models of communication, the academic model for communication is that of free exchange of ideas, and with some exceptions, academics regard academic discourse as an instrument of freedom. Although we have been adept at studying communication

systems in oppressed societies, we have had difficulty recognizing that bourgeois, American, seemingly normal workplace discourse can be severely restrictive or even coercive. On the other hand, we have had difficulty understanding why some openly restrictive writing and writing that does not follow textbook rules still "work" for their audience. As Barabas notes in her study of corporate culture, social construction theory "helps explain why we have clung to our own academically-oriented views of writing and why these views, when transferred to the study of writing in other contexts or communities, often fail to reveal the true nature of the discourse under investigation." For example, the profession must face up to the anti-industry, anti-technology bias found even in industry studies by technical writing specialists. Is it coincidence that the most-developed textbook discussions about corporate power appear in chapters on ethics, invariably pitting the honest individual against unscrupulous management [4, p. 29]?

Technical writing textbooks — themselves models of standard rhetoric — offer other disturbing suggestions that what we are teaching lacks relevance. And, what technical communication majors need is not always covered by rhetoric. For example, most technical communication texts follow a standard rhetorical approach to writing — linear, ordered, efficient, clean, and predictable, where the writer always controls the situation. However, the appearance of an occasional maverick book shows how far off the mark our standard texts can be. Patricia Robinson and Ryn Etter, former University of Wisconsin technical communication faculty members who now work as consultants, provide a refreshing approach in *Writing and Designing Manuals* [34] about how writing is actually done in the workplace. Finding any discussion of "the composing process" similar to the following statement from *Writing and Designing Manuals*, would be unusual in a traditional technical writing text:

> Indeed, many of the major decisions affecting the production of the manual, including both content (information) and schedule (time), are often made by persons in other areas of the company. Deadlines may be set by marketing to coincide with the new model period without regard to the complexity of the writing task. Information needed to meet those deadlines may be held up in engineering because of last-minute design changes. Yet the technical writer is expected to produce usable, accurate manuals, on time and within budget. And in the real world, writing manuals will never be accomplished the way you were taught to write papers in school.
>
> Writing manuals the way you were taught to write school essays is both ineffectual and dangerous. You don't get a manual done, and you might lose your sanity [34, p. 7].

Rather than a neat linear model involving designing, collecting information, outlining, drafting, editing, approving, and printing, you face the following reality:

1. Receiving assignment with nearly reasonable deadline.
2. Begin making some basic decisions.
3. Deadline moved up 2 weeks.
4. Try to get information from engineers. Receive spec sheet with illegible handwritten changes.
5. Receive torn copy of competitor's brochure.
6. Try to get product. Receive outdated model with parts missing.
7. Deadline moved up 2 weeks.
8. Start to write anyway. Receive current prototype. Celebrate.
9. Overheard hall conversation about radical design changes in product. Scrap draft. Begin to read want ads.
10. Deadline moved up 2 weeks.

Writing as it is taught in school assumes two things: complete control and linearity of process—neither of which you have in writing manuals for publications. . . . What you do have, always and forever, is chaos and a deadline. Out of these you create a manual [34, p. 8].

Salaries of technical communicators offer the most convincing support for problems in the technical communication job market. While numerous entry-level positions in technical communication have existed during the past three decades, technical communication is not a power position in organizations. That is, technical communicators are not the "fair-haired children" with high-potential career paths. For example, a national survey of STC members in 1990 by Zimmerman, Muraski and Peterson [35] found that one-third experienced significant frustration about their professional image. Peter Kent's views [36] support those of Scanlon and Coon [28]: technical communicators do not perform well and often do not have the skills required by their clients and employers.

Thus, as Katherine Staples pointed out in her 1999 state-of-the-profession assessment article, "as of 1998 the average salary of a technical communicator was $43,782, and the average age was late thirties" [37, p. 160]. Does that achievement suggest that we are a discipline of power, particularly when many newly-minted 23-year old undergraduates in non-liberal arts fields have starting salaries at that level or higher? Zimmerman, Muraski, and Peterson write about the poor image of technical communicators [35]. The reasons for that poor image—lack of adequate preparation—echo the same problems described by Scanlon and Coon [28] and Hayhoe and colleagues [21].

Has our withdrawal from the utilitarian world of technical communication really helped us? If our students are entering the job market with little promotional future, how can we justify technical communication as a discipline that is simply another humanistic study? A recent article in *College English* by Craig Stroups [38], an American literature Ph.D. who serves as Coordinator of Academic Programs for San Jose State University's Online Campus, suggests that our attempt to play the humanities game has done little but discredit us and the students we purport to prepare for the non-academic community.

Stroups appears unaware of the work done by technical communication faculty in document design. He grudgingly recognizes the possible need for visual presentation in English studies and alludes to technical communication as one of the "marginalized" elements within English studies:

> This encroachment of graphic screen-based display—even into the word-, page-, and book-centered environment of word processing—presents English Studies with choices. The discipline needs to decide not only whether to embrace the teaching of visual and information design in addition to verbal production, which some of the more marginalized elements of English Studies have already done, but, more fundamentally, whether to confront its customary cultural attitudes toward visual discourses and their insinuation into verbal texts. W. J. T. Mitchell has characterized and criticized these attitudes as combining an iconoclastic "contempt" for graphic images as uncritical "idolatry, fetishism, and iconophilia," a "fear" toward visual discourses as a "racial, social and sexual other," and a tendency to see any genre that combines the two discourses, such as theater, as a "battleground between the values associated with verbal and visual codes" [38, p. 608].

Stroups' disdain for technical communication echoes similar condescending remarks about "engineering English," as described by both Kynell and Connors. As Stroups observes,

> To suggest that the loose confederation of scholarly and teaching interests called English studies should consciously visualize itself in these new terms is to argue that those at the discipline's prestigious center follow the lead of its more marginalized or controversial wings: technical communication, cultural studies, film, and popular culture. To pursue such a course would thus lead English to address its internal inequalities through this self-visualization and to recognize the mystified status of the privileged genres, discourses, and cultural narratives on which these inequalities rest. Historicizing these apparent eternal verities, however, also means exposing the political

and pecuniary interests that underlie English studies' investment in and defense of verbal print culture and its customary dismissal of the popular, predominantly visual discourses of magazine and advertising as well as the more iconic media of movies, television, and the Internet [38, pp. 609-611].

Stroups' essay also suggests that efforts of technical communication faculty to survive, fit in, and flourish in many English departments, have been futile. In many English Departments, technical communication faculty struggle for respect or they have become indistinguishable from other humanistic disciplines in academic goals, philosophy, and research. With the exception of a few programs in technical or land grant schools, technical communication is not any more respected than it was, and aside from developing a small group of technical communicators, many underpaid and without power, there is little evidence — no assessment — that shows that our discipline has made any difference in workforce communication.

THE ENGAGED UNIVERSITY— A PARADIGM FOR RELEVANCE

The issue of the utilitarian vs. the non-utilitarian college degree is no longer just a matter of perspective, nor has it been confined to the struggles of technical communication faculty. Alarms have been sounded by major educational groups — from Kellogg and from National Association of State Universities and Land-Grant Colleges (NASULGC) — for land grant universities to return to their roots, to become "Engaged Universities" [39]. The admonition to "return to our roots" means meeting local and national needs through research, service, and teaching which technical communication did so well prior to the late 1980s; creating new knowledge that solves real problems of real people; putting knowledge to work; setting and pursuing research agendas that engage our expertise with our community's problems; finding funding for this research from the community to which we reach out, whose problems we seek to solve. In short, the Engaged University supports integration of service with the development of intellectual capital, teaching, and research, so that faculty become more involved with their communities and forge partnerships to solve problems.

Concomitantly, the Engaged University will develop a reward structure for faculty that recognizes outreach-based research and service. The Engaged University will be accountable to the society that supports it. Rather than just taking financial support from society, the Engaged University will use its expertise to make its communities stronger. The

Engaged University puts knowledge to work in business, government, in the non-profit sector [39]. Technical communication programs in the Engaged University could focus their research on communication problems that plague the non-academic community. From the perspective of technical communication, internships, perhaps multiple internships, would be required of all technical communication majors, with students preparing internship reports that described the communication issues, types, and methods they observed.

Despite the lofty goals of the Kellogg reports, the concept of the Engaged University is alive and well in several land grant universities. Presidents and provosts are working with faculty and deans to restore the civic aspects of teaching and research which were also echoed in the Wingspread Declaration On Renewing the Civic Mission of the American Research University and *An American Imperative: Higher Expectations for Higher Education*. These goals are so refreshing, that several are worth stating here:

- Faculty members have opportunities and rewards for socially engaged scholarship through genuine civic partnerships, based on respect and recognition of different ways of knowing and different kinds of contributions, in which expertise is "on tap, not on top."
- Faculty teaching includes community-based learning and under-graduate action research that develops substantive knowledge, cultivates practical skills, and strengthens social responsibility and public identity for citizenship in a diverse democratic society.
- Faculties' professional service is conceived and valued as public work in which disciplinary and professional knowledge and exper-tise contributes to the welfare of society, and also can occasion the public work of may other citizens.
- Faculty members are encouraged and prepared when they desire to pursue "public scholarship," relating their work to the pressing problems of society, providing consultations and expertise, and creating opportunities to work with community and civic partners in co-creating things of public value.
- Faculty members engage in diverse cross-disciplinary work projects that improve the university and create things of lasting value and significance.
- Faculty are encouraged to mentor students, providing out-of-classroom opportunities to build communities of learning on and off campus. These opportunities have the potential to expose students to the public work of faculty whose own moral imaginations and public talents are vitally engaged in relevant scholarship and work of social significance [40, p. 4].

In short, professional groups within higher education, like Kellogg and NASULGC, are attempting to make university education and research responsive to the public providing these institutions' funding and to achieve responsiveness by ensuring that faculty are rewarded for contributing to relevant education.

ROADBLOCKS TO CHANGE

Technical communication has come too far down the path of academic disciplinarity, which we did to insure our professional survival, to make relevance of our degree programs a central mission—unless a mandate for change surfaces. Because the humanities and the university in general avoid the practical, technical communication as a discipline faces a daunting task: Remain relevant and engaged with the communication needs of non-academic settings or become another humanistic discourse whose research and teaching carry little weight beyond the academy. The latter is easier. Playing the humanities game gets us tenure, promotion, and pay raises. Talking with one another in our ever narrowing "discourse communities" is much easier than trying to worry about the communication problems of the marketplace. Intransigence within universities, bureaucratic faculty governance systems, the desire for prestige, belief that theoretical research is more important than applied research will continue to result in fewer core curriculum courses taught by senior faculty and more use of graduate students and lecturers to handle lower-level courses. Universities, as the Third Report of the Kellogg Commission stated,

> Are so inflexibly driven by disciplinary needs and concepts of excellence grounded in peer review, that we have lost sight of our institutional mission to address the contemporary multidisciplinary problems of the real world. Our departments are self-contained silos, frequently bearing little relationship to the challenges facing society. Agendas of faculty members are so narrowly focused, theoretical, and long-range that they are little more than fingers in the dike behind which are building up vast, complex economic and social pressures requiring immediate attention of the most practical kind [39, p. 20].

To repeat a statement that I made at the beginning, the problems confronting technical communication also face other research university disciplines: Lack of relevance of much of the research that underpins the discipline and indifference to the practical needs of society. Lack of accountability by faculty is nothing new, and many believe that the university exists for faculty rather than for the improvement of society.

The shift in values in technical communication is a cameo of what is happening in universities in general.

A March 24 article in *The Chronicle of Higher Education* argued for charter colleges for the same reasons. As James F. Carlin, former chairman of the Massachusetts Board of Higher Education stated: "There isn't an institution in America less open to new ideas than colleges and universities" [41]. In addition, many administrators as well as faculty are skeptical of any arrangement that suggests loss of control in current higher education governance. Many faculty are more interested in their careers — what is needed for promotions and recognition within their fields — than in providing educational experiences that benefit students. In short, faculty and many administrators are quite happy with the current situation, although demands for accountability, particularly from accrediting agencies, higher education leaders, and governing boards of universities, continue to surface.[4]

Articulation of problems in higher education has increased, with most critiques sharing a similar perspective. As Page Smith, a distinguished historian, stated in *Killing the Spirit: Higher Education in America*:

> The argument advanced here can be simply stated. It is that a vast majority of the so-called research turned out in the modern university is essentially worthless. It does not result in any measurable benefit to anything or anybody. It does not push back those omnipresent "frontiers of knowledge" so confidently evoked; it does not in the main result in greater health or happiness among the general population or any particular segment of it. It is busywork on a vast, almost incomprehensible scale [42, p. 70].

Despite perspectives like those mentioned above, for many academicians in technical communication, it's easier to take the moral high road, to believe that one is doing the right thing by teaching students general rhetorical principles and applications, rather than pandering to corporations' needs by teaching students how to use standard software packages, deal with internal political issues, develop change management communications, develop a general competence with communications

---

[4] See Clark Kerr, *Higher Education Cannot Escape History: Issues for the Twenty-First Century*. New York: SUNY 1994; "Knowledge Ethics and the New Academic Culture," *Change*, pp. 9-15, January/February 1994; Henry M. Levin, "Raising Productivity in Higher Education," *Journal of Higher Education*, 62:3, pp. 241-262, 1991; *Policy Perspectives. Report on the 1994 Pew Higher Education Roundtable*, 5:3, April 1994; James R. Mingle, "Faculty Work and the Costs/Quality/Access Collision," *AAHE Bulletin*, pp. 3-13, March 1993; William F. Massy and Robert Zemsky, "Cost Containment: Committing to a New Economic Reality," *Change*, pp. 16-22, November/December 1991.

technology, and constantly reassess curricular needs [22]. Teaching from a general rhetorical perspective is also easier, particularly if one convinces oneself that rhetoric is omniscient in any age or context. From this perspective, technology can be seen as skills, while rhetoric is "critical thinking." However, when one encounters the kinds of work done by technical communicators in the work place, how can we justify having students take a traditional liberal arts curriculum with a few technical communication courses thrown in? How can we presume that our academic research, prepared with little if any input from the non-academic world of work, can prepare students for a complex world defined by technology?

CATALYSTS OF CHANGE

Is refocusing technical communication toward utilitarian research possible? Movement in some areas suggests that the answer is "yes," particularly within land grant universities. The University of Wisconsin Council on Outreach in 1997 developed a rationale which has contributed to campus-level guidelines for promotion and tenure to produce more positive guidance regarding outreach and extension. Oregon State, Michigan State, Washington State, and the University of Georgia have also taken steps to encourage outreach efforts. Higher education professional societies, along with accrediting agencies, are continuing to argue for accountability and outcome-based education.[5] These groups want to know how graduates are perceived outside the academy. The American Association for Higher Education, along with many other foundations, such as Sloan, Pew, and NSF, recognize the problem of disciplines and programs that are not responsive to society's needs. These foundations are making grants as well as guidelines available to nurture improved, cost-effective core curriculum and to revamp doctoral programs that can produce graduates who can operate effectively in a non-academic environment.

What are the results of allowing technical communication to become just another form of discourse that yields theoretical discussion? As Katherine Staples [37], citing Boyer [43] and Meyer and Bernhardt [44] warns:

> Perhaps to meet the disciplinary responsibility of preparing students to meet citizenship and workplace responsibility with integrity as well as with knowledge and skill. . ., we need to broaden our

---

[5] See, for example, G. R. Evans, *Calling Academia to Account: Rights and Responsibilities.* Buckingham, United Kingdom: Open University Press, 1998; Frank Coffield and Bill Williamson (eds.), *Repositioning Higher Education,* Buckingham, United Kingdom: Open University Press, 1997.

research agenda to welcome the scholarship of teaching, the scholarship of cross-disciplinary integration, and the scholarship of application. . . . In distancing ourselves from the achievements of our disciplinary past, we may risk the ability to meet, support, and influence a changing educational and professional future [37, pp. 161-162].

More specifically, we risk loss of support from business and industry, where technical communication is practiced. Thus, we risk opportunities for funded research, scholarships for technical communication students, and graduate programs that have respect outside the humanities. In departments where technical communication is often a sub-group, we risk diminution when funding is reduced and when tenure lines are decreased, particularly when program assessment shows that our students get jobs but don't have career development.

WHY CHANGE IS NECESSARY

In the previous discussion, a sense of urgency underpinning reform in higher education is clearly evident. In a 1993 issue of *Daedalus: Journal of the American Academy of Arts and Sciences*, Donald Kennedy, President Emeritus of Stanford [45], Kenneth Prewitt, Senior Vice President of the Rockefeller Foundation [17], and Jonathan Cole, Provost of Columbia [46] all recognized that universities can no longer continue to expand as they did during the years of the Cold War economy.[6] As Jonathan Cole observed, higher education is no longer rapidly expanding because of large influxes of government funding that made the 1950s-1980s the golden years. Because of massive funding during this era of Cold War education expansion, "the research universities were able to live with the illusion that they could remain 'full service universities' without having to make many difficult choices about which new areas of knowledge would take programmatic form and would be supported at a level needed to achieve true distinction; which currently supposed areas would have to be phased out" [46, p. 5]. Similarly, Donald Kennedy argued that a new kind of university will have to emerge from the new economic constraints, which "will be even harsher and more permanent than we now imagine" [45, p. 155]. This new "terrain map "will identify which areas are suitable for cultivation and which should be left fallow in defining the institution's identity" [45, p. 154].

---

[6] For an academic's perspective of the results of this shift, see Stuart Rojstaczer, *Gone for Good: Tales of University Life after the Golden Age*, New York: Oxford, 1999.

These 1993 predictions are beginning to make universities more efficient in the face of rising costs. As reported in *Change*, the major publication of the American Association for Higher Education, many universities are already restructuring. Universities are recognizing that they cannot continue to add costly programs. Fund-raising will become even more critical than it is now. In geographic regions where the need to educate more learners is critical to the economic health of the state, the demand for pragmatic degree programs will continue to increase. In addition to more students, fewer tenure lines [47, 48], and decreased funding, higher education is under fire for not producing students who are prepared with not only critical thinking skills but also relevant job skills. Demands for accountability, evident in the emergence of assessment by accrediting agencies, suggest that governing boards of all types want to know what universities are doing with their funds and whether their work is effective. Survival of many institutions and the quality of programs in others will demand stern management policies that require academic programs to be accountable and find outside funding sources. Because technical communication has fought hard for recognition as a discipline, its implosion into the traditional humanities and liberal arts comes at a time when the pragmatic base of technical communication is most needed. Thus, it is ironic that technical communication, which can easily justify its existence today, just as it did during the 1970s and 1980s, appears to be leaning toward a humanities curriculum model that cannot easily be justified.

If we again focus our research and our teaching on technical communication as it operates in non-academic settings, if we design our courses and programs to prepare students for the challenges of the world of work, we can launch and exemplify the best in assessment. That is, we can show that technical writing is deemed by employers and former students to be one of the best courses they took in college. We can use these assessment surveys to show us what we should teach, where we can improve, how research can help us improve. By delivering a product that is respected outside the university, we can ask for and receive funding to support curriculum-based research as well as support for our programs in general.

The marketplace, the public, and governing boards afford the best sources for mandated change, and the warnings have come from a variety of voices, such as the Pew Foundation [49] and many well-known educators [50, 51]. Corporate training programs are increasing because universities continue to produce many graduates who possess the right credentials but not the competencies needed by society and employers. This situation devalues the college degree. Thus, when credentials become less valued than competencies—and in a number of areas this is happening;[7] when corporate education programs can produce employees who are more competent than many graduates produced by universities; when commercial providers, like the Open University, Jones University, and University of Phoenix, begin producing graduates who are more competent than graduates from traditional universities; when governing boards begin eliminating tenure in their anger at spiraling costs and at faculties who have little to show for their teaching and research; when university governing boards begin to award funding to departments and colleges in terms of quality teaching, useful research, and outreach activities, not just for how much research faculty do, then the shift toward instruction that makes a significant difference in the lives of learners may, once again, be possible.

REFERENCES

1. P. V. Anderson, What Survey Research Tells Us About Writing at Work, in *Writing in Nonacademic Settings*, L. Odell and D. Goswami (eds.), Guilford, New York, pp. 3-82, 1985.
2. E. Tebeaux, Redesigning Professional Writing Courses to Meet the Communication Needs of Business and Industry, *College Composition and Communication*, 36:4, pp. 419-428, 1985.
3. P. J. Pomerenke, Writers at Work: Seventeen Writers at a Major Insurance Corporation, *Journal of Business and Technical Communication*, 6:2, pp. 172-186, 1991.
4. M. Richardson and S. Liggett, Power Relations, Technical Writing Theory, and Workplace Writing, *Journal of Business and Technical Communication*, 7:1, pp. 112-137, 1993.
5. A. Freedman and C. Adams, Learning to Write Professionally: "Situated Learning" and the Transition from University to Professional Discourse, *Journal of Business and Technical Communication*, 10:4, pp. 395-427, 1996.
6. E. Huettmann, Writing for Multiple Audiences: An Examination of Audience Concerns in a Hospitality Consulting Firm, *Journal of Business Communication*, 33:3, pp. 257-273, 1996.
7. P. Goubil-Gambrell, Guest Editor's Column, *Technical Communication Quarterly*, 7:1, pp. 5-7, 1998.
8. Itext Working Group, Itext: Future Directions for Research on the Relationship Between Information Technology and Writing, *Journal of Business and Technical Communication*, 15:3, pp. 269-308, 2001.

[7] For an interesting discussion of the new collaboration between the Council of Graduate Schools and the University Continuing Education Association, see Kohl, Kay and Jules LaPidus (eds.), *Postbaccalaureate Futures: New Markets, Resources, Credentials*, American Council on Education, Oryx Press, 2001.

9. D. Charney, Guest Editor's Introduction: Prospects for Research in Technical and Scientific Communication—Part 1. *Journal of Business and Technical Communication*, 15:3, pp. 267-268, 2001.

10. K. T. Durack, Research Opportunities in the US Patent Record, *Journal of Business and Technical Communication*, 15:4, pp. 490-510, 2001.

11. C. Haas and S. P. Witte, Writing as an Embodied Practice, *Journal of Business and Technical Communication*, 15:4, pp. 413-457, 2001.

12. M. C. Taylor, Useful Devils, *EDUCAUSE Review*, pp. 38-46, July/August 2001.

13. T. Kynell, *Writing in a Milieu of Utility: The Move to Technical Communication in American Engineering Programs, 1850-1890* (2nd Edition), Volume 12, ATTW Contemporary Studies in Technical Communication, Ablex, Norwood, New Jersey, 1999.

14. N. O. Keohane, The Mission of the Research University, *Daedalus Journal of the American Academy of Arts and Sciences*, 18, pp. 101-126, 1993.

15. R. J. Connors, The Rise of Technical Writing Instruction in America, *Journal of Technical Writing and Communication*, 12:4, pp. 329-352, 1992.

16. E. Tebeaux, The Trouble with Employees' Writing May Be Freshman English, *Teaching English in the Two-Year College*, 15:1, pp. 9-19, 1988.

17. K. Prewitt, America's Research Universities Under Public Scrutiny, *Daedalus Journal of the American Academy of Arts and Sciences*, 18, pp. 85-99, 1993.

18. A. Bloom, *The Closing of the American Mind*, Simon & Schuster, Englewood Cliffs, New Jersey, 1987.

19. J. Klor de Alva, Remaking the Academy: 21st-Century Challenges to Higher Education in the Age of Information, *EDUCAUSE Review*, pp. 32-40, March/April 2000.

20. E. Garber, Coveting Your Neighbor's Discipline, *The Chronicle of Higher Education*, pp. B8-B9, January 12, 2001.

21. G. F. Hayhoe, F. Stohrer, R. Kunz, and S. Southard, The Evolution of Academic Programs in Technical Communication, *Technical Communication*, 41:1, pp. 14-19, 1994.

22. P. Moore, Evolving Paradigms of Communication Analysis: A Defense of Teaching Software Programs in Technical Communication Classes, *TEXT Technology*, pp. 25-58, Spring 2001.

23. P. Moore, Myths About Instrumental Discourse: A Response to Robert R. Johnson, *Technical Communication Quarterly*, 8:2, pp. 210-222, 1999.

24. S. G. Southard and R. Reaves, Tough Questions and Straight Answers: Educating Technical Communicators in the Next Decade, *Technical Communication*, pp. 555-565, Fourth Quarter, 1995.

25. M. G. Barchilon and D. G. Kelley, A Flexible Technical Model for the Year 2000, *Technical Communication*, pp. 590-598, Fourth Quarter, 1995.

26. R. O. Barclay, T. Pinelli, M. Keene, J. Kennedy, and M. Glassem, Technical Communication in the International Workplace: Some Implications for Curriculum Development, *Technical Communication*, pp. 324-335, Third Quarter, 1991.

27. S. Feinberg and J. Goldman, Contents for a Course in Technical Communication: Results of a Survey, *Technical Communication*, pp. 21-25, Second Quarter, 1995.

28. P. M. Scanlon and A. C. Coon, Attitudes of Professional Technical Communicators Regarding the Content of an Undergraduate Course in Technical Communication: A Survey, *Technical Communication*, pp. 439-446, Third Quarter, 1994.

29. L. R. Smeltzer and J. E. Suchan, Guest Editorial: Theory Building and Relevance, *Journal of Business Communication*, 28:3, pp. 181-186, 1991.

30. E. Tebeaux, Nonacademic Writing into the 21st Century: Achieving and Sustaining Relevance in Research and Curricula in Nonacademic Writing, *Social Theory and Technology*, A. H. Duin and C. J. Hansen (eds.), Lawrence Erlbaum, Mahwah, New Jersey, pp. 35-55, 1996.

31. E. Tebeaux, Teaching Professional Communication in the Information Age: Problems in Sustaining Relevance, *Journal of Business and Technical Communication*, 2:2 , pp. 44-58, 1988.

32. E. Tebeaux, Technical Communication, Literary Theory, and English Studies: Stasis, Change, and the Problem of Meaning, *Technical Communication Quarterly*, 18:1, pp. 15-28, 1991.

33. P. Moore, When Persuasion Fails: Coping with Power Struggles, *Technical Communication*, pp. 351-359, Third Quarter, 1999.

34. P. A. Robinson and R. Etter, *Writing and Designing Manuals* (3rd Edition), CRC Press, Boca Raton, Florida, 2000.

35. D. E. Zimmerman, L. Muraski, and J. Peterson, *Who Are We? A Look at the Technical Communicator's Role*, Center for Research on Writing and Communication Technologies, Colorado State University, Fort Collins, Colorado, 1992.

36. P. Kent, *Making Money in Technical Writing*, Macmillan, New York, 1998.

37. K. Staples, Technical Communication from 1950-1990: Where Are We Now? *Technical Communication Quarterly*, 8:2, pp. 153-164, 1999.

38. C. Stroups, Visualizing English: Recognizing the Hybrid Literacy of Visual and Verbal Authorship on the Web, *College English*, 62:5, pp. 607-632, 2000.

39. Kellogg Commission on the Future of State and Land-Grant Universities, *Returning to Our Roots: The Engaged Institution*. Third Report. National Association of State Universities and Land-Grant Colleges, February 1999.

40. The Wingspread Declaration on Renewing the Civic Mission of the American Research University, June 1999. See also Wingspread Group on Higher Education, *An American Imperative: Higher Expectations for Higher Education*, Johnson Foundation, New York, 1993.

41. S. Hebel, States Start to Consider the Idea of Charter Colleges, *The Chronicle of Higher Education*, 46:29, pp. A36, A38, March 24, 2000.

42. P. Smith, *Killing the Spirit: Higher Education in America*, Viking, Penguin, New York, 1990.

43. E. L. Boyer, *Scholarship Reconsidered: Priorities of the Professorate*, Carnegie Foundation, Princeton, New Jersey, 1990.

44. P. R. Meyer and S. A. Bernhardt, Workplace Realities and the Technical Communication Curriculum: A Call for Change, *Foundations for Teaching Technical Communication: Theory, Practice, and Program Design*, K. Staples and C. Ornatowski (eds.), Ablex, Greenwich, Connecticut, pp. 85-98, 1997.

45. D. Kennedy, Making Choices in the Research University, *Daedalus Journal of the American Academy of Arts and Sciences, 18,* pp. 127-156, 1993.

46. J. R. Cole, Balancing Acts: Dilemmas of Choice Facing Research Universities, *Daedalus Journal of the American Academy of Arts and Sciences, 18,* pp. 1-36, 1993.

47. Y. T. Moses, Scanning the Environment: AAHE's President Reports on Trends in Higher Education, *AAHE Bulletin, 53*:10, pp. 7-9, 2001.

48. M. J. Finkelstein and J. H. Schuster, Assessing the Silent Revolution: How Changing Demographics are Reshaping the Academic Profession, *AAHE Bulletin, 54*:2, pp. 3-8, 2001.

49. *Policy Perspectives. Report on the 1994 Pew Higher Education Roundtable, 5*:3, April 1994.

50. C. Kerr, *Higher Education Cannot Escape History: Issues for the Twenty-First Century,* SUNY Press, New York, 1994; Knowledge Ethics and the New Academic Culture, *Change,* pp. 9-15, January/February 1994.

51. H. M. Levin, Raising Productivity in Higher Education, *Journal of Higher Education, 62*:3, pp. 241-262, 1991.

CHAPTER 3

Points of Reference Contributing to the Professionalization of Technical Communication

Elizabeth Overman Smith

The texts of technical communication professionals form the *transmit* — "the set of concepts representative of a historically developing discipline" [1, p. 158]. The transmit, which I will refer to as a knowledge base and identify as points of reference, is a group of texts that record the conversations of the members of the discipline and their use of the concepts and the procedures that make up the discipline's activities. The points of reference represent the "intellectual genealogy" [2, p. 328] of the discipline. Members of the profession define problems and create and transmit the common terms, metaphors, and models for discussing the problem, the methods for exploring the problem, and the practical application of the concepts and procedures to the problem situation. With each problem solved, the technical communication professional builds power, status, and legitimacy that is recognized not only within the technical communication community but also by those outside the community. The knowledge base for the community evolves from the conversations and descriptions of the problems addressed.

Much of the knowledge base is recorded in our professional journals. Dale Sullivan suggests that the journals are "rhetorical displays" — they are tangible artifacts that show "one has the right to contribute to disciplinary discussions, that is, that one has legitimacy" [3, p. 222]. Legitimacy extends beyond recognition by colleagues to recognition by those not in technical communication. In this study, points of reference are selected from the intertext—the citations—of the conversations by technical communication professionals recorded in five journals.

The knowledge base is malleable, shifting its content to adjust for current workplace and research activities. New points of reference become part of the knowledge base as conversations about new problems are recorded. Professionals "share, to differing extents, communal assumptions and projects as well as a familiarity with the disciplinary literature . . . [and] these individuals are also driven by their own active projects and view the communal legacy through their own interests and schema" [1, p. 325]. The points of reference provide "knowledge that is generally accepted but is open to revision"—what Sullivan calls "an open canon" [3, p. 230]. The points of reference illustrate the last 30 years of conversations and have become significant in the technical communication knowledge base. Identifying the topics represented by selected points of reference calls attention to the problems technical communication scholars and practitioners work on and solve. The topics may be broadly defined, such as the professional issues surrounding pedagogy, research, and defining technical communication, the rhetoric of communities, and document design.

The topics of the points of reference parallel the keywords from the title of this anthology, *Power and Legitimacy in Technical Communication*. Descriptions of pedagogy, research, and defining technical communication discuss issues of status: who are the professionals, what is technical communication, how does technical communication contribute to a community's actions, and what is the relationship of technical communication to other professions. The power of technical communication is found in the technical communication community's use of rhetoric. The "power" of rhetoric—the persuasive and instrumental power of language—is its role in shaping the activities of a community. Technical communication professionals understand language and its rhetorical characteristics (from stylistic and grammatical issues to its persuasive and instrumental features) as they participate in communities. However, it is document design (defined in its broadest sense and much more than deciding where text and visuals go in a document) that gives the profession an identity, its legitimacy. Technical communication professionals are authorities on document design and text production—not the only authority (but one group of professionals that study document design and can offer reasons backed by research for constructing a document). Technical communication professionals are the subject matter experts on the integration of text and visuals and document production.

In this chapter, I focus on 26 points of reference and how they have contributed to the professionalization of technical communication. They are part of technical communication's knowledge base. I will first summarize the method of the collection of citations before giving a brief overview of the 26 points of reference selected for this discussion. Many readers may be familiar with the authors' works listed in Table 1. These intertextual references are a significant part—but certainly not the only texts—of our conversations and intellectual genealogy. In the final section, I suggest that the power, status, and legitimacy of technical communication are represented in the points of reference.

SELECTION OF POINTS OF REFERENCE

The points of reference described in this essay are part of an extended study of the technical communication transmit developed from a database of citations for 1988 through 1997. The citations were collected in two 5-year sets, 1988-1992 (Set I) and 1993-1997 (Set II). Over 25,000 citations were collected from five technical communication journals: *IEEE Transactions on Professional Communication* (IEEE), *Journal of Business and Technical Communication* (JBTC), *Journal of Technical Writing and Communication* (JTWC), *Technical Communication* (TC), and *Technical Communication Quarterly* (TCQ) (formerly *The Technical Writing Teacher* [TWT]). Details for the method of collection and citation analysis research are provided in two earlier articles [4, 5]. Bazerman notes that the "explicit intertextuality" of citations gives the writer a body of works from which to build an argument and "opportunities for persuasive restructuring of the literature" [2, p. 325].

Table 1, first presented in "Points of Reference in Technical Communication Scholarship" [4], identifies the points of reference at the center of this discussion. The 26 selected points of reference offer an important, magnified view of the 163 points of reference identified in the earlier study [4] and, I suggest, they are a representative view of the professionalization of technical communication. The points of reference are the 16 texts most frequently cited from Set I 1988-1992 (the first column) and Set II 1993-1997 (the second column). There are 26 different texts. When Set I and Set II are combined, Set B (the last column) is formed. (Set A is the 163 most frequently cited texts for Set I and Set II combined [4]. Set B, this study, is the top 17 most frequently cited texts.)

The points of reference represent a good distribution of topics, a manageable number of texts to discuss, and each was cited a minimum of 21 times, suggesting that they each had some influence in the development of technical communication. For example, "Writing at Exxon ITD" [6], a workplace study; "A Humanistic Rationale for Technical Writing" [7], a framework for defining technical communication; and *The Structure of Scientific Revolutions* [8], a study of the rhetoric of science, were cited 52,

Table 1. A Comparison of the Top 16 Frequently Cited Text. The Table Illustrates Evolution (Comparing Set I and Set II) and Knowledge Building (Combining Set I and Set II to Form Set B) for Scholarship in Technical Communication. Set III is incomplete: The Text from Set I and Set II were Tracked from 1998-July 2001; Those Listed Continue to be Cited Frequently.

Set I – 1988-1992	Set II – 1993-1997	Set III – 1998-2002	Set B – 1988-1997
Humanistic Rationale — C. Miller	*Shaping Written Knowledge* — Bazerman	*Shaping Written Knowledge* — Bazerman	Writing at Exxon — Paradis, Dobrin, R. Miller
Writing at Exxon — Paradis, Dobrin, R. Miller	Writing at Exxon — Paradis, Dobrin, R. Miller	Humanistic Rationale — C. Miller	Humanistic Rationale — C. Miller
Structure of Scientific Revolutions — Kuhn	*Singular Text/Plural Authors* — Ede, Lunsford	*Structure of Scientific Revolutions* — Kuhn	*Structure of Scientific Revolutions* — Kuhn
What We Learn from Writing — Faigley, T. Miller	Humanistic Rationale — C. Miller	*Nurnberg Funnel* — Carroll	*Shaping Written Knowledge* — Bazerman
Writing . . . Emerging Organization — Doheny-Farina	What Survey Research Tells Us — Anderson	*Visual Display* — Tufte	What Survey Research Tells Us — Anderson
What Survey Research Tells Us — Anderson	*Designing/Writing Online* — Horton	*Designing/Writing Online* — Horton	Writing . . . Emerging Organization — Doheny-Farina
What's Technical About — Dobrin	Ethics of Expediency — Katz	Writing at Exxon — Paradis, Dobrin, R. Miller	*Singular Text/Plural Authors* — Ede, Lunsford
New Essays — Anderson, Brockman, C. Miller	*Structure of Scientific Revolutions* — Kuhn	What's Technical About — Dobrin	What We Learn from Writing — Faigley, T. Miller

Beyond the Text Odell	Writing . . . Computer Documentation Brockmann	Writing . . . Computer Documentation Brockmann	Writing . . . Computer Documentation Brockmann	Writing . . . Computer Documentation What's Technical About Dobrin
Cognitive Approach to Readability Huckin	**Writing . . . Emerging Organization** **Doheny-Farina**			Writing . . . Computer Documentation Brockmann
Revising Functional Documents Flower, Hayes, Swarts	*Writing and Technique* Dobrin		Data for Set III incomplete.	Composing Process of Engineer Selzer
Nonacademic Writing Faigley	What's Practical About C. Miller			*Visual Display* Tufte
What Experienced Collaborators Allen, Atkinson, Morgan, Moore, Snow	Construction of Knowledge Winsor			Nonacademic Writing Faigley
Composing Process of Engineer Selzer	Political-Ethical Implications Sullivan			What Experienced Collaborators Allen, Atkinson, Morgan, Moore, Snow
Collaborative Learning Bruffee	*Nurnberg Funnel* Carroll			*Writing and Technique* Dobrin
Shaping Written Knowledge *Bazerman*	*Visual Display* Tufte			Beyond the Text Odell
				Collaborative Learning Bruffee

Note: The text are listed in order of frequency of citations with the most frequently cited at the top of each column. The shading indicates text common to Set I and Set II. The boxed texts do not appear on the combined list Set B. (See the Works Cited for complete bibliographic information.)

51, and 50 times, respectively. The shaded points of reference in Table 1 are common to Set I and Set II and appear in Set B. The boxed points of reference do not appear in Set B although in most cases they just missed the cutoff for this study.

The different points of reference in Set I and Set II confirm that looking at just the sets of citations combined (Set B) or just one set (Set I or Set II) captures only one picture of the scholarly conversations and does not show the evolution of technical communication. Studying the changes among the sets offers observations about the professionalization of technical communication and how it evolves.

The next collection of citations will cover the 5-year period 1998-2002 (Set III). However, to confirm that the 26 points of reference are still influential and to ensure that the argument here is as current as possible, I reviewed the articles in the five journals and scanned the citations at the end of each article. I noted which of the 26 texts were cited and if the authors have made additional contributions to the profession's conversations. For example, Carolyn Miller, Thomas Huckin (with Carol Berkenkotter), and Dorothy Winsor have texts that will more than likely appear in Set III when the collection is complete. This update does not add new references to the collection—that will be done in 2003. This collection only confirms the extent of the influence for the 9 of the 26 points of reference singled out for this article (third column).

TOPICS OF THE POINTS OF REFERENCE

The 26 points of reference may be grouped into three topical areas: professional issues; the rhetoric of communities; and document design. These topical areas parallel our claims of professional status, power, and legitimacy. Technical communication professionals develop and design documents for getting things done and solving problems in the workplace. They study and report on the rhetoric different communities use in communicating and solving problems. Together the points of reference contribute to the technical communication knowledge base and professionalization of technical communication. The following three sections provide an overview of each.

Professional Issues and Status-Building

Professionals define themselves. They establish their status—their place—among other disciplines with their definitions and discussions of disciplinary activities; for example, the content of technical communication courses or the value added with a technical communicator on the project. The discussions often appear as internal debates and struggles (for example, the responses in the October 1996 issue of *JBTC* to Patrick Moore's "Instrumental Discourse Is as Humanistic as Rhetoric" [9]). The self-examination and critical evaluation keep the concerns of the profession in the forefront. The authors reveal their struggles with professional identity and at the same time suggest an identity. The identity provides a measure of status for the profession. Status has been established in the academy in the 1990s: there are undergraduate and graduate programs and promotion of faculty to tenured positions. This status parallels the increased demand for technical communicators in the workplace.

Seven of the nine points of reference, Table 2, present theoretical discussions that define technical communication and the pedagogical responsibilities of developing an awareness in students of ethical technical communication. Miller [7] in 1979 articulates the major points, and David Dobrin [10, 11], Steven Katz [12], and Dale Sullivan [13] continue the discussion. Kenneth Bruffee [14] contributes a description of the theory of social construction for studies of collaboration in the classroom and workplace. Two points of reference, Lester Faigley's "Nonacademic Writing: The Social Perspective" [15] and the anthology *New Essays in Technical and Scientific Communication: Research, Theory, Practice* [16], provide support for disciplinary activities in research and professional development.

Miller's [7] and Dobrin's [10, 11] texts offer defining statements about the nature of technical communication. Miller and Dobrin dispute the definitions of technical communication in the 1960s and 1970s for their "positivistic assumptions" [7, p. 613] and "list of features" [11, p. 31]. Miller focuses on the teaching of technical writing with her direct questioning of how technical writing is taught, but her more important purpose is to move the thinking of professionals from positivism to "communal rationality" [7, p. 617]. "Humanistic Rationale" marks a significant shift in thinking among technical communication professionals in the late 1970s and the changes are seen in the 1980s and 1990s. Practitioners redefine their roles from translators of information to developers of information. Teachers work with students to balance the final product with the process of developing the information in the document. Miller does not define technical writing; she establishes a philosophical framework for defining it that rests on the theory of the social construction of knowledge. Miller continues to be an influential member of the profession. "Humanistic Rationale," for example, continues to be cited in pedagogy-related articles such as discussions of service courses [17, 18] and technical communication in English departments [19].

Dobrin defines technical writing: "Technical writing is writing that accommodates technology to the user" [10, p. 242; 11, p. 54]. In "What's

Table 2. Points of Reference Focused on Professional Issues
and Status-Building

	Professional issues	I	II	III	B
Anderson, Paul Brockmann, John Miller, Carolyn	*New Essays in Technical and Scientific Communication: Research, Theory, Practice*	✓			
Bruffee, Kenneth	Collaborative Learning and the "Conversation of Mankind"	✓			✓
Dobrin, David	What's Technical about Technical Writing?, *New Essays*	✓		✓	✓
Dobrin, David	*Writing and Technique*		✓		✓
Faigley, Lester	Nonacademic Writing: The Social Perspective, *Writing in Nonacademic Settings*	✓			✓
Katz, Steven	The Ethic of Expediency: Classical Rhetoric, Technology, and the Holocaust		✓		
Miller, Carolyn	A Humanistic Rationale for Technical Writing	✓	✓	✓	✓
Miller, Carolyn	What's Practical About Technical Writing?		✓		
Sullivan, Dale	Political-Ethical Implications of Defining Technical Communication as a Practice		✓		

Technical About Technical Writing?" and *Writing and Technique,* Dobrin expresses social constructionist and humanistic goals similar to Miller's. He focuses on "local knowledge" because "at any time, anything about the situation or context can affect the meaning crucially" [11, p. 10]. Dobrin also acknowledges the relation of technology and technical communication. *Technology* is "more than an array of tools or procedures. It extends to the way human beings display themselves in the use and production of material goods and services" [11, p. 55]. Miller, echoing Dobrin's title in "What's Practical about Technical Writing?" suggests that technical writing as "practical rhetoric . . . provides what techne cannot: a locus for questioning, for criticism, for distinguishing good practice from bad" [20, p. 23]. Miller and Dobrin raise the level of significance in studying the rhetoric of communities by aligning technical communication with the technological community. Miller's "What's Practical" [20] and Dobrin's "What's Technical" [10] continue to be cited in articles discussing pedagogy. They are among the earliest to discuss the rhetoric of technology.

Katz and Sullivan caution that aligning with the technological community does not excuse unethical actions for solving problems. Katz uses an extreme — but very real — example from the Holocaust to emphasize the importance of ethics in technical writing and to warn against the technological expediency: "technical writing . . . always leads to action, and thus always impacts on human life" [12, p. 259]. Sullivan, focusing mainly on Miller's texts, asks "if we enculturate our students . . . by teaching technical genres that reinforce the dominance of the technological system, how can we then call them to responsible social action?" [13, p. 377]. He suggests that political discourse and a public audience should be incorporated into courses — for example, having the class explore a public policy issue. In "Collaborative Learning and the 'Conversation of Mankind'" [14], Bruffee argues for collaborative learning in the classroom. Scholars and researchers incorporate social constructionist theory into their analyses. The context and relation among collaborators become as important as the text produced.

Studies of the rhetoric of discourse communities contribute significantly to technical communication professionals' research activities and illustrate the power associated with rhetorical adeptness — a characteristic of a good technical communicator. Faigley's essay, "Nonacademic Writing: The Social Perspective," in the anthology *Writing in Nonacademic Settings* [21], calls for studies of *discourse communities* [15, p. 238]. Faigley defines the social perspective: researchers must "view written texts not as detached objects possessing meaning on their own, but as links in communicative chains, with their meaning emerging from their relationships to previous texts and the present context" [15, p. 235]. His research with Thomas Miller, discussed in the next section, illustrates research from a social perspective — as do all of the studies described in the next section.

The anthology *New Essays in Technical and Scientific Communication: Research, Theory, Practice* [16], edited by Paul Anderson, R. John Brockmann, and Carolyn Miller, gives a view of the state-of-the-art of the discipline in the early 1980s. The frequency of citations not only for the anthology but for seven of the essays within the anthology (two of them are discussed here) reinforce its contributions to understanding of the profession. The anthology begins with three reports of empirical research; reviews readability, a key topic in technical communication (see Huckin's essay, described below in the Document Design, Technology, and Legitimacy section of this chapter); presents four studies on rhetoric; gives historical perspectives from the Renaissance that influence technical writing; and concludes with Dobrin's "What's Technical" [10]. The number of references to essays and to the anthology itself signals that the purpose of the editors met their goals to

> build further theory, which is the foundation of a coherent and vigorous discipline . . . [to] support and correct teaching strategies and curriculum design. . . [and to] inform the practices and problem-solving strategies of the communication professional [16, p. 10].

New Essays in Technical and Scientific Communication and the other points of reference described in this section laid the foundation for defining and giving status to technical communication since the late 1970s.

Power in the Rhetoric of Communities

The power of technical communication resides in the rhetorical abilities of those who write instructions, proposals, online help screens, and so on. The rhetorical skills (particularly an awareness of the audience and of the influence of genres) give technical communicators the power to participate alongside subject matter experts in developing documents such as policy statements, computer documentation, and Web sites. The communities studied by the authors of the points of reference included in this section (Table 3) offer glimpses of different communities and their rhetoric—for example, studies of engineers at work, a business plan for a startup company, and communication in a social service agency. The researchers "consider issues such as social roles, group purposes, communal, organization, ideology, and finally theories of culture" [15, pp. 235-236]. The points of reference represent rhetoric of science studies but also studies of communities other than scientific communities.

Researchers in the rhetoric of science apply the rhetorical canons in studies of the construction of scientific knowledge. Charles Bazerman's *Shaping Written Knowledge* [2] and Thomas Kuhn's *The Structure of Scientific Revolutions* [8] describe the context including the social and political forces influencing the text's development. For example, Bazerman describes the publication history of Isaac Newton's findings on optics to illustrate that as "writing choices are realized and become institutionalized, they shape the kind of things we consider contributions to knowledge" [2, p. 15]. Kuhn describes scientific findings as not the objective, apolitical data that many perceive them to be but socially constructed texts that shift paradigms. Bazerman and Kuhn continue to be

Table 3. Points of Reference Focused on Power of the
Rhetoric of Communities

	Rhetoric of communities	I	II	III	B
Allen, Nancy Atkinson, Dianne Morgan, Meg Moore, Teresa Snow, Craig	What Experienced Collaborators Say About Collaborative Writing	✓	✓		✓
Anderson, Paul	What Survey Research Tells Us About Writing at Work, *Writing in Nonacademic Settings*	✓	✓		✓
Bazerman, Charles	*Shaping Written Knowledge: The Genre and Activity of the Experimental Article in Science*	✓	✓	✓	✓
Doheny-Farina, Stephen	Writing in an Emerging Organization	✓	✓		✓
Ede, Lisa Lunsford, Angela	*Singular Texts/Plural Authors: Perspectives on Collaborative Writing*		✓		✓
Faigley, Lester Miller, Thomas	What We Learn from Writing on the Job, *Writing in Nonacademic Settings*	✓			✓
Kuhn, Thomas	*The Structure of Scientific Revolutions*	✓	✓	✓	✓
Odell, Lee	Beyond the Text: Relations Between Writing and Social Context, *Writing in Nonacademic Settings*	✓			✓
Paradis, James Dobrin, David Miller, Richard	Writing at Exxon ITD: Notes on the Writing Environment of an R&D Organization, *Writing in Nonacademic Settings*	✓	✓	✓	✓
Selzer, Jack	The Composing Process of an Engineer	✓	✓		✓
Winsor, Dorothy	The Construction of Knowledge in Organizations: Asking the Right Questions about the *Challenger*		✓		

cited for their contributions in exploring the rhetoric of science and expanding technical communication's initial positivistic views to an awareness that knowledge is socially constructed.

Lee Odell and Dixie Goswami teamed with other researchers to produce one of the earliest, most extensive, and most influential studies of workplace writing. They interviewed selected members of a state agency (a social services department), analyzed documents, and asked members of the organization to judge the writing style of other members of the organization. They report findings from their study in three frequently cited texts: "Writing in a Non-Academic Setting" in *Research in the Teaching of English* [22], "Studying Writing in Non-Academic Settings" in *New Essays* [23], and "Beyond the Text: Relations Between Writing and Social Context" in *Writing in Nonacademic Settings* [21]. Their findings emphasize the importance of the audience and the context in determining what the writer said and how the writer presented the information.

The Odell and Goswami research set the standard for workplace studies by technical communication researchers; their edited collection *Writing in Nonacademic Settings* [21], is the forum for three points of reference:

> "Writing at Exxon ITD: Notes on the Writing Environment of an R&D Organization" [6]
> "What We Learn from Writing on the Job" [24]
> "What Survey Research Tells Us About Writing at Work" [25]

Each is empirical, descriptive research employing social science procedures to study writing in the workplace. James Paradis, David Dobrin, and Richard Miller surveyed 33 professionals and then spent one week conducting interviews and observing writing in the research and development operation of a Exxon ITD. Their findings focus on how writing responsibilities match with position in the company, productivity, and dissemination of information. Lester Faigley and Thomas Miller surveyed and interviewed 200 workers in Texas and Louisiana from across professions, focusing their questions on the time spent writing, the type of writing, and whether the writing was collaboratively produced. Paul Anderson's meta-analysis of 50 surveys and the numerous conclusions he draws from the results reinforce the importance of writing for different readers and the variety of writing tasks in which professionals participate.

Reports of research into professional writing activities are also found in Jack Selzer's [26] case study of one engineer and Stephen Doheny-Farina's [27] study of a start-up company. Selzer found that his subject spent more time at the invention stage ("analyzing audiences, reading, consulting colleagues, brainstorming, and reviewing previously written documents" [26, p. 181]), with arrangement dictated by client require-ments, and little time spent on revision. Doheny-Farina studies the collaborative writing effort of a company's officers. His ethnographic study traces a company's business plan from its drafting by the company's president to the involvement of the vice presidents to such an extent that they discovered while writing the business plan that the president wielded more power than they realized and that he had mismanaged the finances of the company. Doheny-Farina witnessed firsthand the collaborative efforts of the vice presidents and the president in reorganizing the company.

Two studies of collaboration continue the studies of the rhetoric of communities. Nancy Allen, Dianne Atkinson, Meg Morgan, Teresa Moore, and Craig Snow interviewed 20 professionals participating in collaborative projects. They found that for professionals "revision, like planning, was a group activity . . . and it often involved renewed planning" [28, p. 79]. Lisa Ede and Andrea Lunsford found a hierarchical mode of collaboration: "carefully, often rigidly, structured, driven by highly specific goals, and carried out by people playing clearly defined and delimited roles" [29, p. 133]. They did not find the dialogic mode as prevalent in professions where problems required immediate response. The authors of the points of reference collected data in several ways to get as complete a picture of the community as possible. Finally, Winsor's "The Construction of Knowledge in Organizations" [30] cautions that researchers, including herself, may oversimplify the rhetorical process and the role communal knowledge plays in decision making. She reviews studies of the *Challenger* disaster that focus on the problems in com-municating information within the hierarchy of an organization and among organizations.

Studies of the rhetoric of different communities are central to tech-nical communication research on professional activities. These studies and theoretical discussions give legitimacy to the academic side of the profession and illustrate the power of understanding rhetoric.

Document Design, Technology, and Legitimacy

Document design gives technical communication its public identity and purpose, particularly beyond the academy. It legitimizes the role of technical communicators as they develop documents for disseminating information. The points of reference changed the most between Set I and Set II in document design (Table 4). The evolution of technical com-munication must occur quickly here; otherwise, the profession will fall behind in its contributions to a community's communication activities. The points of reference represent three strands of influence: cognitive

Table 4. Points of Reference Focused on Document Design,
Technology, and Authority

	Document design	I	II	III	B
Brockmann, John	• *Writing Better Computer User Documentation: From Paper to Hypertext* • *Writing Better Computer User Documentation: From Paper to Online*		✓	✓	✓
Carroll, John	*The Nurnberg Funnel: Designing Minimalist Instructions for Practical Computer Skills*		✓	✓	
Flower, Linda Hayes, John Swarts, Heidi	Revising Functional Documents: The Scenario Principle, *New Essays in Technical and Scientific Communication*	✓			
Horton, William	• *Designing and Writing Online Documentation: Help Files to Hypertext* • *Designing and Writing Online Documentation: Hypermedia for Self-Supporting Products*		✓	✓	
Huckin, Thomas	A Cognitive Approach to Readability, *New Essays in Technical and Scientific Communication*	✓			
Tufte, Edward	*The Visual Display of Quantitative Information*		✓	✓	✓

psychology, rhetoric of visuals, and technology. Each considers the audience and the context within which the end user works and documents are constructed.

One strand represents the influence of cognitive psychology in document design. A study by Linda Flower, John Hayes, and Heidi Swarts [31] and a survey of reading theories by Thomas Huckin [32] appear in *New Essays in Technical and Scientific Communication*. Both studies, written to help technical communication professionals understand the reader, are far less theoretical than might be found in a psychology forum. Moreover, the jargon from psychology is defined for readers of *New Essays*. The scenario principle, explained and tested by Flower, Hayes, and Swarts, "states that functional prose should be structured around a *human agent* performing *actions* in a particularized *situation*" [31, p. 42]. In addition, the authors identify revision strategies and focus on task completion centered on the writer's actions. Huckin [32] reviews the key theories and document design features recommended by cognitive psychologists before he reviews readability. He does not discard readability formulas, but he favors process descriptions from cognitive psychology.

Edward Tufte contributes to discussions of the rhetoric of visuals, the second strand of document design represented by the points of reference. In *The Visual Display of Quantitative Information*, Tufte gives a history of graphics before proposing a series of principles that "provide a language for discussing graphics and a practical theory of data graphics" [33, p. 9]. Data graphics "help people reason about quantitative information" [33, p. 92]. Tufte continues to build his theory of visuals in *Envisioning Information* (1990) [34] and *Visual Explanations: Images and Quantities, Evidence and Narrative* (1997) [35]. Visuals are no longer simply support features in documents; their importance is now equal to verbal features. Tufte's work has contributed to this development.

Documentation of technology—all technology, not just personal computers—represents a third strand of document design. Changes in technology require change in how technical communicators present materials to their audience—particularly computer and software documentation. John Carroll's *The Nurnberg Funnel: Designing Minimalist Instructions for Practical Computer Skills* [36] provides background and empirical research support for developing instructions that "obstruct as little as possible the learner's self-initiated efforts to find meaning in the activities of learning" [36, p. xvii]. Carroll describes instructions that work with user's errors to respond to the user's need for information. *Minimalism* is the keyword associated with Carroll. (I am currently exploring how the concept of minimalism reaches beyond computer documentation to the relatively recent increase in computer-generated presentations in Microsoft PowerPoint or Lotus Freelance, for example, and the emphasis on a minimum use of text and increased use of visuals [37].)

William Horton [38, 39] and John Brockmann [40, 41] each contribute two books to the documentation of technology. Brockmann takes us from paper to online to hypertext in developing documentation for computer use. Horton focuses on online documentation and help files as hypertext documents. Brockmann and Horton provide guidelines for developing

computer documentation (often presented in workshops for practitioners) that continue to be cited in *Technical Communication* articles such
as "Re-engineering Online Documentation: Designing Examples-based
Online Support Systems" [42] and "The Logical and Rhetorical Construction of Procedural Discourse" [43].

The studies "test" the rhetoric of a community's action and tie
the findings to teaching and practice activities. While none of the studies
of the rhetoric of communities look specifically at computer documentation, they do study collaboration and the development and use
of documents. There may be several reasons for this. Studies of computer documentation appear in journals such as *Journal of Computer
Documentation* and *Human-Computer Interaction,* which were not a part of
my study. Studies focused on computer documentation have quickly
become out-of-date and thus had a short citation life with the rapid
technological changes of the 1980s and 1990s. Finally, points of reference tend to involve more theoretical discussions and more broadly
applied research findings. The topics included in the points of reference
as part of the technical communication knowledge base illustrate
diversity in documents and communities studied but they also
demonstrate a common interest in the study of the rhetorical, social
context of genre use.

POWER, STATUS, AND LEGITIMACY IN
THE KNOWLEDGE BASE

Bazerman suggests that understanding the conversations of our
profession gives us "sufficient voice to assert [our] projects, particularly
if the projects are conceived and carried out well within the standards of
the community" and "occasionally, . . . establishing new social relations
can have revolutionary impact on the community" [2, p. 326]. All the
points of reference (Table 1) represent a significant portion of the community's standards. Comparing Set I, Set II, and Set III illustrates the
evolution of the profession while Set B illustrates a strong knowledge base
for technical communication.

Our power, status, and legitimacy lies in two areas of the knowledge
base: the rhetoric of communities and document design. First, our
research and theory-building on the rhetoric of communities have become
more prominent in our scholarship and composition theory has become
less influential. Emerging out of the studies are a rhetoric of technology
and a rhetoric of visuals. Discussions of ethical issues have become less
prominent.

Our primary research involves onsite studies of the rhetoric of
a community, particularly workplace writing, and our theories are

developing out of rhetorical theory, genre analysis, and activity theory to form a rhetoric of technology. Much of the foundational work lies in Kuhn's *The Structure of Scientific Revolutions* [8] and Bazerman's *Shaping Written Knowledge* [2] with two works added from Set III: Carolyn Millers' "Genre as Social Action" [44] and Carol Berkenkotter and Thomas Huckin's *Genre Knowledge in Disciplinary Communication: Cognition, Culture, Power* [45]. (Miller's "Genre" just missed the cutoff criteria for Set II, but it received a significant number of references in Set III. Its influence cannot be overlooked. *Genre Knowledge* was picked up and cited frequently in the review for Set III because of Huckin's earlier contributions.) Studies of specific professional communities dominate academic research and theoretical studies in technical communication—or at least those published in the five technical communication journals reviewed for this study. For example, Paradis, Dobrin, and R. Miller's [6] study of Exxon is still prominent. Winsor's contributions go beyond "Construction" [30] to include references to several of her other works, all focused on a community of writers and their work, for example *Writing Like an Engineer* [46] and "Invention and Writing in Technical Work: Representing the Object" [47]. Technical communication researchers study communication activities as catastrophic as the *Challenger* (one of Winsor's studies) or as routine as the writing environment at Exxon in an attempt to understand and develop more effective workplace communication.

The rhetoric of technology is evolving from studies of the rhetoric of different communities. It is concerned with the communication of daily activities frequently developed collaboratively and in response to explicit need. One indication of the developing rhetoric of technology is a recent special issue of *JBTC* (July 1998) and the attention of Carolyn Miller, Bazerman, Winsor, and others working through the intricacies of theory building. Another example is the formation of the IText Working Group, also described in a recent *JBTC* article (July 2001) and on the Web site www.ItextNext.org. The founding members are many of the authors of points of references discussed here (Bazerman, Doheny-Farina, Lunsford, and Miller). They are joined by authors Cheryl Geisler, Laura Gurak, Christina Haas, Johndan Johnson-Eilola, and David Kaufer. The group focuses on "information technologies with texts at their core—the blend of IT and texts that we call *ITexts*" [48, p. 270]. They are studying, for example, the World Wide Web (WWW) and personal digital assistants (PDAs) because these technologies "have initiated social and material changes that appear to be altering the very character of texts and the interactions of those who use them" [48, p. 270]. The authors identify their theoretical and research methods as based in the rhetoric of science, genre analysis, activity theory, literacy studies, usability research, and workplace writing. A rhetoric of technology is emerging.

Understanding of the rhetoric of visuals also is emerging in technical communication texts. At least one of Tufte's three books are referred to in almost every article discussing visuals since 1997 (see, for example, "A Cross-Cultural Comparison of the Use of Graphics in Scientific and Technical Communication" [49]). Most of the references to Tufte are found in the practitioner-based journals *Technical Communication* and *IEEE Transactions on Professional Communication*, which is the main reason I placed Tufte's *The Visual Display of Quantitative Information* with the document design texts (Table 4). However, his theory forms a framework for discussing the rhetorical characteristics of visuals. Tufte's *Visual Display* [33] is an example of how technical communication professionals reach outside of technical communication for help explaining technical communication. Much of the discussion before Tufte's work entered our conversations concerned the various types of visuals (i.e., bar graph, line drawing). This strand of rhetorical study has direct implications for technical documents (see for example, Ty Herrington [50] and Sam Dragga and Dan Voss [51]). It will be interesting to see if the full collection and analysis of Set III (1998-2002) yields points of reference on visual communication by technical communication professionals.

Professional ethical standards have evolved in part out of the rhetorical studies and discussions of professionalism and in part out of the workplace activities and responsibilities of technical communicators. The range of documents and their different purposes require good judgment by the technical communicator. Fair and ethical behavior gains respect and power in communication activities. The points of reference by Katz [12], Sullivan [13], and Miller [7] directly address the power of rhetoric and the responsibility technical communicators have. These discussions are directed toward teachers of future technical communicators. It appears that discussions of the ethics of technical communication are receiving less attention (only Miller's text appears in Set B and in the Set III collection). Or perhaps, ethical behavior is a professional standard that no longer needs acknowledgment in a citation.

Second, computer documentation has a prominent place in the practice-based discussions frequently cited. More general discussions of document design are not referred to as often but are very much a part of our conversations. The prominence of computer documentation in the points of reference should be no surprise. Rapid developments in the computer industry over the past three decades have provided technical communicators with increased responsibilities and visibility. Technical communicators have become authorities on computer documentation. The extent of the influence of three authors—Brockmann, Carroll, and

Horton in the practice-based journals *IEEE Transactions on Professional Communication* and *Technical Communication* — is signaled by the frequency of references to each. What is missing are discussions of other document design issues — those issues that change quickly with developments in business and industry. Citation collection requires sustained influence, difficult to capture in a rapidly changing environment. To compensate for this, readers should review sources such as STC's *Technical Communication*, the "Recent and Relevant" section in *Technical Communication*, and the "ATTW Annual Bibliography" found in the fall issue of *Technical Communication Quarterly* to get a better view of the practice-based genealogy of technical communication.

The power, status, and legitimacy of technical communication professionals reside in their understanding of rhetoric in its different settings and uses. The points of reference serve as examples of conversations in the profession — its intellectual genealogy. The texts of Set B continue to contribute to the discussion after 10 years, and Set III identifies the continued influence of some of the points of reference. Technical communicators exert their power as professionals who understand rhetorics of technology and visuals and contribute to the construction of documents. New, and at times revolutionary, projects will also contribute to a solid knowledge base; however, they are more difficult to recognize and are lost in a study based on citations such as this one.

The focus of this chapter has been on the 26 points of reference. They are a part of our intellectual genealogy that gives technical communication a legitimacy and a knowledge base to build upon. Our power and legitimacy continue to be in understanding the rhetoric of documents and the analysis of genres and the contexts in which they are used. While computer documentation is a significant portion of our work, it is certainly not the only document or communication activity we make significant contributions to. Our status allows technical communicators to work with those not in our profession who do not have an understanding of the power of rhetoric in the development of documents.

REFERENCES

1. S. Toulmin, *Human Understanding: The Collective Use and Evolution of Concepts*, Oxford, Clarendon Press, 1972.
2. C. Bazerman, *Shaping Written Knowledge: The Genre and Activity of the Experimental Article in Science*, Madison, University of Wisconsin Press, 1988.
3. D. L. Sullivan, Displaying Disciplinarity, *Written Communication*, 13:2, pp. 221-250, 1996.
4. E. O. Smith, Points of Reference in Technical Communication Scholarship, *Technical Communication Quarterly*, 9:3, pp. 427-453, 2000.

5. E. O. Smith, Strength in the Technical Communication Journals and Diversity in the Serials Cited, *Journal of Business and Technical Communication*, 14:3, pp. 131-184, 2000.

6. J. Paradis, D. Dobrin, and R. Miller, Writing at Exxon ITD: Notes on the Writing Environment of an R&D Organization, *Writing in Nonacademic Settings*, L. Odell and D. Goswami (eds.), Guilford, New York, pp. 281-307, 1985.

7. C. R. Miller, A Humanistic Rationale for Technical Writing, *College English*, 40:6, pp. 610-617, 1979.

8. T. S. Kuhn, *The Structure of Scientific Revolutions* (2nd Edition), University of Chicago Press, Chicago, 1970.

9. P. Moore, Instrumental Discourse Is as Humanistic as Rhetoric, *Journal of Business and Technical Communication*, 10:1, pp. 100-118, 1996.

10. D. N. Dobrin, What's Technical about Technical Writing, in *New Essays in Technical and Scientific Communication: Research, Theory, Practice*, P. V. Anderson, R. J. Brockmann, and C. R. Miller (eds.), Baywood, Amityville, New York, pp. 227-250, 1983.

11. D. N. Dobrin, *Writing and Technique*, National Council of Teachers of English, Urbana, Illinois, 1989.

12. S. B. Katz, The Ethic of Expediency: Classical Rhetoric, Technology, and the Holocaust, *College English*, 54:3, pp. 255-275, 1992.

13. D. L. Sullivan, Political-Ethical Implications of Defining Technical Communication as a Practice, *Journal of Advanced Composition*, 10:2, pp. 375-386, 1990.

14. K. Bruffee, Collaborative Learning and the 'Conversation of Mankind,' *College English*, 46:7, pp. 635-652, 1984.

15. L. Faigley, Nonacademic Writing: The Social Perspective, in *Writing in Nonacademic Settings*, L. Odell and D. Goswami (eds.), Guilford, New York, pp. 231-280, 1985.

16. P. V. Anderson, R. J. Brockmann, and C. R. Miller (eds.), *New Essays in Technical and Scientific Communication: Research, Theory, Practice*, Baywood, Amityville, New York, 1983.

17. N. W. Coppola, Setting the Discourse Community: Tasks and Assessment for the New Technical Communication Service Course, *Technical Communication Quarterly*, 8:3, pp. 249-267, 1999.

18. C. David and D. Kienzler, Towards an Emancipatory Pedagogy in Service Courses and User Departments, *Technical Communication Quarterly*, 8:3, pp. 269-283, 1999.

19. M. S. MacNealy and L. B. Heaton, Can This Marriage be Saved: Is an English Department a Good Home for Technical Communication? *Journal of Technical Writing and Communication*, 29:1, pp. 41-64, 1999.

20. C. R. Miller, What's Practical About Technical Writing?, in *Technical Writing: Theory and Practice*, B. E. Fearing and W. K. Sparrow (eds.), Modern Language Association, New York, pp. 14-24, 1989.

21. L. Odell and D. Goswami (eds.), *Writing in Nonacademic Settings*, Guilford, New York, 1985.

22. L. Odell and D. Goswami, Writing in a Non-Academic Setting, *Research in the Teaching of English, 16*:3, pp. 201-223, 1982.
23. L. Odell, D. Goswami, A. Herrington, and D. Quick, Studying Writing in Non-Academic Settings, in *New Essays in Technical and Scientific Communication: Research, Theory, Practice*, P. V. Anderson, R. J. Brockmann, and C. R. Miller, Baywood, Amityville, New York, pp. 17-40, 1983.
24. L. Faigley and T. Miller, What We Learn from Writing on the Job, *College English, 44*:6, pp. 557-569, 1982.
25. P. V. Anderson, What Survey Research Tells Us About Writing at Work, in *Writing in Nonacademic Settings*, L. Odell and D. Goswami (eds.), Guilford, New York, pp. 3-83, 1985.
26. J. Selzer, The Composing Process of an Engineer, *College Composition and Communication, 34*:2, pp. 178-187, 1983.
27. S. Doheny-Farina, Writing in an Emerging Organization, *Written Communication, 3*:2, pp. 158-185, 1986.
28. N. Allen, D. Atkinson, M. Morgan, T. Moore, and C. Snow, What Experienced Collaborators Say About Collaborative Writing, *Journal of Business and Technical Communication, 1*:2, pp. 70-90, 1987.
29. L. Ede and A. Lunsford, *Singular Texts/Plural Authors: Perspectives on Collaborative Writing*, Southern Illinois Press, Carbondale, Illinois, 1990.
30. D. A. Winsor, The Construction of Knowledge in Organizations: Asking the Right Questions about the *Challenger, Journal of Business and Technical Communication, 4*:2, pp. 7-21, 1990.
31. L. Flower, J. R. Hayes, and H. Swarts, Revising Functional Documents: The Scenario Principle, in *New Essays in Technical and Scientific Communication: Research, Theory, Practice*, P. V. Anderson, R. J. Brockmann, and C. R. Miller (eds.), Baywood, Amityville, New York, pp. 41-58, 1983.
32. T. Huckin, A Cognitive Approach to Readability, *New Essays in Technical and Scientific Communication: Research, Theory, Practice*, P. V. Anderson, R. J. Brockmann, and C. R. Miller (eds.), Baywood, Amityville, New York, pp. 90-108, 1983.
33. E. R. Tufte, *The Visual Display of Quantitative Information*, Graphics Press, Cheshire, Connecticut, 1983.
34. E. R. Tufte, *Envisioning Information*, Graphics Press, Cheshire, Connecticut, 1990.
35. E. R. Tufte, *Visual Explanations: Images and Quantities, Evidence and Narrative*, Graphics Press, Cheshire, Connecticut, 1997.
36. J. M. Carroll, *The Nurnberg Funnel: Designing Minimalist Instructions for Practical Computer Skills*, MIT Press, Cambridge, Massachusetts, 1990.
37. E. O. Smith, *Reports to Presentations – Explanations to Visuals*, Association for Business Communication Annual Convention, Atlanta, Georgia, October 2000.
38. W. Horton, *Designing and Writing Online Documentation: Help Files to Hypertext*, Wiley, New York, 1990.
39. W. Horton, *Designing and Writing Online Documentation: Hypermedia for Self-Supporting Products* (2nd Edition), Wiley, New York, 1994.

40. R. J. Brockmann, *Writing Better Computer User Documentation: From Paper to Hypertext*, Wiley, New York, 1990.
41. R. J. Brockmann, *Writing Better Computer User Documentation: From Paper to Online*, Wiley-Interscience, New York, 1986.
42. M. D. Tomasi and B. Mehlenbacher, Re-Engineering Online Documentation: Designing Examples-Based Online Support Systems, *Technical Communication*, 46:1, pp. 55-66, 1999.
43. D. K. Farkas, The Logical and Rhetorical Construction of Procedural Discourse, *Technical Communication*, 46:1, pp. 42-54, 1999.
44. C. R. Miller, Genre as Social Action, *College English*, 70:1, pp. 151-167, 1984.
45. C. Berkenkotter and T. N. Huckin, *Genre Knowledge in Disciplinary Communication: Cognition, Culture, Power*, Erlbaum, Hillsdale, New Jersey, 1995.
46. D. A. Winsor, *Writing Like an Engineer: An Rhetorical Education*, Erlbaum, Mahwah, New Jersey, 1996.
47. D. A. Winsor, Invention and Writing in Technical Work: Representing the Object, *Written Communication*, 11:2, pp. 227-250, 1994.
48. C. Geisler, C. Bazerman, S. Doheny-Farina, L. Gurak, C. Haas, J. Johnson-Eilola, D. S. Kaufer, A. Lunsford, C. R. Miller, D. Winsor, and J. Yates, IText: Future Directions for Research on the Relationship between Information Technology and Writing, *Journal of Business and Technical Communication*, 15:3, pp. 269-308, 2001.
49. W. Quiye, A Cross-Cultural Comparison of the Use of Graphics in Scientific and Technical Communication, *Technical Communication*, 47:4, pp. 553-560, 2000.
50. T. K. Herrington, Ethics and Graphic Design: Rhetorical Analysis of the Document Design, in *The Report of the Bureau of Alcohol, Tobacco, and Firearms Investigation of Vernon Wayne Howell also known as David Koresh*, *IEEE Transaction on Professional Communication*, 38:3, pp. 151-157, 1995.
51. S. Dragga and D. Voss, Cruel Pies: The Inhumanity of Technical Illustrations, *Technical Communication*, 48:3, pp. 265-274, 2001.

PART II

Strategies for Contemporary Practice

CHAPTER 4

Shaping the Future of
Our Profession*

Marjorie T. Davis

A few years ago I was in a group of STC members who are primarily contractors. One of them turned to me and asked, "What's the next tool I have to learn to stay employed—is it RoboHelp, or HTML, or what?" When I answered that I was not convinced that just tools were the answer, he obviously thought I had lost my mind. The tool's the *only* thing, he probably thought. What else is there?

The common lament heard among technical communication practitioners today is their struggle to keep up with the tools. Almost every job advertisement lists advanced software that technical communicators need to know, and that list changes frequently. It is no wonder that many of us feel that the tail is wagging the dog.

None of us would deny the importance of knowing the tools. Mercer alumni who are technical communicators report that they are usually the first in their company to learn and use a tool, and the first to recommend discarding one that has become obsolete. If you are not able to use at least one tool in each major software category, you are at a distinct disadvantage in the job market.

*This essay originally appeared in *Technical Communication*, 48:2, 2002. It is reprinted with permission from *Technical Communication*, the journal of the Society for Technical Communication, Arlington, Virginia, U.S.A.

The future of the technical communication profession is obviously tied intimately into the future of technologies. But unless technical communicators want to remain in a servant role, we must become more than tool jockeys. We must complete the evolution from craftspersons to professionals. As we do so, we follow the same kinds of patterns that such professions as medicine and engineering have followed: from apprenticeships, through developing college degree requirements, to establishing peer review and professional standards. This view of the future frightens many of those practicing today, just as it must have frightened those in the developing days of medicine or engineering. Their paths to professionalism may be instructive for us.

THE RISE TO PROFESSIONAL STATUS

"Professional" is a term that is used rather loosely. In common parlance it sometimes means simply one who makes a living by a particular trade—as in a "professional hairdresser" or "professional wrestler." The status to which we aspire is rather more difficult to obtain and has certain standards, as described by the development of medicine as a profession: ". . . professional status for the individual is achieved only after long training, ordinarily in a manner prescribed by the profession itself, and . . . this training is enforced by the state or other outside agencies" [1, p. 2]. The extensive training or education is intended "to initiate the candidate into a set of professional attitudes and controls, to give him [or her] a professional conscience, and to develop a feeling of group solidarity" [1, p. 2]. Probably the most widely respected profession is medicine.

Medicine was not always held in such high regard; prior to its full development as a profession, it evolved from what Lewis describes as the age of "magic and faith" (1000-1492 A.D.), through "surgery and a shave" (1492-1776), to its current basis in clinical science [2, pp. 8-13]. Tebeaux gives us a fascinating glimpse of medical practice in the English Renaissance, when the newly literate public, who could not afford doctors, sought out technical manuals describing folk wisdom, practices passed down through families, and superstition [3]. It would be years before medical schools were established, degree programs accredited, and practitioners licensed. The first medical schools in America were the College of Philadelphia (1765) and New York's King College (1768); the first to be designed around a modern medical concept was Johns Hopkins in 1876. The first U.S. school to offer degrees in medicine as well as sciences and engineering was The University of Michigan at Ann Arbor [4]. Today, medical schools must be accredited by their professional organizations and doctors must be certified by boards before they can practice.

Steps toward Professional Status

So how did medical doctors achieve the prestige they currently enjoy? How did their profession evolve? Bullough's description of the tasks associated with developing the medical profession outlines these steps:

1. Developing a specialized body of knowledge
2. Institutionalizing this knowledge in universities
3. Relying on professional societies to qualify practitioners
4. Developing ethics codes
5. Enjoying increased status (including money, power, and respect)
6. Being viewed by members as a "terminal occupation" (i.e., members did not leave) [1, pp. 4-5].

Engineers have followed a similar path to professional status. As with medicine, engineering has always incorporated practice as well as education. In America, engineers were able to take advantage of two European models from France and England. The first formally organized school of engineering in the world was École des Ponts et Chaussées, established in 1775. France thus provided engineers from this academic model. By contrast, tradesmen coming from England were trained by a formal system of apprenticeships. Americans aspiring to become engineers blended these two approaches. By the early nineteenth century, both mechanics institutes (such as Franklin Institute in Philadelphia) and college degree programs (at West Point and Rensselaer) were in existence. As America moved into settling the West and constructing railroads and industries, the demand grew for a systematic engineering education grounded in both theory and practice. Engineering education gained tremendous impetus when the Morrill Land Grant Act was passed in 1862, the same year that Congress charted the transcontinental railroad, signed the Homestead Act, and fostered the rapid expansion of the telegraph [5]. Today, engineers who expect to practice their profession must graduate from a college program judged by professionals as accredited — that is, meeting at least the minimum standards for degrees [6]. In some fields, engineers must also be certified by their state's Board to earn the Professional Engineer (PE) license.

Professions Require Education and Practice

What both of these professions have in common is a dual focus on practice and education: "education affects practice, and practice affects education; the two progress hand in hand and their histories are so intertwined that neither can be understood fully without knowledge of the other" [4, p. 7]. Additionally, both medicine and engineering evolved from humble beginnings as trades learned from practitioners or on the job. As they evolved into true professions, they went through a process of 1) establishing professional minimum competencies, 2) establishing and accrediting degree programs, and 3) testing or licensure of professionals to practice. It is my premise that technical communication is poised to achieve professional status, if we are willing to take the steps medicine and engineering took.

RISE OF PROFESSIONALISM
IN TECHNICAL COMMUNICATION

Those of us who have been in technical communication careers for at least a decade came from other career fields. We were either technically educated people who learned to communicate, or communicators who learned to deal with technology. What we knew in the early days came from formal training in fields other than technical communication, plus what we learned from on-the-job-training, or apprenticeship. We tended to think of ourselves primarily as writers, though we acquired additional skillsets as the jobs advanced. We sometimes complained that we were treated as second-class citizens, especially in highly technical industries. Almost no one would have described us as professionals. With the proliferation of degree programs and the escalating demands of information technology, however, we may be already undergoing a significant change.

A Small Illustrative Survey

Snapshots of those currently studying technical communication at the master's or doctoral level can provide a glimpse of where we are. An informal ethnographic survey of master's degree students in one recent graduate class at Mercer was done to determine the backgrounds, degrees, and job titles of the 20 students. While the data are not taken from a large enough sample to draw significant conclusions, we can still make some observations about these practitioners who are taking an advanced degree in technical communication.

The class of 20 students consisted of 8 males and 12 females. Eleven of them had earned bachelor of science degrees, eight bachelor of arts, and one BBA. Their majors in undergraduate school were Social Sciences (8), Humanities (6), Sciences/Engineering/Computer Science (4), Technical Communication (2), and Music (1), with one person holding a double major. Three students already held master's degrees (English,

Human Resource Development, and Library Science). Their average age was mid-thirties.

Their career paths leading them into technical communication were varied:

- Undergraduate major or emphasis in technical communication (4)
- Teacher or trainer (4)
- Journalist or public relations (4)
- Engineering (3)
- Sales and marketing (2)
- Technical writer (2)
- Librarian (1)

At the time of the survey, these were their job titles:

- Trainer or educator (7)
- Designer or developer (5)
- Manager or director (4)
- Writer or Editor (2)
- Sales and marketing (1)

One person was not employed full time at the time of the survey, but had worked in documentation prior to the course.

Their employers ranged from computer-related companies, to technical communication companies, to government/defense industries, to education, to banking or business, to manufacturing.

The New Professionals

It is significant to us that for the first time, in 1998-99, we had young graduate students entering our MS in Technical Communication Management program with undergraduate technical communication degrees. Those young professionals saw themselves quite differently from many of the older students who had drifted into technical communication: they had a firm grasp of the field and knew why they were there. Most importantly, they saw themselves as participants in a separate profession, while some of the older students informally called themselves by titles related to their "old" discipline. It is obvious that the paradigm is shifting year by year as more undergraduates holding technical communication degrees enter the job market and graduate programs.

In Mercer's graduate programs, we note that graduates from strong technical communication programs see themselves as new kinds of professionals: not writers, not programmers, not engineers, but *technical communicators.* Armed with an arsenal of theory wedded to practice, they are entering the workforce with competence and confidence. The profession will never be the same again.

Degree Programs in Technical Communication

Rensselaer Polytechnic Institute offered the first graduate degree in technical communication in 1958; today, more than 220 programs are offered in colleges and universities [7, 8]. These degree programs grew by the work of faculty who had a strong commitment to technical communication. They were located in a number of disciplinary settings and reflect a number of different disciplinary influences: English, Journalism, Communication, Engineering, Agriculture, or Business programs. Because academic promotion and tenure rules require us to fit into our departments, we grew differently depending upon where we were planted. Our research has tended to be shaped by the standards of scholarship of whatever discipline we belonged to — sometimes with good results for the emerging profession, sometimes not. As Keene points out, technical communication faculty attempting to become tenured in traditional academic departments such as English often find a disconnect: for technical communicators, "industry demands applied research, while academe rewards pure research" in a traditional literary field. The kind of practice-based research and teaching needed in engineering and medicine is also needed in technical communication, yet few academic departments embrace this professional approach [8].

In the last 10 years, technical communication has begun to emerge from other disciplines as an identifiable field of its own. We are beginning to develop core knowledge that transcends our own disciplinary locales. Technical communication graduates entering the field are beginning to define themselves in new, more professional ways. Unfortunately, degree programs have not kept pace with the evolution towards professionalism. In fact, a large portion of practitioners have not kept pace either. A quick review of proceedings from recent professional society conferences will reveal a serious deficit in understanding and using the very good knowledge that is being developed in our field. As Hackos says, technical communication is rapidly moving from a cottage industry to a more demanding, more professional field; we must decide whether we want to lead or be left behind [9].

FROM TECHNICIAN TO PROFESSIONAL

Engineers make a distinction between technicians and engineers that could be useful for us: *technicians* are skilled in the technology and can fix something that is broken, but *engineers* can do the original design work to create a new product. That image is instructive for technical communicators: as long as we remain at the end of the product cycle, reacting to the design work of others, we remain in the lower status of technicians. When we assume the role of information creators and designers—team members and equals with engineers, programmers, and others—we are functioning as professionals.

New Knowledge Domains

If we choose to move into the wider arena as knowledge creator, knowledge manager, or information designer, we will be called upon to master a number of new concepts that have not traditionally been part of our education. Creating usable information calls upon the ancient rhetorical base established by Aristotle; yet relying only on ancient rhetorical theory will seriously impede our professional progress. As one colleague asked, how many of us who claim to be in the persuasion business (rhetoric) have read the recent empirical research in psychology or political science? The multidisciplinarity (cross-functionality) of today's tasks demands that we build a broader base of knowledge than we have gained within a single discipline.

One new knowledge domain is that of practice:

> . . . academic programs in technical communication must, whatever else, be grounded in the writing and communication that real people—engineers, architects, social workers, etc.—do outside the classroom and beyond the campus [8, p. 194].

Most likely, a majority of those teaching technical communication have never worked in business or industrial settings. Even if we cannot work as technical communicators outside academe, we can develop student projects and research projects that extend our knowledge base. Research into best practices within different communities is an area that is receiving deserved attention. On-site studies of technical communication often reveal important insights into knowledge management and development that industry finds very valuable [see 10].

Another new knowledge domain is technical subjects. Many articles have been written about the two halves of knowledge implied by the name *technical communication*, yet many practitioners and academics focus almost solely on the communication aspects.

> We need more than a basic understanding of the technology, science, or other specialized information we convey to the users of the documents we create. Without the insights and experience gained by

specialized domain knowledge, we can't transfer that knowledge effectively to our audiences. Even more importantly, without a thorough grounding in the domain, we lack the ability to ask the right questions of subject matter experts and to understand their answers [11].

Again, academics can extend our knowledge base by working directly with colleagues in technical disciplines and by learning from them. Additionally, we can take advantage of the many opportunities to learn about technical subjects by searching the Web or reading specialized journals or magazines. Devoting the same kind of attention to technology as we do to texts can yield impressive gains in this knowledge domain.

Because usability is one of the most important knowledge domains, technical communicators must be able to understand and apply the important principles of human behavior and capabilities. For example, William Gribbons has pointed out that knowledge of human factors is essential. The program he helped design for Bentley College offers a master's degree in Human Factors and Information Design that

- emphasizes human behavior relative to learning, understanding and effectively implementing new technologies;
- defines information design broadly to include documentation, the user interface, training systems, the World Wide Web, and e-commerce;
- develops localization strategy, emphasizing design, communication, and training; and
- explores the integration of information and technology while also promoting the long-term goal of engineering knowledge-based technology products.[1]

Human factors such as cognition and perception dramatically affect the way we should design information, yet few programs are incorporating this knowledge. A few individuals in academic leadership positions are beginning to define core knowledge in ways that will significantly affect the capabilities of their future practitioners, and others can learn from them.

The ever-widening field of knowledge for technical communications certainly includes tools and rhetoric, but it is much larger: best practices, user interface design, the life cycle of software development, the engineering design process with its iteration and optimization, technological trends, internationalization, cross-functional teams, etc.

---

[1] Bentley College. http://www.bentley.edu/graduate/mshfid/hfidprogram.htm

Most of these knowledge areas are a result of the powerful influence of information technology on our lives. When we look at our profession in this way, just keeping up with the tools seems to be the least of our worries.

EDUCATING FUTURE PROFESSIONALS

To the extent that we understand and integrate information technology in all its aspects into our programs, we can be successful in contributing to the growth of the profession and to the greater status and capabilities of our graduates. If we remain locked into the image of educating writers who lack the broad-based technical grounding to succeed in the next 50 years, then we are shortchanging the future of technical communication.

The technical communicator with a degree in field is widely becoming the preferred employee in industry; yet employers complain that there is no consistency among graduates and very little assurance that a graduate has a minimum set of capabilities. Perhaps, as George Hayhoe has suggested, that is why most of the job advertisements resort to listing software tools [11]. Without a set of academic standards for degreed professionals, employers haven't much other choice.

Setting the Bar

Professional societies have a significant role in addition to that of academics. In professions such as medicine and engineering, professional societies are responsible for setting standards and establishing minimum qualifications for practice. A number of STC committees over the years have discussed the issues of accreditation of academic programs and of certification of individual practitioners. After long hours of work and some outlay of funding, these groups have not yet suggested workable ways of managing the self-assessment of our profession—perhaps because they have been debating *whether* to do so, not *how*. Let's move on to implementation. While the issues are many, thorny, and difficult, surely we can use the models developed by engineering (or law, or medicine) to set forth standards and to devise the ways to assess achievement.

As long as societies attempt to keep the profession open to anyone who wants to hang out a shingle, practitioners will remain on a level with amateurs or apprentices. The young people walking across graduation stages and into the workforce, and eventually into graduate study, have a right to demand that colleges and universities prepare them widely, deeply, and well. Practitioners who join professional societies have a right to expect that the society will help equip them for practice in careers that are wider and more rewarding than just tool-jockey.

Professional societies have a critical, pivotal role in helping us to shape the future of the discipline and to move our practice into professional levels. It is time for academics, leading practitioners, and representatives of the major professional societies to address the issues of defining core knowledge sets which are far broader than traditional humanities-based degrees. Indeed, this work in establishing professional standards may well be the most important task in our century for the profession of technical communication.

Two Sets of Standards Needed

Two sets of recommendations must be developed: standards for academic programs and standards for those who practice. Both of these efforts will require that we develop consensus on core knowledge, learning outcomes, and levels of proficiency. No academic organization exists that is deep and broad enough to establish such a consensus alone. The professional societies must be the primary agents to initiate the broader discussion.

The Accrediting Board for Engineering and Technology (ABET) exemplifies one model that works. Its predecessor, the Engineers' Council for Professional Development, was established in 1932 as the first "agency to set standards and inspect engineering schools for compliance with such standards." The agency reviewed curricula, faculty qualifications, industry needs, and opinions of alumni [5]. Today, ABET establishes the core competencies every engineer needs, then provides accreditation processes to assure that graduates have these competencies. ABET has the same flaws as any large and diverse organization and is probably plagued by as many conflicts of interest, values, and personalities; yet it accepts the leadership in assuring that American engineers are educated to appropriate professional standards. (For more information on this accrediting agency, see www.abet.org.)

Licensing of individual professionals to practice is usually done by state boards who administer examinations for many professions (such as law, medicine, and engineering). Members of the state boards typically sit in the agency that is reviewing academic programs. Once a professional body agrees upon knowledge, standards, and evaluation methods, then creating and administering an examination should be (comparatively) simple. Working toward a set of standards for accrediting academic programs, therefore, is the first step.

The task will not be easy—but neither has it been easy for law, or medicine, or engineering. Some practitioners will be left by the wayside, and some academic programs will have to dramatically change what and how they teach technical communicators. Even more difficult will be opening our minds and ranks to include people from fields traditionally regarded as far from ours — people who probably do not belong to Society for Technical Communication, or IEEE Professional Communication Society, or Association of Teachers of Technical Writing. In short, what we need is a strong, knowledgeable, cross-functional team to develop the initial set of broad program recommendations.

CONCLUSION

The predictions made by Elizabeth Tebeaux more than a decade ago in "The High-Tech Workplace" are amazingly accurate: information technology has changed our work, the skills we need, the way we communicate and with whom, and the way we should be educating technical communicators [12]. If we fail to recognize and respond to the challenges, we will be abdicating leadership to others and giving up our chance to secure technical communication's place in the future.

REFERENCES

1. V. L. Bullough, *The Development of Medicine as a Profession*, Hafner, Inc., New York, 1966.
2. C. Lewis, Medical Milestones of the Last Millennium, *FDA Consumer, 34*, pp. 8-13, 2000.
3. E. Tebeaux, *The Emergence of a Tradition*, Baywood, Amityville, New York, 1997.
4. J. Bordley, III and A. M. Harvey, *Two Centuries of American Medicine, 1776-1976*, W. B. Saunders, Philadelphia, 1976.
5. L. P. Grayson, *The Making of an Engineer*, John Wiley & Sons, New York, 1993.
6. T. C. Kynell, *Writing in a Milieu of Utility*, Ablex, Norwood, New Jersey, 1996. See also, Technical Communication from 1850-1950: Where Have We Been? *Technical Communication Quarterly, 8*, pp. 143-151, 1999.
7. K. Staples, Technical Communication from 1950-1998: Where Are We Now? *Technical Communication Quarterly, 8*, pp. 153-164, 1999.
8. M. L. Keene, *Education in Scientific and Technical Communication: Academic Programs that Work*, Society for Technical Communication, Arlington, Virginia, 1997.
9. J. T. Hackos, Trends for 2000: Moving Beyond the Cottage, *Intercom, 47*, pp. 6-10, 2000.
10. S. A. Bernhardt and G. A. McCulley, Knowledge Management and Pharmaceutical Development Teams, *IEEE Transactions on Professional Communication/ Technical Communication, 47*, pp. 22-34, 2000.

11. G. Hayhoe, Toolkit for the New Millennium: Communication, Domain, and Software Knowledge, *Proceedings, STC Atlanta Currents 2000,* Mercer University, Atlanta Campus, March 4, 2000.
12. E. Tebeaux, The High-Tech Workplace, in *Technical Writing Theory and Practice,* B. E. Fearing and W. K. Sparrow (eds.), MLA, New York, pp. 136-144, 1989.

CHAPTER 5

Reconfiguring the
Professor-Practitioner Relationship*

Louise Rehling

It is time for the field of technical communication to kiss complacence goodbye. Perhaps the worst sign of current complacence is the puzzling circumstance, identified by Katherine Staples in her summary of where "we" are now as a discipline, of the academy reporting research that practitioners then seem to ignore [1, p. 161]. This speaks less of "we" than of an "us" *versus* "them" dichotomy (or at least "us separate from them"). That is an attitude perhaps best summed up by a long-experienced technical communication practitioner, then a chapter president in the Society of Technical Communication, who assured me, "I never take the plastic wrap off" of that organization's quarterly research journal because "it's all just academic stuff in there."

But there also are signs of complacence on the academic side, in which technical writing programs tend to become "training departments for corporate 'clients'" [2, p. 177], so such programs offer their students only "an empowerment . . . thoroughly mediated . . . by the values of corporate culture" [3, p. 172]. For example, even in an article in which a professor argues for the importance of academic and industry collaborations, the list of potential benefits for industry partners includes

*This chapter is an expansion of the author's article Exchanging Expertise: Learning from the Workplace and Educating It, Too, *Journal of Technical Writing & Communication*, 28:4, pp. 385-393, 1998.

"teaching the academic world about corporate environments," but makes no mention of what practitioners might actually be able to learn in return [4, p. 614].

As Rachel Spilka has documented in some detail [5, pp. 207-208], the prevailing ideology seems to be that the workplace knows best—an ideology that lulls both professors and practitioners into feeling comfortable with a seriously lopsided relationship.

This is dubious progress for a discipline that was born, early in this century, in part due to worries about the "perception of 'training for a trade'" [6, p. 145], yet had moved by mid-century to reliance on workplace practice as the basis for instruction [1, pp. 154-155]. While it still may be true that applied disciplines, such as ours, typically hold lower status than that of abstract, theory-dominated areas of study, the higher status accorded related disciplines, such as engineering and journalism, suggests that technical communication could improve its lot.

To do so, however, would require legitimizing the work of the academy for non-academics in the workplace, which could redress the power imbalance between the two. Only when those in the field show full respect for everyone in it, and for the contributions that they make, can we have any hope for the opinion of others to change. The key to being seen as professionals may well be expanding the notion of professional development to include a higher level of scrutiny of our values: an ethic of not being complacent about the standards that we already hold.

Of course, it already has been asserted (even assumed) that professional development is a critical component of ethical behavior for our field [7], but that means can be defined narrowly. For example, tools training, or standards based on competitions that judge publications divorced from understandings of complex rhetorical context, may provide useful information or enhance careers. But these are not likely methods for encouraging the kind of critical thinking skills that Jack Bushnell recommends for technical communication students [2, p. 185]. What we need to counter our field's current dilemma of complacence is a new point of view that sees practitioners and professors as partners in creating status, legitimacy, and power for all of us whose work associates them with technical communication.

POINT OF VIEW

In arguing, as I will here, that professional communication specialists in the academy should be equal partners in exchanges with professional communication specialists in the workplace, I acknowledge the observation that both are "practitioners" who deserve each others' collegial respect and appreciation [8]. As someone who has had a career as a practitioner (conventionally defined), then settled into a second career as an educator, and since has moved (during a university leave of absence) back into industry, I use those terms to distinguish primary spheres of professional activity and influence, not to imply hierarchy. However, as I will discuss, common academic practices do assume a hierarchy — one that is both false and unhelpful. Revising or supplementing those practices, in ways that I will suggest, to better balance the roles and contributions of both practitioners and educators would be a positive change for our field.

ONE-WAY ASSUMPTION

Professional communication programs prepare students for careers as writers, editors, document designers, presentation developers, and information managers in technology industries, other businesses, government, and nonprofit organizations. As a result of this focused and pragmatic orientation, what is often termed "real world" input is important for helping to define curricula. The need for communication in this direction — from the workplace to the academy — is particularly important for programs that have grown out of traditional departments of English or of Rhetoric and Composition studies. Without outside influence, such programs might otherwise be too divorced from practices in the workplace to usefully prepare students for its realities.

Therefore, educators have rightfully asked workplace practitioners to assist in developing academic programs. However, as a result, practitioners often just learn from academic programs about what those programs need from practitioners. And the range of favors requested is extensive, including:

- Student needs for internships, jobs, and networking contacts.
- Faculty needs for workplace examples, guest speakers, and internships for their own professional development.
- Needs for technology updates, either in the form of information — needing to know which tools are in use and how they are used — and/or in the form of donations or partnering in the purchase of software and equipment.
- Needs for examples and cases to be used in textbooks and for scholarly research — to test generalizations and models against local specifics and to be sure that academic perspectives are grounded, not out of touch, or too theoretical.

The justification for the academy to look to the workplace for help in filling these needs is obvious. Still, when sharing such needs dominates the discourse between educators and practitioners, the result can be that both parties see practitioner accommodations as the goal of their exchanges. For example, a recent report on discussions of the Academe-Industry Advisory Committee of the Society for Technical Communication (STC) reflects just this kind of view: "academics identified support needed from industry" and "industry called for academia to produce technical communicators" who are "trained" to suit industry expectations. To that end, "educators must understand the job market and employers must explain their needs fully" [9, p. 2]. This conclusion suggests only one-way communication: practitioners should talk to educators, and educators should listen.

Such communication is not a bad thing in itself, but as a primary focus, it is problematic: as if "real world" endorsements are what legitimize academic course work in professional communication.

DOWNSIDE OF A ONE-WAY VIEW

Privileging workplace perspectives overwhelmingly devalues both education and professionalism in professional communication.

First, education—a rich experience that contextualizes specific knowledge and encourages focused intellectual development—can seem to compare unfavorably to training, with its emphasis on transferable skills for immediate, narrow applications. Of course, the discredited theory-practice dichotomy does not apply, because the best examples of education and training in professional communication may have much in common in terms of both complexity and pragmatism. Still, the training model, based on apprenticeship practices, typically does not address long-term goals nor provide the necessary range to build foundational competencies or judgment based on principles. Unfortunately, as has been warned [10, p. 254], when practitioners exercise one-way influence on educators, "quick and dirty" course designs might be validated, simply because they suit immediate needs in the workplace.

Second, identifying practitioners' relationship to educators in terms of what practitioners can provide may send a message to those practitioners that they have nothing to learn from scholarly research and teaching. Perhaps some academics send that kind of message out of lack of self-confidence: those trained in the belletristic tradition that is foundational to many English doctoral programs may feel uncertain about tackling the demands of professional writing coursework, so they rely on industry resources as a crutch. Other professors may feel as intimidated and impressed as their students by the material success of industry practitioners or may be influenced by our general culture's worship of the wisdom of the marketplace. And others in the academy simply may find relying on practitioners for curriculum ideas and materials to be the easy way out of the labor required to develop a more comprehensively researched course plan.

Whatever the reasons, the effect of passive acquiescence to practitioner points of view is unfortunate: If the academy is seen just as a corporate convenience—a first step in shortening the on-the-job training process—then it is not a resource for professionals, since, at best, it only reflects back their views. Professionalism becomes defined solipsistically. Therefore, if educators simply go hat in hand to practitioners, who respond either in hopes of recruiting with reduced training costs or simply with generous condescension (as a professional form of noblesse oblige), these dangers can result:

Disservice to Students

Students may be directed to immediate job skill development. Yet, their interests might be better served by developing foundational knowledge and attitudes, as well as skills. Larger perspectives can help students to build careers and to prepare for professional lives that are likely to involve multiple job changes and adaptations to new technologies.

Denigration of Faculty Expertise

Upstaged by practitioners, faculty may be seen as naïfs or dilettantes. This effect is evident, for example, in the claim of a recent article, aimed at encouraging practitioners to develop college courses, that "preparing to teach a course [in technical communication] is not hard" [11, p. 163]. If educators do not trust the value of their knowledge concerning rhetoric, composition, and related studies, there is a danger that they will accept reductive advice and rule-making from the "real world." Yet, while anecdotal learning, based on inefficient trial and error, is often the norm in workplaces, courses that respect academic methods benefit from systematic accumulation of knowledge and from teaching specifics within a larger framework.

Elevation of Technology Above Other Legitimate Concerns

Advice from practitioners to educators often comes in the form of recommendations for training in specific tools and technologies that are "hot" in the job market. This can lead to inferiority complexes on the part of colleges that cannot keep up with such trends. Students, in turn, may become impatient with anything but the latest revision level of the newest software application. Such a focus on currency and branding has an overall negative effect on the profession as well, by reinforcing a mindset that professional communicators are defined by the tools that they use. This attitude is unhealthy and stressful, requiring constant catch-up.

Limited Spheres of Influence

One-way communication from practitioners to educators does not help the workplace toward the popularly espoused business goal of *kaizen* or "continuous improvement," because such communication simply reinforces the status quo. Absent feedback to practitioners that provides higher level generalizations about their work and helps to develop standards for quality, practitioners may exercise Panglossian logic to determine that whatever is, is right.

TWO-WAY REALITY

For all these reasons, I suggest that the "real world" needs outside perspectives from the academy, at least as much as educators need to hear from practitioners. Practitioners' perspectives on their work can be very limited. I worked at several kinds of writing jobs in different industries, at differently sized companies, and in different geographic areas. Still, despite those experiences, my knowledge of professional communication barely scratched the surface until I began reading scholarly research that helped me to learn much more.

Educators who turn to practitioners for advice on developing programs also should be aware that practitioners' "real world" standards might be disappointingly low. For several years I have judged for the Northern California Technical Communication Competition (the largest regional publications competition of the STC). I have found surprising how much of what professionals submitted, presumably as work that they were proud of, was not only not ideal, but also extremely weak and ill-conceived. This may be partly a result, of course, of workplace pressures of time and budget.

Yet it also seems possible that many professionals simply do not feel held to high standards, perhaps, in part, because the academy has not helped to articulate and/or to share them. In any case, though practitioners may glorify their "in the trenches" mentality, educators should know that it may not set a high benchmark for quality. This is a critical warning, given that recent studies recommending that college composition courses replicate the "embeddedness" [12, p. 235] and "immersion" [13, p. 180] of workplace practices in coursework seem not to recognize that much professional communication may be less successful than its authors claim.

This has been particularly evident in debriefings with student interns and alumni from the technical and professional writing program that I direct. Many of them have reported being disappointed at the mediocrity of publications at their new workplaces. Several have gone on to tactfully "turn teacher" on their experienced practitioner sponsors or bosses, raising internal standards for document production.

Similarly, I have witnessed how little practitioners typically understand about how much students can learn in the academy that applies to their work on the job. For example, one practitioner, who volunteered to mentor our program's graduates, disappointed many of them by recommending two years of menial copyediting work before they applied for "real" jobs. Yet the reality, based on often surprised feedback from those who supervise student interns and new hires, is that many of our program's graduates quickly function at approximately a two-year experience level. They simply need an orientation to "the way we do things here" — company-specific tools and procedures. This type of misunderstanding about academic preparation suggests that practitioners, many of whom may have completed their formal education before many programs in professional communication existed, need to learn from educators about what such college programs offer.

Publications processes in the workplace, too, often do not provide good models. Sessions on career issues at professional association conferences suggest that many practitioners are frustrated, because they hold lowly and relatively powerless positions within management hierarchies. Still, these same practitioners often demonstrate complacence about weak surveying, minimal testing of products, and other signs of ad hoc publication systems, maintained by default. In today's workplace, the "Tina the Tech Writer" badge of martyrdom (based on "Dilbert" cartoons) appears to be more familiar (and perhaps more comfortable) than the notion of writers traversing a management career ladder.

Practitioners whom educators may solicit for advice also often may not have experienced much in the way of professional development. An informed estimate is that "probably fewer than one-third of the practitioner community receives formal training in their discipline each year by attending professional society conferences or in-service courses" [14, p. 19]. Perhaps partly as a result, practitioners often may not have sophisticated approaches to share on broader issues in professional communication, but instead, for example, offer stereotyped responses on internationalization or dismiss ethical concerns.

While, in recent decades, educators in professional communication have had to ramp up their knowledge in response to changes in the field, many of today's practitioners may not have taken much or any professional communication course work in college. Although programs and degrees in the field have been around for upwards of 20 years, they were much less common before the 1990s and still are not omnipresent. And, while taking one or two classes in technical or business writing is a requirement for many majors, such survey courses typically do not cover advanced studies in the field. And, of course, anyone out of school for more than several years who has not returned to learn about current research and academic emphases also might not appreciate the larger impact of contemporary trends. Educators could help practitioners, too, to ramp up.

MUTUAL INFLUENCE AND EXCHANGE

In making this case for transforming existing one-way communication channels into opportunities for dialog, I do not mean to imply that hard-working practitioners are not helpful informants, but rather to more properly value the complementary work that educators can do. If I seem to paint practitioners with too broad and black a brush, it may be in reaction to Lady Bountiful types from industry that I have encountered since crossing over from the workplace to the academy. Yet I know that I did not have a big enough picture of the field of professional communication when I was a practitioner only; and now that I am again working in industry, I find academic scholarship of tremendous help on the job. So I hope to empower other educators to recognize the value of what they can bring to exchanges with practitioners.

In the academic program that I direct, I am just beginning to recognize how much of what educators typically establish as one-way communication channels has potential for a two-way effect. Consequently, I would like to share some of my ideas, biases, experiments, and hopes for the future.

Practitioner-Faculty and Faculty-Practitioners

Based on both my own experience and that of other faculty whom I have worked with, when those who are primarily practitioners take on assignments teaching professional communication, those practitioners have a powerful opportunity to recognize the value of academic studies. Unlike guest speaker gigs—in which educators cede power and authority to practitioners anointed as experts because of their "real world" associations—teaching positions allow for more collegial sharing.

Of course, as Kaaren Blom has discussed, placing practitioners in teaching roles can be problematic, making support from conventional faculty essential [15]. However, full-time educators can support practitioners in new roles as faculty: not only by assisting them with pedagogy, but also by exposing them to the best relevant scholarship. Then, when such instructors—or educators who do faculty internships or consulting stints—share research with colleagues in the workplace, there can be a substantial ripple effect.

At the same time, this kind of collaborative experience can help educators to feel less of the disjunction that Peter Elbow identified as "being a writer" *versus* "being an academic" [16]. Going further, when academics take a step that complements that of practitioners who become faculty by being faculty that become practitioners, through research or employment in industry, those academics can both "dispel a common assumption that academics can teach only so much about industry writing" and also "dispel the myth that some aspects of workplace writing are so mysterious that they can't be taught before students begin jobs in industry" [5, p. 217].

Feedback on Student and Faculty Mentorships and Internships

Both professional communication students and faculty can be acute, informed observers of the workplaces that they experience through mentorships and internships. Currently, well-designed programs ask sponsors and supervisors to evaluate interns and mentees, and those learners also may be asked to reflect on their learning experiences in ways that contribute to curriculum development. However, I have not encountered models for giving feedback to supervisors and sponsors about their workplace practices and their role in training newbie technical communicators. Of course, this could be a delicate proposition, because of the internalized hierarchy of practitioners as gift-givers when sponsoring internships and mentorships.

Still, the opportunity for the academy to provide a helpful service is there. For example, professional technical communicators may sometimes feel forced to hire expensive experienced personnel, rather than less costly entry-level employees, because of uncertainties about how to complement education with on-the-job training. Similarly, a review of job descriptions in the field suggests that hiring managers need help in defining position requirements more fully, rather than simply by listing needed tools.

Advisory Boards and Alumni Associations

Graduates of professional communication programs may well be not only the academy's best ambassadors, but also the best hope for future improvements in the profession. Such graduates can fulfill an ethic of continuous improvement in the workplace and serve as a perhaps less complacent bridge back to the academy. By educating hiring managers who have not experienced professional communication course work about the nature of today's programs in the field, students can help practitioners to see educators in a new, more respectful light.

. COLLABORATIONS THAT WE LEAD

In addition to opening channels for two-way communication, educators can go even further by setting new partnership goals for their interactions with practitioners. To do so would require only emphasizing and developing several existing practices that have the potential for educating professional communication workplaces, such as:

Service Learning

As service learning course work becomes established in professional communication programs, it provides a model of how external organizations can help nonprofit groups that are strapped for staff and expertise. Service learning also helps to educate community organizations about the role of technical communicators [17, p. 400], and so helps to create a more respectful image with the public at large, both of our academic programs and of the profession. If college programs could develop service learning projects jointly with industry, that could provide additional benefits (including, perhaps, funding). In turn, community service work could help practitioners to develop ethical thinking about their profession, by illustrating its social influence and the power of partnerships that extend beyond corporations.

Trends Analysis and Workplace Research

Through their scholarly research, educators are often better positioned than practitioners within smaller company and industry cultures to see the bigger picture of how trends may affect professional communication practice. For full value, however, practitioners must be open to research in their workplaces that does not just document what is done, as is common for current workplace-based research. The next step for professionalism in our field is to go beyond supporting received opinions to analyzing and critiquing those in an unbiased way. For example: Journalism is another applied writing field, but one in which most professionals have college degrees in the field. This discipline has matured enough that research and criticism arising from journalism schools balance practice. The academy has managed to at least tackle the dilemma, identified by Cesar Ornatowski, of the inherent conflict between serving employers and being objective in research [qtd. in 18, pp. 310-311]. Institutions, such as the Columbia Journalism Review and the Center for the Integration and Improvement of Journalism, influence practices in the field. Similar independence on the part of the technical communication academy could allow it not just to learn about workplace practices, but also to monitor them reflectively and to serve as a goad for high standards in professional communication.

Workplace Consulting and Training

Educators may be able to come in at a higher level to share with practitioners insights about processes and technologies that are based on a range of experiences reported through research. Similarly, by providing training services in the workplace, educators may be able to showcase what they do best which could, in turn, earn them greater respect from practitioners. Although training is not education, its goals may be complementary.

Reviewing and Judging

Regional and national publications competitions provide additional opportunities for educators to show informed leadership in articulating and developing quality standards for professional communication. Most importantly, they can provide educators with a forum for developing the neglected or misunderstood perspectives of composition as socially constructed, by pointing out the limitations of formal, product-based criteria as a method of determining context-specific usability or worth. Actively shaping and/or establishing such competitions could be useful for educators who want to give direct feedback to practitioners.

Presenting to Practitioners

Exposing practitioners to academic research is a critical first step toward encouraging them to apply it. But, at conferences for technical communicators, professors often find themselves presenting to one another, rather than to a more mixed group. One approach for improving this situation might be for academics to device pragmatically-focused topic titles and more appealing presentation formats, recognizing that practitioners may not be so inured to the often abstruse and pedantic style popular at academic conferences. Another approach might be to lobby for abolition of presentation ghettos, such as the Education and Research stem at the Society for Technical Communication conferences. Such segregation keeps professors ineffectually penned together, while most practitioners attend talks elsewhere. Education and research, of course, should inform all of the threads in any conference dedicated to knowledge exchange.

EXCHANGING EXPERTISE

The goal of the kind of leadership that I am suggesting is not to rearrange a hierarchy in favor of educators, but rather to have them work as peers with practitioners with a common purpose of improving professional communication. Others have limned the relationship between educators and practitioners as one of mutual antagonism, mistrust, and arrogance [8, 14]. But, while some educators may indeed have tried to assert superiority over practitioners, the practices of the academy reflect the opposite view.

Tipping the balance by helping practitioners to value the role of the academy less narrowly and more effectively could improve academic programs, workplace practice, and the profession as a whole. As Gerald Savage has explained, the existence and influence of academic programs is, in part, what can make technical communication become and be recognized as truly a mature profession [19, p. 357]. So, how practitioners are seen and valued may depend upon how they see and value their partners in the academy. The programs of professors who specialize in technical communication can help to legitimize the profession of practitioners. And academic studies that demonstrate added value or that establish standards of excellence for communication processes and documents can help practitioners to expand their own roles.

By acknowledging such possibilities, and then reconfiguring their relationships with professors to support academic research and teaching, practitioners can gain status (and its associated power) — to the benefit of all who specialize in *our* field. There is no threat to those in the workplace from recognizing the legitimacy of work done in the academy. It is as partners, presenting a united front to the world outside, that we can best develop the value of technical communication.

Of course, changing the perceptions that technical communication specialists inside industry and inside the academy have of each other will not automatically change the opinions of the larger public. But as long as the community of practitioners remains smugly sure that it has little to learn from academics, while professors continue to be comfortable taking their lead from industry, our field will face others with a low profile, not a progressive one. To the extent that power, status, and legitimacy are based on perceptions, as well as verifiable outcomes, we all need to arm ourselves with balanced and balancing critical perspectives.

REFERENCES

1. K. Staples, Technical Communication from 1950-1998: Where Are We Now? *Technical Communication Quarterly, 8*:2, pp. 153-164, Spring 1999.
2. J. Bushnell, A Contrary View of the Technical Writing Classroom: Notes Toward Future Discussion, *Technical Communication Quarterly, 8*:2, pp. 153-164, Spring 1999.
3. M. J. Killingsworth, Technical Communication in the 21st Century: Where Are We Going? *Technical Communication Quarterly, 8*:2, pp. 153-164, Spring 1999.
4. D. S. Bosley, Collaborative Partnerships: Academia and Industry Working Together, *Technical Communication, 42*:4, pp. 611-619, November 1995.
5. R. Spilka, The Issue of Quality in Professional Documentation: How Can Academia Make More of a Difference? *Technical Communication Quarterly, 9*:2, pp. 207-220, Spring 2000.
6. T. Kynell, Technical Communication from 1850-1950: Where Have We Been?" *Technical Communication Quarterly, 8*:2, pp. 153-164, Spring 1999.
7. L. Allen and D. Voss, *Ethics in Technical Communication: Shades of Gray*, Wiley, New York, 1997.
8. K. Schriver, New Literacies: New Challenges for Communicators, keynote speech: *Joint Conference of ACM-SIGDOC/IEEE-IPCC*, Snowbird, Utah, October 22, 1997.
9. T. Teich, STC Sponsors Focus Group on Improving Technical Communication Education, *ATTW Bulletin, 8*:2, pp. 2-3, Spring 1998.
10. S. C. Geonetta, Designing Four-Year Programs in Technical Communication, in *Foundations for Teaching Technical Communication: Theory, Practice, and Program Design*, K. Staples and C. Ornatowski (eds.), Ablex, Greenwich, Connecticut, pp. 251-258, 1998.
11. A. M. Suray, Professional Writers Have a Classroom Role, *IEEE Transactions on Professional Communication, 39*:3, pp. 163-165, September 1996.
12. P. Dias, A. Freedman, P. Medway, and A. Paré, *Worlds Apart: Acting and Writing in Academic and Workplace Contexts*, Erlbaum, Mahwah, New Jersey, 1999.
13. A. Beaufort, *Writing in the Real World: Making the Transition from School to Work*, Teachers Press, New York, 1999.
14. G. Hayhoe, The Academe-Industry Partnership: What's in It for All of Us, *Technical Communication, 44*:1, pp. 19-20, February 1998.
15. K. Blom, *Practical Research: Practical Outcomes: Report for the Faculty of Communication and Community Services*, Canberra Institute of Technology, Canberra, Australia, 1999.
16. P. Elbow, Being a Writer vs. Being an Academic: A Conflict in Goals, *College Composition and Communication, 46*:1, pp. 72-83, February 1995.
17. C. Matthews and B. B. Zimmerman, Integrating Service Learning and Technical Communication: Benefits and Challenges, *Technical Communication Quarterly, 8*:4, pp. 383-404, Fall 1999.

18. G. J. Savage, The Process and Prospects for Professionalizing Technical Communication, *Journal of Technical Writing and Communication*, 29:4, pp. 355-381, 1999.
19. G. J. Savage, Redefining the Responsibilities of Teachers and the Social Position of the Technical Communicator, *Technical Communication Quarterly*, 5:3, pp. 309-327, 1996.

CHAPTER 6

(Deeply) Sustainable Programs, Sustainable Cultures, Sustainable Selves: Essaying Growth in Technical Communication

Robert R. Johnson

Could my soul once take footing, I would not essay but resolve: but it is always learning and making trial. (Michel de Montaigne, *Of Repentance*)

I don't think there is much argument that technical communication is a field experiencing tremendous growth. Technical communication is a scholarly discipline, a field, a set of national, regional, and local professional associations and academic programs enjoying the good feelings that accompany "growth." The very issues of power, status, and legitimacy that this collection addresses are in themselves potentially linked to growth. Whether you represent an individual, an institution, and/or a greater cultural community, it is difficult to imagine how power and status can be maintained if there is little or no promise for growth. Simply put, growth is good. In the academy, for instance, being a discipline or academic program that is experiencing growth is an enviable position. In a time of budget cutbacks, a drop in the number of tenure-track positions, and other constraints, it is a good feeling to be part of a field that has strong arguments for expanding its present base.

At the same time, however, "growth" can be painful—even more excruciating than the nagging growing pains usually associated with maturity and coming of age. Some of the pain is what John Mellencamp might describe as "hurting so good." Just like teenagers suffering from the inevitable angst of their quickly evolving selves, we know that growth can hurt, but we just can't help ourselves. So, in a variety of ways we continue to grow but we spend little time reflecting on what it means to grow. Hence, we go forward, spending little time questioning the growth of our minds, bodies, and spirits, hopeful that all will be well.

It is this problem of inevitable growth in the field of technical communication that I wish to investigate here: the problem of growing and hoping that rapid growth will be followed by a long life that will, in turn, be sustained well beyond one person's career or one program's development or one professional association's membership rolls. Further, I want to think through the different "types" of growth that our profession is experiencing. I have already mentioned, for instance, the strong material growth that we currently are benefiting from as a result of strong academic and industry interest in technical communication. As we grow in these material ways, however, it is clear that we should be continually pressed to analyze how we are growing (shall I say it?) *spiritually*. By that I mean, a critical sense of who and what we are in terms of ethics and social responsibility should be a constant standpoint from which we can observe and monitor our "upward mobility."

The vehicle that I will use to explore these multiple types of growth will be the metaphor of "sustainability" because it not only suggests growth/life, but it also invokes the inevitable problem of limits. To be sustainable suggests that maintenance *and* reflection are part and parcel of any forward movement we may be contemplating or actually practicing. That is, to sustain means to think *and* to act, to contemplate *and* to practice. This implies that we are charged with the responsibility of constantly looking behind, to the sides, and ahead as we develop our disciplinary and professional identities.

Such multi-directional, active reflection is part of a profession like technical communication. The charge to be continually conscious of the past, critically active in the present moment, and measured about our future actions is in the blood of technical communication professionals. Technical communicators literally are suspended between the proverbial theory/practice binary. Although we often are seen by others as mere practitioners, the reality is that we bring the theoretical (the contemplative) to the various tables of our workplaces (if "they" ask for it or not). Whether we work in industry or the academy, whether we are students in undergraduate or graduate academic programs, we often play the role of productive critic, healthy skeptic, or maybe what sometimes is perceived as trouble-making questioner.

For instance, this role manifests itself when the technical communication specialist asks the software development team to consider the actual users *before* they begin designing and coding the program. This role is carried out by the technical communication academic program director as she prompts the university computing committee to consider whether the new across-the-campus computing initiative (e.g., a laptop in every lap, a server-linked dummy terminal in every dorm room) is actually as efficient and productive as the various decision-makers claim. This role even ripples out to other (often public) contexts as we become advocates for children as we try to influence local school districts to implement technical and scientific communication in the public school curriculum.

To further strengthen and to complicate the notion of sustainability, I will also add the word "deep" to the lexicon. I do this for two reasons (although I'm sure there are others). First, the concept of sustainability is one that has run rampant in recent years with the result of occasionally becoming empty rhetoric: words that often are used in the service of certain agendas, but which in the final analysis hold questionable value. Not unlike the term ecology, sustainability is used by politicians, business consultants, CEO's, scientists, community organizers, academics, and others to denote a concept that on the surface appears to be helpful, but under closer inspection can be problematic and even, paradoxically, harmful.

For instance, the term "ecology" has been used recently by knowledge management consultants [1] and information technology specialists [2] to depict the ways that information and knowledge are distributed, altered, and managed in various human contexts. The ecology metaphor works well for the most part. To talk about "systems," "diversity," and "keystone species" certainly provides a window onto the problems of working in organizations or in information communities. Little discussion, however, is given over to such ecological roles as predators or bottom feeders. Who are the sharks and the alligators? Who eats the heavy metal sediment at the bottom of the metaphorical sea? Put another way, the metaphor is useful as far as one wants it to be useful.

My second reason for choosing the concept of "deep sustainability" is that it has been effectively used by philosophers for over two decades in relation to (what else?) ecology, and in particular to the problems that I mention above regarding the "shallow" use of a metaphor. Further, deep ecology has a social, cultural, and political mission that helps to enrich the dialogue of how to sustain the profession of technical communication beyond merely the simple material aspects mentioned above. Consider the following statement taken from the introduction to a recent collection on the deep ecology movement:

> Why a *deep* [sic] ecology? Perhaps there is a more basic question: What *is deep ecology* [sic]? The Norwegian philosopher Arne

Naess, who coined the term in 1972, originally emphasized a contrast between deep ecology and "shallow ecology"—or what was later termed "reform environmentalism." Reformist environmental policies are concerned mainly with problems, such as resource depletion and pollution, that have adverse effects on the well-being and affluence of human populations in the developed world. These shallow policies attempt to reform human activity regarding the environment without instigating a systematic change in human behavior, attitudes, or institutions. Deep ecology, on the other hand, offers a normative critique of human activity and institutions, and seeks a fundamental change in the dominant world view and social structure of modernity. According to Naess, "The aims of supporters of the deep ecology movement is not a slight reform of our present society, but a substantial *reorientation of our whole civilization*" [sic] [3, p. ix].

Obviously, these are lofty goals. At the same time they are laudable goals: goals that certainly lie at the heart of problems associated with building status, developing authority, and maintaining legitimacy. Thus, I will place these lofty goals out there as ideals we can strive for, if not actually reach to some degree. At the very least, such goals and intentions can serve as beacons into the night so that the terrain is recognizable and we might avoid stumbling too badly as we move forward in disciplinary and professional development.

The remainder of this chapter will focus on the question, What will it mean to sustain technical communication in the coming years and decades? More specifically, I will interrogate the following three issues through the metaphor of sustainability:

1. the inevitable and continual relationship our field has with technology and what it means "to be sustainable" in this relationship,
2. what sustainability means for the future of academic programs, and
3. how technical communicators as individuals might sustain themselves and their communities in the years ahead.

I. DEEPLY SUSTAINING A RELATIONSHIP WITH TECHNOLOGY

Sustainable is currently a difficult word to associate with technology. I don't mean that it is impossible, just difficult because the pace of technological innovation is so incredibly fast. For instance, in popular media we continually see the image of the super highway associated with computer technology. The metaphors of quick, easy entrance ramps and endless roadways to wherever one wants to go are numerous, to say the least. On the surface, these depictions of computer technology are not inaccurate representations of the internet. The idea that the internet is a super highway allows us to imagine computer technology as a fast moving vehicle for traversing the virtual frontiers of the twenty-first century.

Digging a little deeper into this direct analogy between the interstate highway system and the information highway system is useful here. For instance, today we are continually barraged through computer industry marketing with advertisements for faster, sleeker, more advanced computer technologies. Apple Computer, Inc. has recently dubbed their new G4 "cube" a supercomputer that you can have on your desktop. Dell Computer Corporation (as well as other companies) lets you "build your own" computer so that you can be sure to have the most advanced features that you might desire. In short, your computer has a half-life of about 18 months because a newer, faster, sleeker model is soon to come down the virtual road.

Forty years ago, a virtually identical marketing campaign was waged over the automobile. By 1960 the number of individually owned auto-mobiles had trebled in just 20 years. Not only were there many more cars, but they were bigger, faster, and sleeker than their WW II era ancestors. Have you ever looked at the dashboard of a 1960 Chrysler Imperial? The many glowing lights, bulbous glass covered instruments, and other amenities are reminiscent of current computer interfaces and World Wide Web sites that are replete with flashing lights, animated road signs, and even voice-capable instructions. Under the hood you will find a 300+ horsepower engine; inside the Pentium-driven computer you will find 300+ Megahertz of pure information processing speed.

My point here is not to beleaguer the rather obvious marketing con-nections between the computer and automobile industry. In and of itself, the analogy is amusing, if nothing else. Looking more deeply, however, we might learn from the analogous social consequences between these two dominant technologies. As we are all aware, the automobile has not been an unproblematic technology. The efficiency, ease of travel, and convenience of the car has been countered by problems of safety, environ-mental degradation, and the higher costs for fuel and the automobiles themselves. Certainly, there have been many efforts to alleviate these problems. Cars have been engineered to minimize injury in the case of accidents; engines are more fuel efficient, for the most part, and thus pollute less than their predecessors. Such advances are what we generally refer to as "progress," I suppose. We solve such technological problems as they arise, after the fact.

The computer has similar problems associated with its emerging status as a mundane artifact. No longer just for experts, the computer is now as much a part of our culture as a car. With this everyday use comes issues of access, privacy, and even safety (as we see in cases of child pornography and, more grimly, cases of child molesters lurking in virtual chat rooms intent on finding the physical addresses of potential victims). While these connections with the automobile and the interstate highway system are not always direct, they nevertheless are markers of common social and political problems that we potentially are ignoring as we build relationships with information and communication technologies.

Chief among these markers is that communication technologies are becoming what Langdon Winner calls "forms of life." Drawing the concept from Wittgenstein, Winner argues that a technology becomes a "form of life" when "life would be scarcely thinkable without them. . . . As they (technologies) become woven into the texture of everyday existence, the devices, techniques, and systems we adopt shed their tool-like qualities to become part of our very humanity" [4, pp. 11-12]. On the surface, the fact that communication technologies have become indelible parts of our everyday lives is not surprising. Similar to an automobile, inter-networked computer technologies have opened up new possibilities for human exchange, education, and in an increasingly market-driven world, consumer marketing.

Deeper down, however, there is an irony of significant consequence when a technology becomes so embedded in our lives—we become *dependent* on the technology to such a degree that we are essentially leashed to the technology in controlling ways. Such leashing to technologies is nothing new. In her classic text from the history of technology—*More Work for Mother: The Ironies of Household Technology from the Open Hearth to the Microwave*—Ruth Schwartz Cowan has demonstrated how a multitude of household artifacts have leashed women to more intense levels of work than they had been before the advent of devices like washing machines and vacuum cleaners [5].

Similar to Winner's point that such leashing happens invisibly, Cowan closes her book by calling for us to reflect on our use of everyday technologies before we become wedded to their powers. "Many of the rules that tyrannize housewives are unconscious and therefore potent. However, manufacturers and advertisers exploit these unconscious rules, they did not create them. . . . If we learn to select among the rules only those that make sense for us in the present, we can begin to control household technology instead of letting it control us" [5, p. 219].

For technical communicators, communication technology and the information superhighway contain similar problems. Technical communicators work intimately with communication technologies and thus are akin to Cowan's housewives in that we live with these technologies on a day-to-day basis. Computers have become ubiquitous in technical communication and, like vacuum cleaners and washing machines, they are marketed to us (and to our supervisors) as time-saving devices which will allow for greater output with less work. They are clearly forms of life in our professional existence in that they have become inseparable from our everyday work activities. Consequently, we are now leashed to e-mail, faxes, Web sites, and word processors in ways that dictate the very characteristics of our lives. Yes, we can take our work home with us through these new technologies, but even that is fraught with double-edged consequences. It may be nice to work from home, for instance, but it is not always preferable to have work follow you home.

At the same time, however, we have some power in this new relationship. Through the very nature of our work, we have the *potential* to have an impact on the sustainable development of new communi-cation technologies in different workplace and educational contexts: the potential to affect the tautness, length, and, I would argue, occasionally the existence of the leash itself. Further, we are intimately connected with many of the everyday users of communication technologies – students, secretaries, managers, graphic artists, etc. – and therefore have power to affect changes in workplaces and educational institutions when it comes to upgrading systems, implementing new information technologies, or altering workplace and classroom practices. Potential is the keyword here – the power will stay inert if we fail to use it critically.

II. DEEPLY SUSTAINING ACADEMIC PROGRAMS

The growth of technical communication is nowhere more apparent than in the arena of academic program development. Only 20 years ago, a student would have been hard pressed to find many undergraduate programs, let alone more advanced graduate study. Since that time the number of programs at all levels has mushroomed. In a study of academic programs in technical communication published in 1997, it was estimated that the mere handful of programs that existed in 1980 had grown to over 200 by the mid-1990s. The breakdown of these programs by degree shows not only the growth in numbers, but in level and type of degree as well: 13 Ph.D., 24 M.S., 40 M.A., 31 B.S., 52 B.A., 41 Certificate [6]. In light of the numerous mailings and email postings I receive announcing the start up of new programs, it is safe to assume that since the publication of this study the number of programs has increased significantly once again. The growth of technical communication programs appears to be like the proverbial Energizer® rabbit – they just keep on going and going and going. . . .

In addition, with the increase of programs has come a strong demand for faculty to staff them. The 2000 Modern Language Association *October Job Information List* (JIL) database shows approximately 120 faculty positions advertised in technical and professional communication. This number has increased by about 10 percent per year over the past five years (according to my own unofficial count), creating a strong market for qualified applicants (and difficult recruiting situations for those of us trying to lure the best candidates!).

Obviously, this is tremendous growth and is an example of our enviable position; I can easily think of many disciplines that would love to be in this situation. Sustaining such growth, however, will be a difficult task, to say the least. These nearly geometric growth patterns are the kind of stuff that Boom/Bust stories are made of. As I sit in my office in the Upper Peninsula of Michigan, I only need to look out the window to see the remnants of a once tremendous boom: mining and manufacturing sites that once employed thousands are now idle, left to rust and eventually turn to dust. The copper and the iron of the once world famous mines are now virtually gone, the victims of unsustainable growth and development. Many of you, I am sure, could recount similar stories of the places you have lived. Boom/Bust is an often-told narrative in modern, postmodern, or whatever times.

Of course, we don't need to be grandiose and draw histrionic analogies to make the point that sustaining technical communication programs could be problematic. Our English and American literature colleagues are currently living the Boom/Bust reality that has run from the 1960s to the present. The stories of unemployed literature Ph.D.s, bitter graduate students, and programs threatened by precipitous drops in applications are legend. The only thing sustaining some of these programs is the tenure system because literature faculty hold the precious positions, and even that security is tenuous given the current state of budgetary affairs in higher education. The situation has become so severe that the Modern Language Association and the Association of Departments of English now hold regular meetings on what to do about the problem. The productiveness of these meetings is unclear as the potential promise of sustainability may have been lost.

Only time will tell, but at present I believe our best course of action is to learn from examples like literary studies to plan a sustainable course of action for technical communication programs, be they graduate or undergraduate. Technical communicators in the academy must be prepared to dismantle the Boom/Bust binary and think through solutions that use the binary as a tool, instead of as a trap. A wide-ranging plan for disrupting this binary is beyond the scope of this chapter, but in an attempt to start the conversation, I will look at two principal issues that are part of a sustainable future: 1) determining program size (both in terms of student enrollments and faculty lines), and 2) garnering resources for program development.

In the 1994 Fall edition of the *ATTW Bulletin*, there was an interesting debate between Stuart Brown, Cindy Selfe, and Jack Selzer over the question, What is the future of doctoral programs in technical and professional communication [7]? All three of these academics have been intimately involved with technical communication programs for many years—Brown has been involved with the New Mexico State program since its inception and has also played an important role nationally collecting data on rhetoric and composition for *Rhetoric Review* for several years; Selfe was instrumental in the development of the Michigan Tech Rhetoric and Technical Communication doctoral program; Selzer has been a key player in the Penn State program for many years. Thus, the debate was well grounded in the lived experience of three scholars who have vested interests in the future of graduate study.

Interestingly, the debate brought out quite different viewpoints. That is, although these scholars all operate in similar contexts (public institutions with established graduate programs in rhetoric, composition, and technical communication), they had considerably different positions on how programs might prosper (or not) in the coming years. Brown situated himself on an end of the debate spectrum that might be labeled "grim," and even more pointedly he concludes his discussion by simply saying, "I'm not optimistic" [7, p. 6]. Drawing upon cases of students in the Michigan Tech program, Selfe situates herself at the other end of the spectrum as she argues that technical and professional communication Ph.D.'s are a new breed of graduate student who will be able to fill multiple social roles—academic and nonacademic. Further, she argues with a "guarded optimism" that programs will be able to flourish because of the many new possibilities that can exist if we prepare our students for this new landscape of opportunities [7, p. 12]. Finally, Selzer comes down somewhere in the middle of the debate; however, he concludes with a tone that is decidedly reserved,

> Professors of English and the other modern languages are unique, as far as I know, in setting up a system designed to kill off its young, either by denying them jobs, or replacing them at tenure time from the stockpile of equally accomplished but marginally cheaper beginners. . . . I say that the price is too high, much too high, and that we ought to do some things to change before we get ourselves in the same predicament as the other fields in what are known, not without irony, as "the humanities" [sic] [7, p. 9].

Interestingly, even though these three researchers have different views of the problem of growing graduate programs in technical communication, they at least all define the problem as one of "program size." To see the problem in this common way gives us a window through which to view an essential question to consider — How big is big enough? Brown appears to favor fewer and smaller programs; Selzer wants programs to maintain themselves in light of "historical realities"; and Selfe wants programs to grow intelligently: to keep sight of future possibilities in emerging interdisciplinary and electronic marketplaces. All of these viewpoints, of course, have validity, but is there one that promises to insure a *sustainable* future for our programs? In other words, can we at one and the same time grow, yet limit our growth? Will the U.S. academy and the U.S. economic system, allow such a measured approach to growth? Let's take a brief "then and now" look at some data related to technical communication programs.

In the same article, Stuart Brown backed his skeptical stance with both the MLA job listing data and upon reports from the *Wall Street Journal* concerning the "myth" of increased numbers of faculty lines in the near future. He noted that the MLA Job Information List (JIL) in 1993 had only about 10 technical communication positions listed. He further estimated that by 1996 there would be "40 to 50 new doctorates in technical and professional communication on the market annually as existing programs move into full production" [7, p. 6].

But, he queries, will there be places for these new graduates to go, especially in the academy? Quoting Tony Horowitz in *The Wall Street Journal*, Brown points to an interesting paradox in the potential for future jobs in higher education. Horowitz claims that even though there will probably be significant numbers of retirements in the academy over the next several decades, there is no evidence that these permanent faculty lines will be renewed. "Hiring has been preempted by severe retrenchment at most schools because of falling enrollments and state grants, soaring financial aid costs, and other factors, including the end of mandatory retirement rules that allow faculty to teach into their 70's" [7, p. 6]. Further, Brown points to an interesting "rule of thumb" concerning university hiring in Horowitz's article that was provided by a professor from Colgate, Daniel Little: "For every three retirements, only one typically leads to a tenure track position. The second is eliminated. The third is filled on a 'term' (terminal) appointment for a year or two, or by a part-timer hired for a specific course" [7, p. 6].

Have Brown's predictions of 1994 come true? Certainly his MLA *JIL* information has not proven accurate. As I stated earlier, the number of positions in technical and professional communication has risen dramatically. The number of programs has blossomed as well, thus providing potential places for these newly minted Ph.D.s. In addition, my own anecdotal information from colleagues in technical communication indicates that it is extremely difficult to find qualified people to take these positions. This scarcity of human resources has, in turn, led to speculation by some that we now need to create more doctoral programs to fill this need.

Is the problem as clear cut, as black and white, as the numbers claim? Once again, let's dig a little deeper into the problem of sustaining programs in the long-term. Even though the MLA *JIL* is a strong indicator of growth, the overall picture of the academy is less glowing. For instance, the American Association of University professors (AAUP) states that from 1975 to 1995 the number of full-time positions has declined while the use of part-time faculty has more than doubled [8, p. 54]. In addition, most public universities have seen the percentage of support decline dramatically from their respective state legislatures. This decline has been so precipitous that it has even affected the rhetoric of public support for higher education from "state-supported" to "state-assisted" education. We are currently experiencing the material impact of this sort of rhetorical shift through nationwide double-digit increases in tuition and student fees at most public institutions of higher learning.

A major outcome of this drop in state funding has been to turn toward more sponsored research, as well as increased private fund-raising efforts by all institutions of higher learning. We are looking to corporations and individuals to help us build buildings and create professorships, among other things. One recent listserv discussion in technical communication, in fact, had a rather extended discussion considering the potential for technical communication programs to garner corporate support for a Ph.D. program, thus reaping, so to speak, some rewards from those very companies that hire our graduates. This, of course, is common in business schools, and is becoming increasingly commonplace in the sciences and engineering, as we see departments and entire colleges named after individuals or corporations—"The Brand X School of Y."

Such may be the future of not just technical communication programs, but of the university system as well. There are difficulties, though, as we probe even a little deeper into this new age of the university. The most obvious danger is that universities will become the "servants" of private interests and lose an essential element of the "academic freedom" which has been a hallmark of higher education for the last two centuries. A most vivid example of this is the $25 million endowment in 1998 that Berkeley's Department of Plant and Microbial Biology received from Novartis, the large Swiss pharmaceutical company. According to Eyal Press and Jennifer Washburn in an *Atlantic Monthly* article titled "The Kept University,"

> In exchange for the $25 million, Berkeley grants Novartis first right to negotiate licenses on roughly a third of the department's discoveries—including the results of research funded by the state and federal sources as well as Novartis. It also grants the company unprecedented representation—two of five seats—on the department's research committee, which determines how the money is spent [8, p. 40].

It could be called reactionary to argue against the firm installation of corporate interests in the university. Those who stand against such practices will probably be labeled as "old-fashioned," "romantic," or even "obstructionist." The example of Berkeley, however, is too concrete to be ignored. This is one of our country's major research institutions—the type of institution that many other schools emulate on a number of levels. From Carnegie Foundation classification systems to *U.S. News and World Report* rankings of colleges, schools like Berkeley run the show. In addition, institutions of higher learning are not new to this kind of pressure. We have already seen how virtually every major sporting event (collegiate or otherwise) and nearly every major sporting facility has become a marketing attachment for a corporate interest; I wonder if the academic side of the academy might follow suit.

For technical communication programs, this is surely a dilemma. We have pursued increased status and power in the face of formidable odds. Tenure lines have been hard to pry from literature and other disciplines; curriculum development has been slowly lifted above mere service (at least in some places); Full Professor of Technical Communication is no longer an oxymoron. However, is it worth the price of admission (even if the ticket is free) if we must compromise some basic values of what we have long fought to call a "humanistic" discipline?

From a sustainable perspective, we must constantly remind ourselves that we are part of the problem *and* the solution. Put another way, if we go with the flow of current corporate financing to solve our problem, what might be the effect on other members in our academic community? At George Mason University, for example, the president, Alan G. Merten, went after $25 million in new state funds targeting the development of degrees benefiting high-tech industries in Virginia. Merten created new programs in biosciences, bioinformatics, and computer and information science. The price of these new programs was the loss of programs in classics, German, and Russian. When asked to account for these radical changes, Merten replied, "There was a time when universities weren't held accountable for much—people just threw money at them. Today people with money are more likely to give you money if you have restructured and repositioned yourself, got rid of stuff that you don't need to have. They take a very dim view of giving you money to run an inefficient organization" [8, p. 51].

I see in both of these examples, Berkeley and GMU, a strong thread of technological determinism. The system is *heavily* determining the action of the agents [9]. In a proverbial sense, it smacks of fearing the hand that feeds us. For an academic discipline like technical communication—a field that operates in the boundaries between the humanities and the scientific and technological disciplines—we are placed in a compromising position. Do we wave good-bye to our colleagues in the humanistic disciplines, or do we "fight the good fight" and possibly go out the door with them? Again, the problem is certainly not such a blatant either/or decision. We can seek outside funding and at the same time argue for universities to have broad-based educational goals. Nevertheless, the perseverance to sustain our programs, and to anchor our power and status in and out of the academy, will require deep and sometimes painful assessment of who we are and where we want to go.

III. SUSTAINING COMMUNITIES AND SELVES

The Western philosophical tradition has long been taken with the problem and paradox of "the one and the many." "The one and the many" is a problem, some say, because it can be a justification for placing the needs of an individual over the majority. In a democracy we tend to let the majority rule, but sometimes that is problematic, especially when the majority dominates in a colonial fashion (not the way a democracy is supposed to work, I know, but that is part of the problem). "The one and the many" is a paradox because in the absence of one you cannot have many. That is, we all make up the whole, individually, one at a time.

In this section I will confront the issue of the one and the many through the lens of professionalism and status in technical communication. The context I will look at is the quickly emerging specialization known as "knowledge work," or, as Robert Reich calls it, "symbolic analysis" [10]. I have chosen this context for a couple of reasons.

First, the concept of "knowledge work" has had profound effects upon the ways we look at the workplace. The idea that the products of work are intimately tied to knowledge and the production of knowledge refashions fundamental aspects of the human condition. For technical and scientific communicators the fact that knowledge is now a commodity to be invented, designed, and eventually marketed holds great promise for our profession. After all, technical and scientific communicators have always been the inventors and distributors of either their own or someone else's knowledge; to suddenly have the significance of our everyday labor recognized is tantamount to striking a mother lode. In this post-industrial world the transfer of information has become so important that most companies have employees hired specifically as "information managers," or "knowledge specialists," or something of the sort. Thus, it is a timely topic and one of central concern to technical communication because we *are* those information managers and knowledge specialists. The fact that few in the corporate world know this is, well, a problem for another essay.

In addition, I have chosen knowledge management and symbolic analysis because it represents a potential change in the material and social status of technical communicators, particularly in the corporate workplace [11]. A recent article in *Technical Communication* makes this point most bluntly:

> Consider the role of chief knowledge officer. Jay Leibowitz and Thomas Beckman point out that executives in this position command salaries ranging from $600,000 to $1,250,000, with experienced consultants making $30,000 per week when consulting externally. Even if these figures are drastically inflated (say, doubled), they nonetheless indicate that organizations are willing to pay a high premium for executives who can grow and leverage their organizations' knowledge [12, p. 523].

Any technical communicator bringing in those salaries will certainly be at a higher level of status than most technical communicators are at present! If such tales are true, even lower-level knowledge managers will possibly be moving on up from their present status as "mere" editor, writer, project manager, or document designer. This is a virtual new frontier for technical communicators, so to speak.

Unfortunately, there is always a rub, as Shakespeare reminds us, and this rub is not just for the individual who climbs the ladder, but for the entire community, or communities, that the individual technical communicator belongs to. In a sustainable culture we all affect each other on a daily basis with everything we do. More to the point, such a move up the ladder of professional respectability has an impact on all of the rungs, especially the lower ones. As we move up the professional ladder, we, of course, leave behind many who possibly are unable to make this social and economic "upward" transition.

Put another way, as we move up we also move away. In a critique of his own concept of symbolic analysis, ex-Secretary of Labor Robert Reich characterizes both the qualitative nature and the social consequences of knowledge work as a classic problem of the one and the many. "The work this group [symbolic analysts] does is becoming less tied to the activities of other Americans. . . . In contrast with people whose jobs tend to be tedious and repetitive, symbolic analysts find their work varied and challenging. In fact, the work is often enjoyable" [13, p. xviii]. He continues, however, that these high-skilled knowledge workers, who are in the upper fifth of incomes in the United States, ultimately pool "their resources to the exclusive benefit of themselves" [13, p. xxi]. Citing examples of economic disparities in public school systems, urban and suburban neighborhoods, and even the building of libraries and cultural event centers, Reich contends that symbolic analysts are key residents of urban and suburban economically advantaged enclaves with the best schools, libraries, theaters, and so on.

Observing this new world of knowledge work from a technical communicator's perspective—from our new-found perch economically and socially far above the "non-knowledge" workers—we can view these workers for whom we "write-up knowledge" through our technical communication practices: the computer operators, automobile mechanics, nurses, secretaries, and countless others whose professional status is often not as highly regarded as it should be. Yet we are removed from them, and if we continue to "climb the ladder," then we will become even more remote and less accessible to the workers and users for whom we write and speak.

Our status as technical communicators is unique. We have an affinity, even an empathy, with those at the "lower rungs" of the professional ladder. At the same time, we have the power to remove ourselves from that level because of our role as knowledge and symbol transporters. What should be our position on this matter? How can we, as increasingly important players in the knowledge and electronic communication game, come to terms with the consequences of our professional actions?

FRAGILITY AND RESPONSIBILITY: SOME CLOSING COMMENTS

At the beginning of this chapter I took a quote from the French renaissance essayist Montaigne to, in part, excuse myself for writing an essay [14]. After all, in technical communication we often don't talk about the genre of the essay, and for good reason. The traditional genres of technical communication are enough to deal with, and the essay most often just plain does not fit into our daily lives. It is probably the case that I haven't even written what many would consider to be an essay anyway. No matter, I will call it that and be done with it.

My more fundamental reason for quoting Montaigne, however, was to call attention to the fluid and ever-changing nature of life that he alludes to. It is difficult to "take foot" when teaching loads, student enrollments, and administrative costs are continually changing—mostly upward, too. Outside the academy things are probably even more fluid, more affected by change on a continuous basis as knowledge and information morph with every blink of the digital clock. Programs, careers, and even institutions are made fragile through these dynamics: we must be cognizant of those changes — see them before they pass by — and we must also sometimes be the glue that puts the pieces back together again.

Thus, essaying is a good genre for reflecting on the current and future status of technical communication — to essay can help us to see the cracks and fissures, to observe the strong points and new places to explore. Ultimately, however, our roles as advocates and members of a professional community are to move beyond the reflective mode and become productive. Our responsibility is to work back and forth between contemplation and action, constantly expanding the available means of persuasion that enable us to be professionally strong and culturally sensitive. This process, I would say, is at least one way to continually re-invent our professional communities, selves, and spirits. In this spirit of productive scholarship, then, I will "crack" the essay genre by offering some direct guiding thoughts on how we can sustain ourselves in the coming years.

Redefine "Growth" as it Applies to Technical Communication Programs

The propensity to grow technical communication programs is too strongly associated with words such as "bigger, biggest, largest, fastest-growing." This is dangerous because becoming bigger and faster can also make us fragile — less able to control our growth and thus making us susceptible to breakdown. As I have already pointed out, other disciplines have gone this route and there have been dire consequences that threaten the sustainability of those disciplines.

Instead of growing "bigger," we should strive to be sustainable. This does not imply, of course, that some increase in size or scope might be beneficial. We can continue to expand to some degree, but that growth should be measured and strategic. For instance, technical communication programs often attempt to be all things to all people. We often create single programs at individual institutions where students can become just about anything — Web designers, grants writers, publishing industry specialists, usability specialists, medical and environmental writers, marketing specialists, etc. In itself, preparing students to have a wide variety of communication-related skill is laudable. In fact, we currently manage to accomplish much of this in many of our programs.

However, I question whether the pace of this far-flung enterprise can be sustained over extended periods of time. Presently, many programs are understaffed; lone faculty in some cases play the roles of graduate and undergraduate curriculum developer, internship supervisor, classroom teacher, technology administrator, and so on. The human energy involved in sustaining this type of work is great, and the multi-tasking nature of the work is psychologically fracturing and physically taxing.

Although they had their own problems to deal with, our predecessors in other disciplines had more favorable economic conditions that promoted growth, especially in public institutions of higher learning. We will most likely never see the number of faculty that, say, literary studies did in the 1960s and 1970s when institutions were able to hire significant numbers of sub-specialists (e.g., medieval, renaissance, eighteenth, nineteenth, and twentieth century British and American, etc.). Our challenge now is, whether we like it or not, to do what we can do well with less.

One potential solution is for programs to become more focussed and specialized. Each program, in other words, could have distinct and recognizable purposes beyond the pail of general technical communication. In short, we should consider creating programs that present "pockets of specialties": programs where students can go to focus on strong and well developed areas of curriculum and scholarship that will be fruitful for students and faculty alike. There, of course, will always be regional constraints and needs which will call for specific types of programs in certain geographic or cultural arenas. Nevertheless, focussed growth is certainly a viable option to what sometimes appears to be a helter-skelter approach to program development.

Become Stewards of the Technologies that Fall Within the Purview of Technical Communication

We should strive to work both productively and critically with technologies in our everyday contexts. For example, the pressure to adopt the newest versions of software and the fastest computers available is intense — not unlike the pressure that the automobile industry put on the American public during the twentieth century. As I mentioned earlier, the analogy between these two culture-altering industries is not exact, but it is curiously similar. A common impulse in regard to cultural agents like information and automotive technologies is to adopt these technology-driven changes with little or no reflection as to why such adoption is taking place. At the same time, humans have a propensity to work in direct opposition to unreflective stances by taking an equal and opposite position, often called Luddite, that encourages a hand-off and sometimes destructive attitude toward technological innovation.

In contrast to both of these attitudes, a stewardship model encourages engagement with technologies, but it also has ample room for sensitive and appropriate questioning of the use of those technologies in given contexts. Recent agricultural history provides one example of this approach to technology and the results that stewardship can produce.

In the mid-twentieth century, as agricultural practices in the United States became more mechanized and scientific through the use of such things as combustion engines and genetic engineering, advocates of alternative farming methods called for a rethinking of these practices. As they saw lands being over-tilled to produce more crops in shorter periods of time, animals being fed antibiotics to speed their weight gain, and seed crops being increasingly altered through genetic manipulation, these alternative farmers experimented with other technologies to develop more sustainable agricultural methods. Sometimes they tried "older" technologies, such as using manure for fertilizer or rotating crops to lessen the stress on the soil and, at the same time, reduce the amount of chemical fertilizer. At other times, they used "newer" technologies, like computer-generated weather information, to make choices about planting and harvesting.

These stewards of the land see their relationship with technology as crucial, but they don't immediately adopt the newest technology just because it promises more profits or fewer hours worked. Instead, they carefully inspect new technologies and attempt to use only those that meet a specific array of criteria. Technical communicators, as stewards of academic and nonacademic environments, should adopt a similar relationship with technologies that fall within our purview.

Foster a Stronger Sense of Technical Communication's Responsibilities Outside of Our Immediate Academic and Workplace Contexts

This is probably the most difficult to enact because it comes squarely down on central issues of ethics and forces us to look beyond the present moment and anticipate the future. However, the example of the knowledge worker I addressed earlier is too potent an example to ignore. That is, what we do in our working lives has direct impacts on the social and cultural circumstances that often appear far removed from our daily contexts. Some might say that this is like the "butterfly effect" often associated with chaos theory: when a butterfly beats its wings in Singapore, there may very well be an effect upon the weather in New York City several weeks later.

We are all part of an unpredictable network that is difficult to control. Nevertheless, recognition that some controls are possible, even necessary, is our responsibility. To act otherwise, to act with blind disregard as to the greater scheme of things, is not acceptable. As Montaigne points out, we are always learning and making trial. Everything is always changing. To be sustainable, in more modern parlance, means to "go with the flow," but it also implies that we know the speed, direction, and destination of the flow—that we learn and make trial as we go into tomorrow.

REFERENCES

1. T. H. Davenport and P. Prusak, *Information Ecology: Mastering the Information and Knowledge Environment*, Oxford University Press, New York, 1997.
2. B. A. Nardi and V. L. O'Day, *Information Ecologies: Using Technology with Heart*, MIT Press, Cambridge, Massachusetts, 2000.
3. E. Katz, A. Light, and D. Rothenberg, *Beneath the Surface: Critical Essays in the Philosophy of Deep Ecology*, MIT Press, Cambridge, Massachusetts, 2000.
4. L. Winner, *The Whale and the Reactor: A Search for Limits in an Age of High Technology*, University of Chicago Press, Chicago, Illinois, 1986.
5. R. S. Cowan, *More Work for Mother: The Ironies of Household Technology from the Open Hearth to the Microwave*, Basic Books, New York, 1983.
6. S. Geonetta, R. Hirst, M. Keene, and F. Stohrer (eds.), *Education in Scientific and Technical Communication: Academic Programs That Work*, Society for Technical Communication, Arlington, Virginia, 1997.
7. S. C. Brown, C. L. Selfe, and J. Selzer, Interchange: Doctoral Studies in Technical and Professional Communication, *ATTW Bulletin*, 5:4, pp. 5-12, Fall 1994.
8. E. Press and J. Washburn, The Kept University, *The Atlantic Monthly*, 235:3, pp. 39-54, March 2000.
9. R. R. Johnson, *Usercentered Technology: A Rhetorical Theory for Computers and Other Mundane Artifacts*, SUNY Press, Albany, New York, 1998.
10. R. B. Reich, *The Work of Nations: Preparing Ourselves for 21st Century Capitalism*, Alfred A. Knopf, New York, 1991.
11. J. Johnson-Eilola, Relocating the Value of Work: Technical Communication in a Post-Industrial Age, *Technical Communication Quarterly*, 5:3, pp. 245-270, Summer 1996.
12. C. Wick, Knowledge Management and Leadership Opportunities for Technical Communicators, *Technical Communication*, pp. 515-529, Fourth Quarter 2000.
13. R. B. Reich, Everything Has Changed Except the Way We Think, *America's New War on Poverty: A Reader for Action*, R. Lavelle (ed.), KQED Books, San Francisco, California, pp. xvi-xxiv, 1995.
14. M. de Montaigne, *Essays and Selected Writings*, St. Martin's, New York, 1963.

PART III

Strategies for Alternative Futures

CHAPTER 7

Toward a Definition of Best Practices in Policy Discourse

Carolyn D. Rude

ASSESSING WHAT WE KNOW ABOUT COMMUNICATION ON SOCIAL ISSUES

In technical communication, knowledge about communication in social policy and practice has been developed primarily through critique. Examination of flaws in communication practices has revealed the power and importance of communication and the social consequences of flawed practices. Studies have focused on situations ranging from the international to the local and on issues ranging from death and gender and racial abuse to the silencing of citizens. Investigations have targeted the Challenger [1-5], Three Mile Island [2, 6], and Tailhook [7, 8] as well as environmental impact statements [9, 10], the MOVE report [11], Nazi memos [12, 13], mine safety [14], and citizen versus bureaucracy disputes [9, 15]. These critiques, and others like them, have helped to disturb the now-antiquated notion of communication as the accurate transmission of clear information and have confirmed the close connections between communication, culture, and power. Just as important, they have suggested how the knowledge of the field might be valuable in the public sphere. The critiques suggest a role for technical communication beyond industry and beyond computer documentation. They identify communication problems for which this field might have some answers.

Collectively critiques tell a sorry tale of inept communication strategies or powerlessness in the face of custom and bureaucracy. They link flawed communication with disaster and with abuses of power. By

123

exposing failures and their causes, critique heightens awareness of the need for ethical and informed action as well as of the situations that may discourage such action. Sometimes critique identifies practices that could minimize communication failures in the future. However, many critiques focus on national and international catastrophes, such as the Challenger explosion, and the drama of the situation itself may overwhelm the recommendations for changing practice in ordinary circumstances. Furthermore, the work of this field's critiques is concentrated on a few social issues, especially the environment and gender. Many other issues of policy that depend on effective communication remain undiscovered in this field. And, critique that foregrounds issues tends to leave readers with enhanced knowledge of the issue (such as gender or the environment) more than of practices that might be used to ensure effective communication in the future. Although technical communication has established that it may have a significant voice beyond industry, it has not yet found quite how to use that voice in ways that matter beyond consciousness raising within the field.

Practice is intimately linked to critique and depends on it. Critique disrupts comfortable assumptions and practices that may have become counterproductive. Critique analyzes the components of a situation to determine where the problems occur. It can then identify possible solutions. Critique also grounds the analysis in theory, which provides an ideal scheme for the way that communication should occur. Various critiques illustrate methods for research so that knowledge can grow. Critiques such as those cited above link technical communication with its roots in rhetoric and civic discourse. As civic issues are increasingly connected with technology, with its potential for catastrophe and its realignment of power relationships, these roots impel a continuing consideration of how the field might use its knowledge for the public good. Such work has been in progress for the last decade, marked by collections at its beginning [16] and its end [17]. Both of these collections offer not only critique but also case studies that illustrate discourse in the context of policy deliberations. In spite of these efforts, there appears to be more talk than action. There is a gap between knowing that something should be done and knowing what to do and how to do it.

One risk of critique without action is a kind of self-satisfied ivory tower or armchair critique that never moves toward influencing practice. In addition, studies of cases in which communication failed, often for reasons embedded in bureaucracies and other systems, can lead to a paralyzing pessimism about the power of research or teaching or individual actions within organizations to change practice. Another risk of critique without action is that the field talks to itself. A field as small and as little known as technical communication does not attract interest and requests for comment from outside in the way a larger field might. The conversation in technical communication about policy discourse or issues of power fails to engage readers even beyond academic boundaries within its own field. Within technical communication, the voices of critique are largely silenced beyond academe, increasingly dominated by discussion of computer documentation. At the same time, the voices of critique may turn against the workplace instead of outward toward society, widening disciplinary separations. The bifurcation in the field raises questions of identity: whether the critiques of failed communication in the public sphere have anything to do with designing a better manual and vice versa. In fact these disparate areas of inquiry have much in common, and seeing the connections (while respecting differences) can benefit both areas and increase the power of the field of technical communication as a whole.

This chapter assesses what the various case studies and textual analyses have revealed about the practice of communication in the public sphere and within the corporation beyond developing useful product-related materials. With just a few exceptions, it concentrates on work developed by people who identify themselves with technical communication, though parallel work occurs in related fields including rhetoric, communication studies, and social science. Turning to the knowledge of the field, which on the issue of practice is most mature in computer documentation, the article examines the practice of communication in various settings by exploring the concept of "best practices" within industry and how this concept may summarize a goal for the next phase of claiming a space for technical communication in policy discourse. It points to some strategies for using this knowledge in the developing knowledge and influence on communication in the social sphere.

THE EXAMPLE OF COMPUTER DOCUMENTATION: RESEARCH INTO BEST PRACTICES

The example of work in computer documentation, which on the surface seems so alien to the work of social critique and action, can illustrate some directions for the way the field can develop its voice and position in the public sphere. In a way this linking seems counterintuitive, if only because social critique so often challenges custom and hierarchy on behalf of the common good while industry pursues growth and profits first of all for its own good. Other examples might provide equally good or in some ways superior models. However, for the sake of the field's wholeness and health, it makes sense to look first within the field to see what the knowledge of the field can bring to various communication situations.

To see what the industry example may offer for writing with a social or political agenda requires putting aside, at least temporarily, suspicion that employees adopt a technological and capitalistic set of values and avoid responsibility for their actions. (In fact, many of these employees are engaged in community service, working for Habitat for Humanity or developmental disabilities or other community projects.) The interesting history of technical communication within the computer industry is one of increasing power and how it emerged: the change from a marginal and cleaning-up role for writers to new responsibilities for design and development. The increasing respect for technical writers in the workplace is more than an accident of the growth of technology. The writers have been proactive in both constructing a valuable place for themselves and in advocating it. They have unsettled the assumptions that writers are competent with sentences and paragraphs and little else. They have constructed a role for technical communication by analyzing the problems that marginalize writers and that frustrate their achievement. They have engaged users in defining the goals for product materials, and they have tested their materials for usability. They have used this problem analysis to identify goals for research and to improve practice based on new knowledge. The experience gained from these achievements may offer a body of knowledge in technical communication that has application in other contexts.

Twenty years ago computer documentation was universally considered (and probably was) bad. It "documented" programs (a static concept, focusing on the artifact) rather than foregrounding user tasks and how to accomplish them. The writers entered a project at its end without a chance to influence project direction nor even with the time to document. Today, although challenges remain for instructions on increasingly complex hardware and software, and although issues of access and power are understudied in the workplace, the manuals and help systems are significantly better than they were. They incorporate specialized knowledge of best practice in communication, including knowledge of development processes and assessing user needs as well as the structure and display of the resulting documents. As they have influenced practice with measurable results, technical communicators have gained more respected voices in many organizations. These changes were partly driven by industry forces apart from the status of technical communicators: performance goals, the need to defend documentation as a "value" rather than as a "cost," and demands of users. These incentives have forced technical writers in industry to identify and develop best practices, whether these practices relate to user analysis and testing, to management, to collaboration, to production tools, to page layout and media, or to structuring information. Writing practice and products have improved because the situation demanded this improvement.

Knowledge of practice regarding discourse for social purposes seems about a decade behind the work on best practices of writing in the computer industry. We have "documented" poor practices by accumulating multiple examples. Where profits may have compelled workplace improvements, a sense of civic responsibility as it inheres in the rhetorical tradition may compel further work in social and policy discourse. In both domains, disciplinary issues of status influence goals. But any power or disciplinary status beyond industry will depend on the ability to influence and direct as well to critique. Where should we look for best practices in policy making and discourse, and how should we research them? What types of practices apply to settings beyond conventional technical communication? The critiques cited above, and other socially-oriented research both within technical communication and in related disciplines, suggest some directions by identifying issues that recur in case studies. These issues have analogues in industry practice.

STAKEHOLDER PARTICIPATION AND EXCLUSION: INVOKING HABERMAS

The critiques of failed discourse are rooted in social concepts of discourse with the premises that knowledge is constructed, not found, that language can never accurately reflect an absolute and external reality, and that readers or participants are co-constructors of meaning. These views challenge hierarchical systems of decision making with top-down imposition of policy. They also question the privileging of technical data over human and social values.

Participation—and its antithesis, silencing—is a theme that recurs throughout the critiques and case studies. Participation defines who has a voice and therefore power. An imbalance of power means that policies may be distorted to benefit the powerful rather than the common good. Furthermore, failed policies and decisions often result from too narrow an assessment of the issues, which in turn results from the limited perspectives of a few decision makers. Besides inviting multiple stakeholders to participate in decision making, wide participation allows decision makers to balance technical data with human and social goals. Any discussion of best practices in the discourse that affects policies must consider how to involve stakeholders in the decision making. One way to limit participation is to assert the superior reasoning of experts. Expert testimony excludes by being technical and by privileging quantifiable data over discursive reasoning. It argues almost exclusively with appeals to logos and is condescending to ethos and pathos.

The pitting of the social against the technical is common in critique of communication practice in industry and government. For example, Thomas B. Farrell and G. Thomas Goodnight, discussing communication failures after Three Mile Island, write:

> Technical reasoning, interested in prediction and control, employs non-reflexive procedures in order to solve puzzles integral to specialized codes. By contrast, social reasoning focuses upon situation-dependent problems, employing self-criticism in order to inform choice and guide conduct toward a more perfect society [6, p. 97].

A number of researchers [9-11, 15] invoke Jürgen Habermas's social theory to critique practice in policy decisions. Particularly fruitful for the critiques is Habermas's contrast of instrumental rationality with communicative rationality [18]. One difference is in the way communicative and instrumental rationality approach and recognize truth.

Instrumental rationality, associated with bureaucracy and systems, assumes clear connections of causes and effects or means and ends. This is a rationality of facts, order, control, and efficiency. Experts determine a course of action and impose it. Systems are hierarchical. Deviant discourse might be recognized but not particularly accommodated. Instrumental rationality finds its application in goal-oriented "strategic action."

Communicative rationality, by contrast, is participatory and is associated with the "lifeworld." It assumes truth to derive from consensus of participants. Truth is not universal. Participation means involving the public in decision making. Language (argument, rhetoric) is the means of achieving consensus or at least agreements on courses of action that accommodate differences. Communicative rationality is inefficient, messy, and time consuming, but it allows disagreement, critique, and reasons that are not tied strictly to facts. As an alternative to the quantitative and technological measures of instrumental rationality, Habermas identifies four "validity claims" to mark undistorted communication. This communication is meaningful (can be understood), truthful, justified (certain social norms or rights are invoked), and sincere (no attempt to deceive) [18, pp. 305–309].

Flaws in communication practices are explained in Habermasian terms. Wells claims that the commission investigating the government violence against the MOVE group in Philadelphia oversimplifies causes and effects by using instrumental rationality [11]. Although the commission is critical of government, its report, with its gaps and bullet points, tidies up the mess and restores order—an aim of instrumental rationality. Blyler, describing the triumph of bureaucracy over concerned citizens in a hospital expansion case, concludes that technocratic consciousness has usurped communicative action in social life and that communicative action is an unachievable ideal in such cases [15]. Killingsworth and Palmer claim that the guidelines for the environmental impact statement (EIS) impose instrumental rationality on a process that presumably includes the public in environmental decision making [9]. The marginalization of individuals affected by environmental action is built into the values that direct the development and construction of an environmental impact statement. All of these studies point to participation as a condition of effective policy making, and while all claim some generalizable findings, they focus on specific cases, a locus for action.

Dayton [10] both confirms and complicates Killingsworth and Palmer's study [9] of environmental impact statements, comparing two cases with different processes and outcomes. In one environmental impact investigation, the government representatives remained distant from and condescending toward the citizens in a process marked by conflict and distrust. In the second investigation, citizens and planners worked effectively together toward mutual goals in developing a rapid transit system. While the other analyses have focused on problems and the uneven struggle of citizens for power against bureaucracy, Dayton finds some reason for optimism that citizens can participate in policy making and that the EIS guidelines do not preclude this process—assuming that other circumstances (personalities, procedures, common interests) encourage it. Dayton's conditions include an openness to citizen participation during the planning of a major project, not just the opportunity for comment at the end of the process. The successful case he studied involved a series of public meetings on the rapid transit case with adjustments in plans reflecting public wishes, an example of communicative action. This case, along with the Killingsworth and Palmer example of the marginalization of public comments after the draft EIS was developed, suggests that effective participation must be part of the entire process. Participation restricted to the end of the process is likely to be no more than an appendix, both to the document and to the policy-making process. This conclusion echoes growing awareness in computer documentation that users must be consulted during product development and that technical communicators can play a valuable role if they, too, are part of the development process and not just brought in at the end for cleanup.

Hauser, while not writing from the perspective of technical communication, has studied a variety of situations in which an expert elite either accommodates public voices or reduces them to the technological data of polls [19]. Hauser modifies Habermas's theory to emphasize local norms of reasonableness over global norms of rationality. He insists that public opinion is constructed through conversation in informal settings and further that civil judgment regulates power even though it is based on a discourse outside of power [19, p. 75]. His thorough case studies reveal the limitations of processes that exclude public voices. These studies confirm that participant voices will be heard even when they are subverted. He relates the failure of the 1980s report by the Meese Commission on pornography, for example, to exclusion of some perspectives, and he links Jimmy Carter's failure to win reelection to his reduction of public opinion to poll data.

What can these critiques and studies reveal about best practice in policy discourse? One thing they offer is a vocabulary for identifying who gets to participate in policy making. They identify differences between expert and stakeholder perspectives and between communicative rationality and instrumental rationality. They suggest alternatives to the technological reasoning of experts, particularly rhetorical reflection and validity claims that emphasize communication rather than the distortion of technologized answers. That knowledge makes it easier for someone involved in a controversy to recognize what is happening and how different people may be predicted to act. One good practice is to be informed, not just about the issues in the controversy but also about methods by which a resolution may be approached. The critiques tend to be pessimistic about the domination of experts with power, but Hauser is confident that the public voice continues to regulate power, and Dayton's second example [10] illustrates communicative action. Limited examples prove nothing, but they do provide a starting point for evaluating what practices succeed. Perhaps all the examples point to local situations rather than universal practices as sites both for study and for action.

FEMINIST CRITIQUE

Feminist critique also points to issues of empowerment and exclusion in social problems. Several studies note not just the exclusion of voices but also of topics that should influence inquiries and outcomes. Sauer connects rational, objective discourse and the silencing of human suffering to male thought [14]. The perpetuation of power structures takes precedence over health and safety. Orbell and Cargile-Cook both find strategies of avoidance in unsatisfactory reports regarding the status of women in the military. Orbell discusses a series of failed reports on Tailhook 91, each bypassing certain difficult topics or information by the constraints it imposes on purpose or research method [8]. Eventually, the reports and the analyses point not just to events and to particular people but to cultural values, especially values regarding women and power, and to the discourse that constructs as well as reflects these values. The contrast between Orbell's rhetorical analysis of the reports and the reports themselves illustrates the potential of rhetoric in discovery of reasons for ruptures and in defining productive future social action. Some failures in the Tailhook reports result from an antirhetorical stance by the investigators — an insistence on looking only at what could be measured or observed in an "objective" way and the tendency to restrict the inquiry to answering "what happened?" (the forensic question) as opposed to "what should be done to prevent recurrence?" (the deliberative question). Although the investigators skirted questions of values, they inevitably made epideictic statements, which the rhetorical analysis revealed. A rhetorical approach, as provided by Orbell's analysis, reveals more than the scientific, objective approach: it questions the status quo, considers contextual issues, accepts responsibility for looking forward as well as back, and considers values as well as facts. This kind of inquiry suggests ways in which the interests of technical communication and the methods of rhetoric may combine productively to enrich study of the discourse that shapes policy decisions.

Cargile-Cook discovers that Government Accounting Office investigators of complaints of harassment in the military academies, biased in favor of quantifiable data, avoid querying victims or challenging the chain-of-command reporting process that discourages complaints [20]. Although they recommend changes in record keeping of incidents, they maintain the status quo. The goal of investigation and reporting seems to be to address the problems safely, without significant disruption of current processes and organizational structures. Applying postmodern mapping to analysis of the reports, she demonstrates a workable method of identifying gaps in arguments and choices about issues to foreground.

Ranney observes that the supposed neutrality of policy writing and enforcement is a cover for gender blindness [21]. The U.S. national sexual harassment policy works as a "discursive technology," a "verbal prescription of behaviors, violations, and treatments" [21, p. 14]. Countering the sense of policy documents as vehicles to convey rules, Ranney recommends seeing policies as the culmination of investigations into values and choices among alternative options [21, p. 20], investigations in which workers would participate. This "user-centered" approach could accommodate situation, constraints, and unwritten rules. The users or employees would be makers of knowledge, not just consumers.

All four of these writers point to gaps in arguments as well as to silencing. Their analyses require thinking beyond the page, beyond what is given, to what issues might be addressed but are not. Including the relevant issues requires including the relevant voices. The contrast between reasoning that is bound by technical data and reasoning that is broad and discursive appears in the documents and situations that these writers address, as it does in examples discussed in the previous sections. These writers reject the idea that a text may define the scope of an issue.

The participation and inclusion themes that are so prevalent in critique have industry analogues. A major change in the process of developing documentation in industry has been to involve users of products in the design and testing of the products and documentation. Instead of experts delivering products via technical writers to an inexpert public (the translator model, the top-down model), products develop with user participation. Technical communicators are not merely scribes and translators but assume responsibility for articulating user needs to designers and for actively analyzing the design and recommending improvements. "Communication" is more than competence with sentences and paragraphs; it constructs priorities, relationships, tasks, and even technology. The "articulation" concept of author, according to Slack, Miller, and Doak, offers more power than the "transmission" or "translation" concepts [22]. Ranney finds some promise for overcoming authorless regulatory texts in the concept of a user-centered approach to policy making [21].

STUDIES OF STAKEHOLDER PARTICIPATION
IN PRACTICE

Critiques establish participation and inclusion as standards of best practice in policy discourse. What we don't know particularly well is how to integrate stakeholders in policy making and where the knowledge of technical communication contributes. Participation may take various forms, some of which may give the impression of participation without actually giving participants meaningful voices. In their review of 23 empirical studies on public meetings, workshops, and community advisory committees, Chess and Purcell distinguish public participation as "boosterism" to support agency claims and presentation to the public after decisions have been made from efforts that involve citizens while policy is being developed [23]. They encourage evaluation of participation both according to participatory process and outcome of the process. "Participation" is too complex to equate simply with best practice; the concept needs to be refined, analyzed, and placed in context with the documents that enable or discourage this interaction. Some studies have begun this work.

Waddell has both theorized participation and studied it [24]. His four-part scheme for different models of public participation includes the technocratic, a top-down imposition of policy developed by experts; the one-way Jeffersonian model, which involves the public but in which the transfer of knowledge is one way, from expert to public; the interactive Jeffersonian, in which experts might adjust their positions in response to public views; and the social constructionist, in which communication involves an interactive exchange of information. To investigate public participation in practice and its consequences, he studied public hearings and documents in the International Joint Commission on water quality in the Great Lakes by observing the hearings, interviewing representative speakers and commissioners, and analyzing the report. He concludes that public participation probably did influence the commissioners [24, p. 153]. For example, the history of participation over time encouraged a more open opportunity for participation in the hearings that Waddell observed. Although the commissioners were probably convinced by scientific evidence gathered in their investigation, they likely were persuaded to action by the emotional appeals of the speakers telling of human health consequences of pollution in the Great Lakes [24, p. 153]. Waddell also observes that homocentric appeals were far more effective than ecocentric appeals, although the speakers who could link the appeals may have made the ecocentric appeals accessible to a larger audience [24, p. 156]. The commission's report acknowledges the information gathered and shared by public groups. Waddell believes that the social construc- tionist model can expand democratic governance and decentralize political power and that it should be the model for public participation [24, p. 158].

In his research on client involvement in HIV/AIDS local planning councils, Grabill sought procedures to overcome barriers to participa- tion [25]. He identifies boundaries of physical access, time of meetings, transportation, health, and specialized languages of organizations that keep clients from participating meaningfully in planning. Participating on a task force to increase involvement, Grabill and other members persuaded the planning council to give their group committee status, thereby increasing its power. Grabill describes this new structure as an institutional change, inserting client involvement into ongoing decision making. He writes, "In this little way, we have changed the process of client involvement, although we have yet to impact in any significant way how policy is made" [25, p. 45]. Where does technical communication fit in? Grabill defines "documentation" not as a narrow textual practice but as the act of designing processes and describes his project as being about documentation in this broader sense. His definition suggests the "ecological model" of writing that Cooper offered in 1986, in which "writing is an activity through which a person is continually engaged with a variety of socially constituted systems" [26, p. 367]. These systems "are made and remade by writers in the act of writing" [26, p. 368]. The writer is not the solitary author but rather an "infinitely extended group of people who interact through writing" [26, p. 372]. This sense of writing also reflects Miller's concept of practical rhetoric "as a matter of *conduct* rather than of production, as a matter of arguing in a prudent way toward the good of the community rather than of constructing texts" [27, p. 23].

Savage reports the experience of a consultant on health and safety manuals to a company with traditional values [28]. As a consultant, Savage observes, this writer had more direct access to managers than staff employees might have as well as stature resulting from her professional reputation. Although the managers resisted her suggestions of including workers in developing safety policies and procedures, her discussion of her position convinced them to yield in some respects. She feels that through her discussion with managers and with workers, she laid the groundwork for a change from a legalistic, rule-driven manual to one in which the workers participated in developing the policies.

Waddell's, Grabill's, and Savage's studies suggest that the research into the processes that affect participation is an active and engaged research, in the moment of the action rather than afterwards. While some of the research may be textual, it is likely to consider social and organizational issues as well. Savage's consultant considered herself more than a writer: as a consultant with access to managers, she also influenced values and practices. Waddell and Grabill both look extensively at the organizational structures and political contexts of participation. Dayton's work with the environmental impact statement [10] also rests on experiential as well as textual knowledge. This kind of research is central to defining best practices in policy discourse because it examines the processes, not just the results, and it considers the situations in which the texts are produced, not just the texts. The examples also suggest that action and results are likely to happen on a small scale and over time, with a small concession at one point opening opportunities for greater change at a future time.

It is hopeful to acknowledge that citizen participation can have positive effects on policy making, in some circumstances, and that there are established mechanisms (advisory committees, public meetings, workshops and seminars, written materials) for engaging the public in planning future action. Communication mediates and permeates all the processes and results. At the same time, there is more to learn about composition and size of groups, personalities, process management, and communication strategies.

DISCIPLINARY KNOWLEDGE

Critiques reveal the significance of the problems of discourse as it is used in policy making, but they also reveal gaps in knowledge that would be useful in correcting or preventing the problems. These gaps relate not just to the texts but also to the processes of developing them, mechanisms for including public participation, the contexts in which they will be used, and their genres and language. Although the established body of knowledge within technical communication about discourse in policy making may be too limited at present to give technical communication a voice with any power, researchers and practitioners within technical communication potentially have much to offer. Technical communication scholars are comfortable researching processes and management of document development, collaboration, contexts of use, users, genres, and language, and the field has methods for gathering additional information, including rhetorical and discourse analysis, case study, and ethnography. Furthermore, there are theoretical bases for this work, including rhetorical theory; critical theory on the themes of domination, ideology, and the transformation of society; literacy and what constitutes the ability to function in society; and theories of technology in society. There is an increasingly substantial body of work within technical communication on ethics and on risk communication. All of this knowledge has application for best practices in spheres beyond industry.

The field's strength is best developed in understanding of language. Language is powerful in influencing as well as replicating values. The right metaphor can alter the course of a debate and open up possibilities for different policies. A good example is the metaphor of *sustainability* or *sustainable development* in environmental studies. "Ecospeak," as Killingsworth and Palmer define it [9], is the impasse of opponents considering the issues from different perspectives, one pro-environment, the other pro-development. "Sustainable development" yokes the two positions into a shared goal, development with the condition of sustainability, and ecospeak yields to discussion. Waddell offers an expanded definition of sustainability development and suggests that it "illustrates the Social Constructionist Model of environmental-policy formation, in that it draws upon the knowledge and values of both experts and the 'non-expert' public" [29, p. 14]. Another useful metaphor in technical communication is *usability* or *user-centered*. It has come to define not just the way in which people interact with technical artifacts but also more broadly their engagement in determining the goals for the product (system, process, policy, software) and the human measure of whether a product has value. This is the way in which Ranney [21] uses the term in suggesting alternatives to the supposed neutrality of sexual harassment policy. Both *sustainability* and *user-centered* are metaphors that resonate beyond the situations in which they emerged. They also incorporate both social and instrumental values and become a point of contact between opposing viewpoints. Developing and using such metaphors is part of best practices of discourse in the public sphere.

Case studies of communication practices within organizations expand the sense of how situation influences both the construction and interpretation of discourse. These examples become part of disciplinary knowledge and influence the definition of best practices. Studies of flawed practice have revealed unusual demands on corporate communication at times of stress. One lesson of the Challenger is that it is harder to convince a manager of bad news than of good news, and this difficulty is compounded when multiple corporations are involved [4]. Another lesson is that politeness may be misunderstood as reassurance [3]. The memo regarding transportation of Jews to extermination camps that Katz [12] studies is an example of how style embodies the values of the culture that it represents, and the unsayable becomes sayable by the distancing of language conventions that the culture accepts. At the least, students preparing for jobs in corporations or any other organization should be prepared for the ways in which the cultures of these organizations may influence who they become.

PEDAGOGY TO SUPPORT SOCIAL RESPONSIBILITY

The increasing power of technical communicators in the workplace has developed not just in that site but with the support of colleges and universities that have developed robust curricula supporting user-centered, task-oriented documentation and an expanding definition of "writers" as architects and designers. Courses in project management, usability testing, and technology, along with more offerings in the conventional areas of writing and editing, have empowered entry-level writers and have given them some expectations for how they might function in substantial, valuable ways. Academic support for writing in the area of policy will be needed if technical communication is to have any power in the public sphere. Much disciplinary knowledge can be transferred to new settings, but students can contribute more in their alternative worksites if their courses have prepared them specifically. Concentrations on writing in the public sphere also bring visibility to this area of technical communication and help to establish this link between the discipline and the public site of practice.

The critiques of policy and organizational discourse often focus on the limits of the language used in policies or in investigations. Where the discourse produced in the cases is flawed, it is not entirely clear whether the writers (not professional writers) were devious and calculating, inept, or so caught up in the values of the sponsoring organizations that they could not think and write independently. Certainly bureaucratic, neutral, and objective discourse has been linked to the value system that trusts quantifiable data more than intuition, that privileges rationality over communication and male over female, that is more comfortable with the status quo than with change, and that pits technology against humanity. Yet some of the bureaucratic prose that the cases quote often seems more naïve than calculating, somewhat like the weighty prose that undergraduates offer when they are trying to sound smart but don't have the knowledge to do it other than by hiding behind clumsy, overwrought constructions. The (poor) quality of the prose raises questions about whether these writers have had instruction in writing policy and whether they lapse into immature writing and replication of common thought patterns because no one has shown them an alternative. Are these writers "transmitters" or "translators" of the usual thinking because no one has given them the strategies for being "articulators"? A survey of technical communication texts in the mid-1990s revealed that a small minority of the textbooks suggested that investigators recommending actions or making decisions should consider social issues along with technical and managerial issues [30]. The sense that facts acquired by right methods will speak for themselves and that good thinking is marked by distancing oneself from the issue permeates this field. In the vehicle by which the field shares its knowledge beyond its own boundaries (textbooks), issues of policy and decision making are largely absent.

Laying the burden on technical communication of making not only better writers but also better policy makers is asking more than a small field can accomplish. Since most students other than technical communication majors will take no more than one technical writing course, it's outrageous to expect that this field can turn around centuries of thinking patterns. On the other hand, the goals do not need to be that ambitious to begin to make some changes. Most policies that affect individuals do not exist in the life-threatening and dramatic situations that the critiques typically describe. They are local and organizational policies about working conditions, hiring practices, the environment, healthcare, distribution of wealth, transportation, fees, and other such everyday issues. Rather ordinary people, some of whom pass through technical communication classes, make and enforce these policies. Power obviously resides with those who can influence multitudes, but it also resides in small places, with the people who know how to claim it. Claiming power requires using the knowledge of discourse, the values of inclusion, and the thinking that articulation encourages. The classroom is one place where potential policy makers can learn to research, to frame questions, to consider multiple issues, to reason, and to articulate their conclusions and recommendations.

Some courses are dedicated to preparing future policy makers. For example, Smith teaches a practicum in writing public policy at Syracuse University for students of public affairs and policy studies [31]. Her students write various policy documents, including white papers, mission statements, and strategy memos. They interact with elected and appointed policy makers and organization leaders, and they simulate a legislative open hearing to deliberate legislation on a topic such as education reform. In the context of a writing class, they learn research, analysis, deliberation, and debate. Their interactions with individuals already engaged in policy making complicate glib assumptions. And they learn enough of how the genres function to give them some confidence when they have writing tasks as professionals. Perhaps they will not have to default to bureaucratize to cover uncertainty.

In a course on writing to shape public policy, Martin and Sanders invite professionals writing about the same issue of public policy into their classrooms [32]. From the varied perspectives of these professionals, students can see the complexity of the issues, analyze the arguments, and write their own papers on different policy issues incorporating multiple points of view [32, p. 152]. The students consider the possibility that writers "may become agents of change to help bring resolution to potentially conflicted issues" [32, p. 156] and wrestle with the place of personal narrative in investigations that aim to be objective and factual.

In the same spirit of the Smith and Martin and Sanders courses, Bereano teaches a course at the University of Washington on the policy dimensions of genetic engineering [33]. He also teaches a course on analyzing documents of a public character (proposals, environmental impact statements, technology assessments) that aims for understanding of the socio-political milieu in which the documents are planned, organized, and written; and "specialized audiences (e.g., agencies with their missions, guidelines, constituencies; citizen groups; commercial interests)" that the documents serve. This linking of writing with issues and situations suggests the vital way in which writing is engaged with deliberation and decision making. Bereano's courses also suggest ways in which writing, technology, and social issues intersect within technical communication.

Blyler [34] and Herndl [35] would teach courses that foreground ideology, especially the role of language in reproducing the values and power structure of a culture. Blyler argues that narrative lends insight into culture and is a means by which groups are constituted. Herndl would engage the students in reflecting on the politics of writing within the university. Such ideologically-based courses would develop the reflection and critique that influence practice.

Service learning also provides opportunities for offering students some critical tools for thinking about problems and policies, especially if the course requires students to reflect on the values and assumptions that are explicit or implicit in the organizations for which the students work and if students examine the discourse of the organization critically. Students might be assigned to write a reflection paper on the explicit and implicit organizational values and communication practices where they intern. This kind of paper would be appropriate whether students are preparing for careers in the public sector or in industry. Service learning may also open opportunities for research that explores communication in organizations, including issues of power, status, gender, and technology. For example, Grabill's client involvement project [25] began as a service learning project in a technical communication class.

Developing dedicated courses within technical communication on social and policy issues or reframing of service courses are small steps in the direction of developing a voice for technical communication in the public sphere, if only in the indirect way of influencing students who will go out and make decisions. The results will not be dramatic: there will continue to be shocking cases of domination, exclusion, and abuse, and the evidence will be encoded in text as though the text itself bears responsibility apart from the situation in which it was created, but perhaps it is better to start somewhere than not at all. Again the analogy of the workplace is instructive: the increasing power of technical communicators has not happened overnight but rather has been an ongoing process of about two decades that is still ongoing.

CONCLUSION

The pursuit of a role for technical communication in the public sphere seems marked now by a sense of responsibility constrained by pessimism and lack of knowledge about how to put values into practice. In addition, there is no critical mass of people doing technical communication in the public sphere with a sense of shared identity, such as that afforded to workplace writers by the Society for Technical Communication. The evidence of multiple cases in which discourse has failed to prevent catastrophe or has avoided coming to terms with it encourages the pessimism. The story of bureaucracy dominating or excluding citizens occurs too regularly to ignore. But other cases, mostly local and small, offer some insight into the practices that enable citizens to participate in constructing policies that honor and support humanity and the democratic process. Disciplinary knowledge is available to improve practices.

Unless technical communication can identify practices that direct policy discourse so that it will suit the values of the field, it will retain the relatively powerless role of judging after the fact. Furthermore, within the field of technical communication itself, those who care about public discourse will be adjuncts in a field that is already an adjunct to the computer industry. The topic raises multiple questions of power: whether technical communication has a voice and power beyond industry, whether the field can embrace both computer documentation and issues of social policy, and even the place of the field within industry. It raises questions of the scope of the field, a scope that is too narrow, says Whitburn in a recent history of technical communication [36]. Whitburn's study shows diminishment in technical communication over the years as it has rejected the broad Isocratean tradition in rhetoric and accepted a limited role for itself. A healthy, whole field will probably not be defined as a service field but as a field with its own knowledge that applies in multiple arenas. At stake are disciplinary identity and social responsibility.

REFERENCES

1. P. Dombrowski, The Lessons of the Challenger Investigations, *IEEE Transactions on Professional Communication, 34*:4, pp. 211–216, 1991.
2. C. G. Herndl, B. A. Fennell, and C. R. Miller, Understanding Failures in Organizational Discourse: The Accident at Three Mile Island and the Shuttle Challenger Disaster, in *Textual Dynamics of the Professions: Historical and Contemporary Studies of Writing in Professional Communities*, C. Bazerman and J. Paradis (eds.), University of Wisconsin Press, Madison, 1991.
3. P. Moore, When Politeness is Fatal, *Journal of Business and Technical Communication, 6*:3, pp. 262–292, 1992.
4. D. A. Winsor, Communication Failures Contributing to the Challenger Accident: An Example for Technical Communicators, *IEEE Transactions on Professional Communication, 31*:3, pp. 101–107, 1988.
5. D. A. Winsor, The Construction of Knowledge in Organizations: Asking the Right Questions about the Challenger, *Journal of Business and Technical Communication, 4*:2, pp. 7–20, 1990.
6. T. B. Farrell and G. T. Goodnight, Accidental Rhetoric: The Root Metaphors of Three Mile Island, *Communication Monographs, 48*, pp. 221–237, 1981. Rpt. in *Landmark Essays on Rhetoric and the Environment*, C. Waddell (ed.), Erlbaum, Mahwah, New Jersey, pp. 75–105, 1998.
7. B. Orbell, The DoD Tailhook Report: Unanswered Questions, *Journal of Technical Writing and Communication, 25*:2, pp. 201–213, 1995.

8. B. C. Orbell, *Discourse, Power, and Social Ruptures: An Analysis of Tailhook 91,* unpublished doctoral dissertation, Texas Tech University, 1997. UMI order number 9812049.
9. M. J. Killingsworth and J. S. Palmer, *Ecospeak: Rhetoric and Environmental Politics in America,* Southern Illinois University Press, Carbondale, 1992.
10. D. Dayton, Evaluating Environmental Impact Statements as Communicative Action, *Journal of Business and Technical Communication, 16*:3, pp. 355-405, 2002.
11. S. Wells, Narrative Figures and Subtle Persuasions, in *The Rhetorical Turn: Invention and Persuasion in the Conduct of Inquiry,* H. W. Simons (ed.), University of Chicago Press, Chicago, pp. 208-231, 1990.
12. S. B. Katz, The Ethic of Expediency, *College English, 54*:3, pp. 255-275, 1992.
13. P. M. Dombrowski, Nazi Records: The Origin and Use of Information, in *Ethics in Technical Communication,* Allyn & Bacon, Boston, pp. 81-120, 2000.
14. B. A. Sauer, Sense and Sensibility in Technical Documentation: How Feminist Interpretation Strategies Can Save Lives in the Nation's Mines, *Journal of Business and Technical Communication, 7*:1, pp. 63-83, 1993.
15. N. Blyler, Habermas, Empowerment, and Professional Discourse, *Technical Communication Quarterly, 3*:2, pp. 125-145, 1994.
16. W. Martin (ed.), Special Issue on Public Policy and Professional Communication, *IEEE Transactions on Professional Communication, 34*:4, 1991.
17. N. W. Coppola and B. Karis (eds.), *Technical Communication, Deliberative Rhetoric, and Environmental Discourse: Connections and Directions,* Ablex, Stamford, Connecticut, 2000.
18. J. Habermas, *The Theory of Communicative Action,* Vol. 1. *Reason and the Rationalization of Society,* T. McCarthy (trans.), Beacon, Boston, 1984.
19. G. Hauser, *Vernacular Voices: The Rhetoric of Publics and Public Spheres,* University of South Carolina Press, Columbia, 1999.
20. K. Cargile-Cook, Writers and Their Maps: The Construction of a GAO Report on Sexual Harassment, *Technical Communication Quarterly, 9*:1, pp. 53-76, Winter 2000.
21. F. J. Ranney, Beyond Foucault: Toward a User-Centered Approach to Sexual Harassment Policy, *Technical Communication Quarterly, 9*:1, pp. 9-28, 2000.
22. J. D. Slack, D. J. Miller, and J. Doak, The Technical Communicator as Author: Meaning, Power, Authority, *Journal of Business and Technical Communication, 7*:1, pp. 12-36, 1993.
23. C. Chess and K. Purcell, Public Participation and the Environment: Do We Know What Works? *Environmental Science & Technology, 33*:16, pp. 2685-2692, 1999.
24. C. Waddell, Saving the Great Lakes: Public Participation in Environmental Policy, in *Green Culture: Environmental Rhetoric in Contemporary America,* C. G. Herndl and S. C. Brown (eds.), University of Wisconsin Press, Madison, pp. 141-165, 1996.
25. J. T. Grabill, Shaping Local HIV/AIDS Services Policy through Activist Research: The Problem of Client Involvement, *Technical Communication Quarterly, 9*:1, pp. 29-50, Winter 2000.

26. M. M. Cooper, The Ecology of Writing, *College English, 48*:4, pp. 364–375, April 1986.

27. C. R. Miller, What's Practical about Technical Writing?, in *Technical Writing: Theory and Practice*, B. E. Fearing and W. K. Sparrow (eds.), Modern Language Association, New York, pp. 14–24, 1989.

28. G. J. Savage, Redefining the Responsibilities of Teachers and the Social Position of the Technical Communicator, *Technical Communication Quarterly, 5*:3, pp. 309–327, 1996.

29. C. Waddell, Defining Sustainable Development: A Case Study in Environmental Communication, in *Technical Communication, Deliberative Rhetoric, and Environmental Discourse: Connections and Directions*, N. W. Coppola and B. Karis (eds.), Ablex, Stamford, Connecticut, pp. 3–19, 2000.

30. C. D. Rude, The Report for Decision Making: Genre and Inquiry, *Journal of Business and Technical Communication, 9*:2, pp. 170–205, 1995.

31. C. F. Smith, Writing Public Policy: A Practicum, *Technical Communication Quarterly, 9*:1, pp. 77–92, 2000.

32. W. Martin and S. Sanders, Ethics, Audience, and the Writing Process: Bringing Public Policy Issues into the Classroom, *Technical Communication Quarterly, 3*:2, pp. 147–163, 1994.

33. P. Bereano, *TC 408 Public Documents: Proposals, Environmental Impact Statements, Assessments*, University of Washington, September 15, 2000. www.uwtc.washington.edu/courses_and_programs/courses/tc408.htm

34. N. R. Blyler, Pedagogy and Social Action: A Role for Narrative in Professional Communication, *Journal of Business and Technical Communication, 9*:3, pp. 289–320, July 1995.

35. C. G. Herndl, Teaching Discourse and Reproducing Culture: A Critique of Research and Pedagogy in Professional and Non-Academic Writing, *College Composition and Communication, 44*:3, pp. 349–363, 1993.

36. M. Whitburn, *Rhetorical Scope and Performance: The Example of Technical Communication*, Ablex, Stamford, Connecticut, 2000.

CHAPTER 8

Critical Interpretive Research in Technical Communication: Issues of Power and Legitimacy

Nancy Roundy Blyler

In this chapter, I examine the implications of adopting an alternate research perspective to the one common in technical communication. In doing so, I suggest that scholars have the opportunity to reconsider long-held and seemingly foundational assumptions about our research, opening up new directions for our work and providing additional possibilities in the choice of acceptable research sites and methods. Scholars also, I suggest, have the opportunity to reflect on the goals for research, thus rethinking the way power works in our research practices and—ultimately—altering the type of legitimacy sought for our field. Below, I further examine these issues of power and legitimacy.

POWER AND LEGITIMACY IN TECHNICAL COMMUNICATION

Scholars in technical communication recognize the importance of examining issues of power [1-5] and legitimacy. They note, for example, the long-standing connections between technical communication and such traditional sources of power as science, business, and industry [5, p. 59; 6]. They also critique what they feel is a tendency toward domination and exclusion in technical communication practices.

These critiques concern a variety of contexts and bring to bear a number of theoretical perspectives. Sauer, for example, uses feminist theory to examine technical documentation, concluding that investigation reports on mine accidents exclude "alternative voices and thus perpetuate salient and silent power structures" [7, p. 63]. Similarly, the Bartons draw on Foucault to study technical and professional visuals, treating them as "sites of power inscription" [8, p. 138] that can either disempower or empower the viewer. Finally, Slack, Miller, and Doak use Hall's articulation theory to analyze three views of technical communication (as transmission, translation, and articulation), noting that technical communicators "are always implicated in relations of power" [9, p. 31] regardless of the view with which they are identified.

As a profession, then, we are re-examining the links between technical communication and traditional sources of power and legitimacy and critiquing practices that these and other scholars identify as exclusionary. What we are only beginning to study, however, are questions of power and legitimacy as they pertain to our research practices.

In a discussion of ethnographic research, Herndl lays the foundation for this type of critique. Challenging scholars in technical communication to "discover the sources of ethnography's persuasive power," he suggests that we view ethnography as embedded in "institutional discourse." Ethnography becomes, then, not simply a method of study, but also a way for the discipline to "organize and control knowledge and social power." "Its propositions," says Herndl, "must refer to a specific range of objects, belong to a certain theoretical field, and use concepts recognized by the discipline's theoretical model" [4, p. 323]. To Herndl, therefore, ethnographic research is less about a "relationship to fact" [4, p. 322] than it is about power and exclusion.

Herndl's examination of ethnographic research is certainly a beginning, as is Grabill's more recent and more general discussion of technical communication's "critical turn" [10, p. 33; see also 11]. We need, however, to expand on these scholars' work, in particular connecting our research practices to broader issues of power and to the legitimacy of technical communication as a field. We need, for example, to better understand how power operates in our research practices and the ways that, like other technical communication practices, they might be implicated in domination and exclusion. We also need to better understand the kind of legitimacy our current research practices lend to our discipline. And finally, we need to continue to explore alternate research practices that might be available to us, so that—should we choose—we can focus more on empowerment, altering the type of legitimacy sought for our field.

In this chapter, I want to move us in this direction. More specifically, I want to discuss issues of power and legitimacy in connection with both research as it has traditionally been conceived in technical communication and critical interpretive research: a perspective that—in one of its manifestations[1]—employs radically participatory methodologies to effect empowerment and social change [see 13]. Against the backdrop o this alternate perspective for research, I claim that scholars in technical communication who wish to engage in critical interpretive research should rethink issues of power to put a priority on empowerment. In doing so, I also claim, scholars must reconsider the ways both their research and our field are legitimized, arriving at a view of the profession that some scholars may find more socially and ethically appealing.

In order to understand, however, how such rethinking—and change—are possible, we must further explore this notion of power. In the next section, I use theory in cultural studies to undercut our commonplace assumption that power—such as that acquired by our research practices—is inherent in those practices, allowing them to repress and dominate alternatives.

CULTURAL STUDIES AND POWER

Theorists in cultural studies undercut our ideas about power in two ways. First, rather than being merely repressive, power is considered productive. Grossberg, for example, defines power as "the enablement of particular practices"—the "conditions of possibility" that allow "a particular practice or statement to exist in a specific social context" [14, p. 95]. And second, rather than being inherent in or intrinsic to any entity, power is seen as being acquired through links to other entities. As Grossberg says of practices, they are "like chemical radicals; while they may momentarily appear to be free-floating during some disruptive experimental intervention, their identity and power depends [sic] upon their re-entrance into particular relationships" [14, p. 87].

Grossberg's focus on relationships suggests that, in order to understand how our research is implicated in power, we must examine the connections between it and a host of other practices—what Grossberg calls the "interpretive context out of which [practices] emerge, into which they are inserted, and within which their theoretical and political consequences are articulated" [14, p. 87]. Only by thinking of power and our research in this way can we fully understand where its sources

---

[1] The type of critical interpretive research I discuss here is participatory. A second type of critical interpretive research is largely analytical. In this type, researchers attempt to empower audiences by examining the workings of power and the relations of domination and exclusion that they believe exist in various settings, rather than by joining with participants in research projects [see 12].

of power are and how those sources—and hence our research—might be changed.

This type of critique, where the connections (or what cultural studies' theorists, following Hall, call "articulations" [15, p. 53]) among practices are examined within a broad and complex interpretive context, is already being advocated by technical communication scholars. In discussing cultural studies as a research orientation, for example, Blyler and Thralls assert that, instead of studying social practices in isolation, researchers must examine them in all their relations to one another, because significance and meaning result from the connections among practices in specific situations [12]. In addition, when looking at institutions as cultural agents, Longo recommends that technical writing as a practice be placed within "situated relationships of knowledge and power" [5, p. 54] extending well beyond the confines of a single organization. And finally, when discussing the technical communicator as author, Slack, Miller, and Doak claim that "social practices, ideological positions, discursive statements, social groups, and so on are also articulated identities" [9, p. 28] and thus that the meaning of the term "technical communicator" changes depending on the particular complex of linkages or context into which it is inserted.

In the next section, I want to build on the work of these scholars, using this notion of relationships or articulations to examine issues of power and legitimacy in technical communication research as it has traditionally been conceived.

POWER, LEGITIMACY, AND TRADITIONAL RESEARCH IN TECHNICAL COMMUNICATION

Research in technical communication is connected to a host of disciplinary, institutional, and societal and cultural practices. The practice of tenure and promotion, for example, is clearly tied to our research [16], as is the practice of housing technical communication within different administrative units at various universities (e.g., conventional English departments [17, pp. 18-19] versus other units such as engineering [16, pp. 79-82]). Both of these practices, along with others too numerous to mention, shape the research that is connected to them, enabling some possibilities while disempowering others [see, for example, 16, pp. 79-82 for a discussion of the types of research valorized by different administrative units].

I want, however, to examine two other practices integral to technical communication research: our disciplinary discourse about the qualitative research process and seeking funding for research initiatives. Examining these two practices, I believe, reveals the way power operates to enable our traditional conception of research while excluding alternate perspectives from consideration. Further, examining these two practices indicates how closely our research is connected to traditional power sources — science, business, and industry — clarifying the kind of legitimacy our research practices lend to our field. In the next two sections I discuss these issues of power and legitimacy in connection with our research practices as traditionally conceived.

Traditional Research Practices and Power

Both of the practices I identify — disciplinary discourse about the qualitative research process and seeking funding for research initiatives — have a long and venerable history in other fields [see, for example, 18, p. 149 for a discussion of the "uncontested hegemony" of disciplinary discourse in mainstream anthropological fieldwork] and in ours. This long history in our field suggests that these practices are particularly "tenacious" [9, p. 27] — deeply embedded, that is, in our conception of technical communication and highly resistant to change. If, as Grossberg suggests, power is the enablement of particular practices, then these two clearly have acquired considerable sway over our imaginations, becoming "apparently necessary" [14, p. 92] in relation to our research.

With this tenacity and apparent necessity comes the potential for domination and exclusion: As power "draws boundaries" and "delimits complexity" [14, p. 92], alternate research practices are excluded from our consideration as possibilities for choice. Below I examine each of these practices, focusing on this potential for domination and exclusion.

Disciplinary Discourse about the
Qualitative Research Process

Disciplinary discourse is important to any discussion of power because — by "govern[ing] what can be said, by what kinds of speakers, and for what types of audiences" — such discourses "organize a way of thinking into a way of doing" [16, p. 151; see also 4, p. 323]. By these means, they provide norms, stipulating the way research ought to be conducted. Though research practices are never general or abstract but rather are deeply embedded in "the context of the researchers and their interpretations" [18, p. 151], still the normative nature of disciplinary discourse does allow for certain generalizations about the practices of choice in particular disciplines and — given the tendency of fields to borrow practices from other fields — across disciplines as well.

One important normative rule, for example, concerns the distinct roles that disciplinary discourse about qualitative research inscribes for both researcher and participants. The researcher is viewed as "the sole arbiter of knowledge" [19, p. 20], the person with "sole responsibility for the work" [20, p. 150] who has the privilege of deciding how the research will proceed—which research questions to ask, for instance, and what methods to use. As the arbiter of knowledge, the researcher also has the privilege of interpreting the information gathered [19, p. 20]—information about both "the cultural and social practices under his or her gaze" and "those who engage in them" [18, p. 161]. Finally, the researcher has the privilege of using the findings, for a "doctoral thesis, advancement of science, promotion, personal prestige or financial gain" [20, p. 150] or for assisting research sponsors who have an interest in the work [21, p. 124; see 22, p. 130 for a discussion of this privileging in qualitative research in technical communication].

While disciplinary discourse about the qualitative research process gives control and direction of the work to the researcher, scholars in technical communication and in other fields claim that participants are often confined to a "passive" role as informants or providers of information [22, p. 130; 23 p. 45]. There exists, thus, a "subject/object relationship" [24, p. 4]—a distinction or "bifurcation between researcher and those being studied" [19, p. 20; see also 21, p. 121] that may systematically exclude participants from ownership of the work and the knowledge produced [see 22 for a discussion of this exclusion in qualitative research in technical communication].

In addition to inscribing roles for researcher and participants, disciplinary discourse also identifies methodologies of choice, which technical communication scholars Sullivan and Porter call "community frameworks, constituted and agreed upon by researchers" [25, p. 234]. The particular methodologies of choice or community frameworks may change over time. Charney, for instance, traces the shift in attitude toward empirical research in technical communication—from adherence to what Charney terms "demonization" [26, p. 23]—while Spilka identifies the mid-1980s as the time when our field turned to qualitative studies of writing in the workplace [27, p. 209]. And concerning these qualitative methodologies, Herndl discusses the emergence of ethnography as a way to study writing [4, p. 320], while Rentz details the current importance of the "in-depth study of a single case" [28, p. 37]. Methodologies of choice, therefore, do change, but disciplinary discourse directs this privileging, enabling certain possibilities while excluding others.

This potential for excluding methodologies concerns scholars in other fields who believe that the methods currently privileged in research are often the province of the researcher as expert. As a result, the researcher's—and, by extension, the academy's—control over the production of knowledge are solidified [20, p. 151]. Excluded as possibilities, however, are alternate methods that might be more accessible to participants [24, p. 8; 29, p. 211] — what Fals-Borda terms "a common people's science" and "popular science," which use methodologies not traditional in academe [20, p. 151].

Tied to this exclusion of methodologies is a third element inscribed by disciplinary discourse: the kind of findings that will be acceptable. Currently, for example, technical communication appears to set a high priority on "valid and grounded claims" [4, p. 322]. This priority may be linked in part to our field's desire for research results that we believe can be translated into effective and proven pedagogy [4, p. 320; 27, p. 215; 30, p. 65] or into reliable solutions to business and industry's problems [1, p. 292]. Though what constitutes validity in technical communication research is undergoing scrutiny [5, p. 62; 22; 31, pp. 260-261], nonetheless valid and grounded claims currently appear to be favored.

This focus on valid claims, however, raises the potential for excluding alternate forms of knowledge not intended to meet such a test [21, pp. 128-129; 29, p. 243]. Fals-Borda, for example, points to the academic mistrust of "popular knowledge" such as "common sense" and "folk knowledge," which "do not come in the form of isolated facts known to specific individuals" but instead "[come] in packets of cultural data gathered by social groups" [20, p. 150; see also 21, pp. 126-129]. "The legitimacy of such knowledge," says Gaventa, "is constantly being devalued and suppressed" [21, p. 128]. Like the "painted lines on a tennis court," this "valourization" of academic knowledge limits the kind of findings a field will accept [29, p. 243].

Disciplinary discourse about the qualitative research process, then, enables some possibilities, in terms of roles for researcher and participants, methodologies, and acceptable findings, while excluding others [see 10, pp. 32-35 for a general discussion of these issues in technical communication]. The same potential for domination and exclusion occurs with the connection of technical communication research to a second practice: seeking funding for research initiatives.

Seeking Funding for Research Initiatives

Like disciplinary discourse about the qualitative research process, seeking funding for research initiatives has a long and venerable history. This is particularly true in scientific and social scientific disciplines, where such support has been considered crucial. Seeking funding, however, is also becoming more common in fields that fit under the broad rubric of English studies. As one example, in English as a Second Language (ESL) — a field that in my department has close ties with technical communication — grants may be viewed as "[speaking] to the faculty member's productivity and [indicating] that the faculty member has done something significant in the field" [32, p. 109]. This high regard for sponsored research is hardly surprising, since work that connects with universities' economic interests is considered especially valuable [16, p. 83]. And given this value placed on sponsored research, it is also not surprising that scholars in technical communication—like those in ESL and other fields—may desire to secure more funding for research initiatives.

As with disciplinary discourse about the qualitative research process, however, seeking funding for research initiatives may lead to domination and exclusion. For example, to be considered for funding, research must usually address the problems sponsors find significant and generate findings that will solve those problems [27, p. 210]. Excluded from consideration, however, are alternate problems and findings that might benefit other interests. Mumby, for example, points to the difficulty of "articulat[ing] an agenda that challenges the fundamental power structure of an organization," which could "result in a withdrawal of funds and termination of the project" [33, p. 153]. In addition, problems and findings of concern to groups normally outside the dominant power structure and often unable to support or sometimes even conduct research (e.g., demographic entities such as the poor, minorities, and women; nonprofit or community organizations; arts and cultural groups) may also be excluded.

These two practices, then—disciplinary discourse about the qualitative research process and seeking funding for research initiatives— function to narrow possibilities and delimit choice, raising the potential for domination and exclusion. Moreover, these two practices also underscore how close the connection is between our research and traditional sources of power such as science, business, and industry, clarifying the kind of legitimacy our traditional research practices lend to our field.

Traditional Research Practices and Legitimacy

From very early in its history, technical communication has been closely connected to science, business, and industry. In early attempts to conceptualize the field, for example, scholars stressed its ties to science, labeling technical communication "the rhetoric of the scientific method" [34, p. 137] and claiming that the "type of thought processes involved" in technical communication were akin to those in mathematics and science [35, pp. 10-11]. More recently, scholars note that our field has long valued the objective rhetorical stance common in the sciences [36, pp. 355-358; 35; 36]. "Traditionally defined technical communication," claims Lay, associates itself with "scientific positivism" [36, p. 358] and with "the quantitative and objective scientific method" [36, p. 355], where communication is viewed as "the objective transfer of data, truth, and reality" [36, p. 358]. Though now commonly recognized as a rhetorical strategy or what Lay calls a "deceptive ethos" [36, p. 356], this stance of objectivity — and its link to science — are still attractive to scholars and teachers in the field: As Miller claims, "teachers of technical and business writing" have a high regard for "scientific objectivity" [38, p. 64; see also 17, pp. 13-15].

Along with this connection to science, technical communication also has long-standing ties to business and industry, as is clear from the early influence of Taylorism. In this scientific approach to management and the study of work, workers' jobs were systematically analyzed, creating the need for "prescribed and objectivist" communications through which management could exercise control [17, p. 13]. Though the obvious influence of Taylorism may have diminished, as with our field's links to science, this early connection to business and industry continues today. As Lay says, "the mission of most technical communication scholars is to prepare technical writers to enter industry and to improve the industrial processes that produce communications" [36, p. 365].

These long-standing connections to science, business, and industry are then made more tenacious by our practices of disciplinary discourse about the qualitative research process and seeking funding for research initiatives. Our disciplinary discourse about "more scientifically modeled research" [5, p. 69], for example — with the role it inscribes for researcher and participants, its methodological stipulations, and its focus on valid claims — solidifies the connection to science, where disciplinary discourse about the research process is particularly strong and normative rules intended to ensure objectivity and validity have an extensive history [5, pp. 64-65; see also 29, p. 179 on empirical-analytic and interpretive inquiry]. Moreover, this connection is further strengthened when, as a field, we turn to practices in scientific and social scientific disciplines as models for seeking sponsored research. Finally, since business and industry represent obvious sources of sponsorship — as well as places of employment for many technical communicators who conduct research — our field's connection to these sources of power is further solidified as well.

As a discipline, technical communication gains status and legitimacy by allying itself with highly valued fields and endeavors such as those in science, business, and industry. Describing this process of legitimization, for example, Lay asserts that, in order to remain close to "patriarchal institutions of power," "traditionally defined technical communication" affiliates itself with "scientific positivism" where the rhetorical stance of objectivity is valued. In this way, she claims, the "legitimacy" of our field is "enhance[d]" [36, p. 358].

Examining these two practices, then—disciplinary discourse about the qualitative research process and seeking funding for research initiatives—reveals how close the connection remains between technical communication and traditional sources of power. Indeed, despite recent critiques, the cast of our disciplinary discourse about the qualitative research process and the influence of external funding on our research suggest that the connection may now be more tenacious than it previously was.

Should we choose, however, we can rearticulate our research. That is, because connections among practices are "nonnecessary" [9, p. 26], we can link our research to alternate practices than those I describe. In the next section, I discuss practices connected to critical interpretive research as one such alternative, while also re-examining issues of power and legitimacy.

POWER, LEGITIMACY, AND CRITICAL INTERPRETIVE RESEARCH

As a perspective relying on radically participatory methodologies to effect empowerment and social change, critical interpretive research is a broad term that includes under its rubric a number of more specific theoretical approaches (for example, participatory action-research or PAR [29, 39, 40]; feminism [41, 42]; Freirian radical pedagogy [18]) that cross disciplinary boundaries.[2] Though critical interpretive research is certainly conducted in academe [e.g., 18, 19, 33], purely scholarly work is often not its focus [29, p. 176]. Rather, it combines research, education, and "sociopolitical action" [24, p. 3] in an "overtly political" approach aimed at "chang[ing] the status quo where unjust social, economic, and decision-making structures exist, to break free of constraints and open up possibilities" [29, p. 177].

Because of this overtly political nature, critical interpretive research is not suited to all researchers or to all research sites. However, as Grabill mentions, under the guise of PAR it has been used successfully in organizational settings [10, p. 34; see also 43]. It has also been used in everyday life [29, pp. 173, 244], when—at times with the help of a facilitator—groups of "socially interdependent" [29, p. 175] people collectively identify problems they want to solve and pursue the research they believe is necessary. These groups proceed by researching or "examining their

[2] Despite differences among theoretical approaches, I believe that research included under the umbrella of the critical interpretive perspective is characterized by certain broad principles. Given this commonality, I draw on the work of scholars from across this broad spectrum who are interested in radically participatory research.

reality" — "asking penetrating questions, mulling over assumptions related to their everyday problems and circumstances, deliberating alternatives for change, and taking meaningful actions" [29, p. 173; see also 24, p. 3]. In doing so, such groups are working to alter in significant ways the structures and practices of domination and exclusion that they believe have a significant impact on their lives.

Though a research site connected to everyday life might seem far removed from the traditional concerns of scholars in technical communication, in fact our profession has for some time been exploring alternate research sites. Grabill, for example, takes research into the arena of public policy, urging us to examine "the local institutional systems" [10, p. 48] that greatly affect people's existences. Similarly, feminist scholars have long advocated focusing on women's everyday lives, expanding technical communication by studying, for example, the "business of living" for a nineteenth century landlady [44] and the birth narratives of midwives [45].

Similarly, I want to expand our notion of possible research sites by describing a critical interpretive research project in which I participated. This project took place in Ames, Iowa, where a group of local people — graduate students at Iowa State University (Iowa's land-grant institution), activists interested in a new approach to agriculture, and small family farmers — came together to address what they perceived as a problem in their everyday lives: agribusiness's increasing control over the production of the food they ate. Collectively, these people decided to establish a community supported agriculture organization or CSA.[3] Though this project certainly addressed technological and business issues (specifically, agricultural technology and marketing strategies), the focus of the project was on the meaning of these technological and business

---

[3] A CSA is a relatively new agricultural marketing strategy, as well as a means for altering notions of acceptable agricultural production and for fostering community. Briefly, a CSA loosens agribusiness's control over food production by directly linking local farmers — often organic vegetable producers — and community residents as CSA members. In exchange for a prepaid fee that covers the farmer's expenses up front, the members receive a weekly market basket of produce throughout the growing year. In this way, the farmer gains, since the financial risk associated with this kind of farming is shared by the CSA's members. If a growing season is poor, for example, the farmer can still make a decent living and thus remain on his or her land. The CSA's members gain as well: They know exactly by whom, how, and where their food is grown. They also receive produce — usually grown by organic means — that has been harvested just hours or days before rather than produce grown with herbicides and pesticides that has traveled many hundreds of miles, such as the produce distributed through supermarkets. And finally, the entire community — both CSA members and farmers, as well as the community at large — gains from the bonds among people and between people and the land that a CSA attempts to strengthen and perpetuate.

issues to this group of people and the social action that they perceived would improve the lives they lived together.

So that you can better understand the overtly political, local, and collective nature of critical interpretive research, here is what Shelley, a graduate student in agronomy and rural sociology and a member of the group that started the CSA, had to say about the problem group members wanted to solve, which for them was epitomized in the name they chose for their organization:

> During some discussion later, we talked about a name for our group. Actually, it was Jeff Hall [another member of the group] who said, "It seems pretty obvious to me—the Magic Beanstalk." . . . We went out the next week and got a copy of that story, "Jack and the Beanstalk," and really ended up feeling like it was a very symbolic story for what we were doing. For us, Jack sort of symbolized the small farmer who was marginalized by big agribusiness. In a lot of ways the giant symbolized big agribusiness, and this giant was wanting more and more and more. And Jack was trying to reclaim some resources or, in our case, some local production, allowing us to create a local food system that we have some control over what we grow and what we eat [46].

As Shelley describes, acting collectively, this group of local people identified a problem in their lives and did the research and the work necessary to solve it.

Critical interpretive research of this kind may not have as long and venerable a history as more traditional approaches. Mumby, for example, links this perspective in organizational communication to the "interpretive, linguistic turn" of the late 1970s and 1980s [19, p. 19]. Like more traditional research, however, the meaning of critical interpretive research emerges from its connection to a host of practices.

Primary among these practices, for my purposes, are discourse about the critical interpretive research process and seeking funding for projects aiming at empowerment. Both of these practices contrast greatly with their counterparts in traditional research. In addition, these practices connect critical interpretive research, not to traditional sources of power such as science, business, and industry, but to grassroots movements that attempt to alter the status quo [see, for example, 24, p. 3 and 29, pp. 173-174 on PAR]. In critical interpretive research, then, issues of power are redefined in a way that sets a priority on empowerment, altering the kind of legitimacy this research confers. In the next sections, I examine these issues of power and legitimacy in connection with critical interpretive research.

Critical Interpretive Research and Power

Scholars who are committed to critical interpretive research are acutely aware of issues related to power, in particular the tendency toward domination and exclusion that they believe occurs with traditional research [e.g., 18, pp. 152, 162-163; 29, pp. 175-176]. Advocating intense reflexivity in their work [18, pp. 150, 152], they attempt to resist this tendency by engaging in what McLaren terms "theoretical decolonization" — "unlearning," that is, "accepted ways of thinking" and "refusing to analyze in the mode of the dominator" [18, p. 152]. Though these scholars are also acutely aware of the difficulty they have in escaping the "controlling cultural mode of [their] research" [18, p. 162], they try to do so by rearticulating their research practices—including their discourse about the critical interpretive research process and the funding they seek—within a perspective that focuses on empowerment.

Discourse about the Critical Interpretive Research Process

Discourse about critical interpretive research openly addresses the kind of exclusion—what Smith calls "operat[ing] stiffly within finite boundaries" [29, p. 244]—that critical interpretive researchers claim characterizes more traditional research. These researchers wish to be open and flexible, following a research process that they see as "evolving" [29, p. 173] and "experiential" [24, p. 3]. In doing so, they attempt to avoid "imitation or replication of techniques" and to take actions based "on the specific conditions and circumstances of each experience" [20, p. 149]. They also endorse what has been termed "popular action" [21, p. 124]: the collective commitment of groups of ordinary people to "undertak[e] and sustai[n] inquiry" [29, p. 244] that is relevant for solving their problems. By these means, critical interpretive researchers believe "opportunities for empowering moments of truth and action" can be created [29, p. 173].

Given this flexibility and this focus on popular action and empowerment, the discourse guiding critical interpretive research constructs very different roles for researcher and participants than those that occur in traditional research, as well as suggesting different views of both methodologies and findings. Regarding roles, for example, in critical interpretive research, the researcher does not have the privilege of deciding which research questions will be asked, how the research will be carried out, or how the findings will be used. Instead, this type of research "is characterized by a lack of control by the external researcher over the problem, the methods, and the timing" [29, p. 182]. As Mumby says, "the researcher gives up the pretence of a closed authority" [19, p. 20; see

10, pp. 39-40 for a discussion of this lack of researcher control in a technical communication research project].

Given this diminishing of the researcher's authority in critical interpretive research, the participants have a much more active role. As McLaren asserts, they have a "hermeneutical privilege in naming the issues" and "in developing an analysis" that will be "appropriate" [18, p. 161]. Smith echoes McLaren's assertion: "The participants' questions belong to them — they develop ownership over what is pursued and how" [29, p. 211]. "People," claims Smith, "are not 'objects' to be studied (as in conventional empirical or interpretive methods) but are full 'subjects' in the research process. They are actively involved in decision making and in taking actions, with ownership of the resulting consequences and knowledge" [29, p. 178]. In critical interpretive research, then, researchers are "doing research *with* and not *on* a group" [18, p. 154; italics in original].

In my critical interpretive research project with the Magic Beanstalk, for example, I was a member of the group on an equal footing with all other members — as Smith notes, "a participant in an evolving group process" [29, p. 231]. In fact, I joined the project in its third year, so I was not at all instrumental in defining the problem group members wanted to address, gathering the necessary information on community supported agriculture, or setting up the Magic Beanstalk. Since critical interpretive research is evolving and experiential, deliberately resisting exclusion, this shifting nature of groups is not uncommon. As Smith says, involvement is key: "So long as an involved group remains intact," its membership can change and the research project can continue [29, p. 185].

For over a year, I participated along with the other group members in ongoing work that Smith identifies as a "shared struggle" [29, p. 183], where the goal is "the creation of movement for personal and social transformation" [29, p. 181]. I pitched in to help with the ongoing tasks of the CSA, such as running the weekly distribution of vegetables and planning celebrations (visits to the local farm where members' vegetables were grown, spring and fall festivals). I also participated in the group's research, and, when appropriate, brought my own expertise in rhetoric to our work.

Smith calls this kind of participation a "permanent dance with yourself," as the researcher "reconnect[s] the self with others and with the universe" [29, p. 218]. "Individuals," she continues, "are willing to invest *of* themselves in the group and are open to challenge and movement. . . . This resolution promotes active learning: the transformative processes that develop people's capacities as they discover and use new-found abilities" [29, p. 226; italics in original].

Such involved participation, Smith asserts, can cause "inner and methodological turmoil" for researchers used to a more distant and objective stance toward their research and its participants. Further, given the lack of external control over the research process and the fact that critical interpretive researchers may have to admit "they do not know what to do next," such participation may well be "a troubling plight for those reporting to or dependent on agency support and/or funding" [29, p. 232]. Nonetheless, since "*any* hint of manipulation of the group" — by the researcher or by any of the participants—"will result in mistrust and breakdown of the process" [29, p. 241; italics in original], the kind of participation where both researcher and participants invest in and are fully included in the group is central to critical interpretive research.

This same kind of inclusiveness informs the critical interpretive perspective on methodologies. In particular, all methods are possibilities for choice, whether or not they produce valid findings in the conventional sense of the term [14, p. 87; 24, p. 10]. Researcher and participants can, for example, "rearticulat[e] the practices of the so-called empirical tradition into their own theoretical and political projects," drawing on "the full range of sophisticated methodological tools available" [14, p. 87] and using such widely accepted methods as interviews, surveys, direct observations, and statistical analyses [24, p. 10].

Alternatively, researcher and participants can employ methods not usually accepted within the empirical tradition—for instance, using "video productions, popular theatre, dramas, community radio, role-playing, dancing, . . . songs, and story-narratives." "All of these," claims Smith, "generate data in differing forms" [29, p. 211]. "Sometimes the objective is to deliberately and carefully obtain systematic information but, at other times, people want more spontaneous, inventive ways to express what is happening in their heads and hearts" [29, p. 212]. Fals-Borda adds to this list of alternate methods use of the oral tradition and witness accounts, "designed to stimulate the collective memory" [24, p. 8].

Finally, in oppositional situations, researcher and participants can use what Gaventa terms "guerilla research" — an approach that "draws heavily upon the investigative research tradition in the United States and upon the public interest research movement championed by Ralph Nader" [21, p. 123]. They can, for example, gain access to information about the power structures of their communities through government records, uncover information available in the public sector about corporations, and use the Freedom of Information Act and right to know movements to find out about issues affecting the public's interest.

This experiential, nontraditional approach to selecting research methodologies is clear from my critical interpretive project with the Magic Beanstalk. In this project, the group did use some standard, social scientific methods to gather information they needed to make decisions. For example, I drew on my training in technical communication to help develop a questionnaire, sent to all members of the CSA at the close of the Magic Beanstalk's third season, where the goal was to collect member input so the group could plan for the next year. At that same time, the group also had the assistance of a sociology professor and a graduate student in sociology at Iowa State University, who conducted in-depth telephone surveys and focus groups to evaluate the project.

Other useful methods, however, were far less codified—as Smith says, "arising from the group's context, questions, and interactions" [29, p. 212]. For example, in order to help identify why members of the initial group were at odds with food production as it existed, they drew on their collective memories of a past that many of them felt had since slipped away. Here is Shellie articulating the kind of collective under-standing and memory that group members talked about and that came to guide their actions:

> People think back to their own experiences in the garden, the flavor of the food they tasted when they were younger. . . . People really do look back to a more simple time, when our lives were more focused on food and community and extended families getting together on Sunday for a meal together. It doesn't happen any more, and I think people realize there was a value to that. . . . It's not so much remembering how it was fifty years ago, but it's sort of strengthening the remaining threads that are there and reweaving a little bit of the area that had been pulled apart [46].

Then, to further clarify why these initial group members were dis-contented with the present system of food production and what they could do about it, they held a retreat that included a visioning session. The written vision statements from this session helped group members conceptualize their community supported agriculture project. Finally, once group members had decided to undertake this project, they drew on the narrative of Jack and his magic beanstalk to give a name to their new organization and to invest it with meaning. As Shellie says, "at a potluck dinner and meeting for those interested in the community farm idea," people passed around a jar filled with beans that had been grown in Iowa, "so that everyone could take one when it was their turn to share an idea for the farm." These beans and the story of "The Magic Beanstalk" became "a symbol of our ideas and process to create a community farm. Everyone took a bean home with them to keep as a reminder of our potential to grow this magic beanstalk community" [47, p. 4].

Just as inclusiveness is important with methodologies, it also marks the critical interpretive view of research findings. Specifically, participants welcome any findings they believe can be useful, despite the fact that some of these findings may not be valid in the traditional sense. Indeed, the exclusion of such nontraditional findings has been called "expert domination" [21, p. 129]—the result of improperly imposing "external rationally based criteria about acceptable standards and requirements" [29, p. 245].

Critical interpretive researchers recognize instead that "the production of scientific knowledge by scientists" is just "one type of knowledge production that is not inherently superior to others" [21, p. 129]. Thus, these researchers redefine the concept of validity in participatory and experiential terms [29, p. 245], setting a priority on considerations intrinsic to a given project. The findings necessary to solve a group's problem, then, are validated by members' collective wisdom rather than by external criteria. Says Smith, "Individual knowledge accumulates to become social knowledge as the group verifies what it knows and understands" [29, p. 215]; "content that was 'subjective,' held as an opinion or belief by an individual, gains 'objectivity' when it moves to being held in common by group members" [29, p. 212]. In this way, "who controls knowledge, the type of knowledge produced—and, indeed, the very definition of what constitutes knowledge"—are altered [21, p. 131].

In my critical interpretive project with the Magic Beanstalk, for example, the understanding gained from the narrative about Jack and his beanstalk became part of the collective wisdom of the group. While an understanding of this kind may not be a "valid claim" in Herndl's sense of the term, in critical interpretive research such a finding is not excluded but instead is welcomed for its powerful contribution to a group's "popular knowledge" [21, p. 128].

Even this cursory treatment of discourse about the critical interpretive research process indicates how fully this discourse is rearticulated within a perspective that values empowerment. The same is true of the funding critical interpretive researchers may seek for projects aiming at empowerment.

Seeking Funding for Projects Aiming at Empowerment

Seeking funding for critical interpretive research projects may not be particularly common, perhaps because of the experiential nature of this type of research where the researcher does not control the process [29, p. 232] or the uses of results. Nonetheless, certain businesses and organizations may be willing to engage in or sponsor critical interpretive research, believing that it best serves their interests in terms of reaching solutions to problems that all can accept [see 38; also see 10 in technical communication research]. In addition, certain foundations and granting agencies focus on projects aiming at empowerment and therefore represent sources of funding for critical interpretive research projects.

As an example, the group that founded the Magic Beanstalk received help in their work from two grants. The first was from a cooperative effort called Shared Visions, supported by the W. K. Kellogg Foundation, Iowa State University Extension, and two sustainable agriculture organizations—Practical Farmers of Iowa and the Leopold Center for Sustainable Agriculture. The grant from Shared Visions, intended to encourage grassroots initiatives for developing community-based, sustainable farming systems, was used to fund the group's visioning retreat. The second grant was from the United States Department of Agriculture's Food Security program. Although the Magic Beanstalk formed only a part of the funded project, which focused on developing a broad-based, local food system, the CSA received financial assistance with several initiatives, such as transporting surplus vegetables from each week's distribution to local food pantries and holding a community-wide harvest festival.

As with discourse about the critical interpretive research process, then, this practice of seeking funding for projects is rearticulated within a perspective that values empowerment. This rearticulation of practices suggests that, should scholars in technical communication choose to adopt critical interpretive research, this perspective would lend a very different kind of legitimacy to scholarly work and thus to technical communication as a field.

Critical Interpretive Research and Legitimacy

Because critical interpretive research aims to empower people, at times in their organizational but also in their everyday lives, this type of research could weaken the links between technical communication and traditional power sources such as science, business, and industry. For example, the role critical interpretive research constructs for researcher and participants may pose a difficulty. Since the researcher cannot control the research questions asked, the methodologies employed, or the kinds of findings generated and their uses, it is possible that critical interpretive research will not provide solutions to science, business, and industry's problems. Further, given this perceived gap between critical interpretive research and their needs, certain organizations and granting agencies might not be available as sources for funding.

In place of these links to traditional sources of power, however, critical interpretive research establishes connections to grassroots movements for empowerment. Critical interpretive research projects have occurred in the less developed countries of the world, as well as in the United States and other more developed countries [21, p. 122]. Such projects have also occurred in organizational as well as in everyday life. Smith, for example, describes projects that took place in Mexico, Canada, Honduras, Uganda, India, and Chile [29]. Gaventa lists research in "rural areas" such as Appalachia; research with "groups whose interests are not well represented within the knowledge elite—minorities, women, workers, the poor"; and research conducted by "community groups, labor unions, and minorities involved in concrete, grassroots-based action" [21, p. 122]. McLaren discusses his work in a Catholic school in Toronto, Canada [18], while Whyte, Greenwood, and Lazes cover research done in the Xerox Corporation in an attempt to reduce costs and preserve jobs [40]. Finally, in technical communication, Grabill explains his project with an AIDS policy-making body in Atlanta [10].

Clearly, being linked to grassroots movements for empowerment would confer a different kind of legitimacy on technical communication than that conferred by links to traditional sources of power. Based on the radical participation of people in solving problems they identify, critical interpretive research would legitimize our field through the value of what Gaventa terms a "knowledge democracy" and the common commitment this sharing of knowledge and power entails [21, p. 121]. Smith describes the result: "When we struggle together to meet challenges, we add to our complexity as individuals, our abilities to care for and be cared for, our sense of rooted connectedness, and our capacity to rehumanize our world" [29, p. 252].

For some scholars in technical communication, this kind of legitimacy—one based on the common struggle of local people to empower themselves, to re-establish ties that bind them to one another, and to rehumanize their world—may be more socially and ethically appealing than the legitimacy conferred by an alliance with traditional sources of power. As Gaventa asserts, "the believer in popular participation must hope that the vision and view of the world that is produced by the many will be more humane, rational, and liberating than the dominating knowledge of today that is generated by the few" [21, p. 131].

Despite its social and ethical appeal, however, the choice to engage in critical interpretive research has profound implications for technical communication, in terms of power and legitimacy. I close by reviewing those implications.

IMPLICATIONS FOR POWER AND LEGITIMACY

If scholars in technical communication are to undertake critical interpretive research, they must recognize that this perspective calls on them to redefine power and to rethink the kind of legitimacy desired for our field. Specifically, scholars must be prepared to relinquish control of the research process, changing their "usual notions of participation" [29, p. 232] so that the privileges of selecting research questions, deciding on methodologies, and identifying and using findings belong, not to the researcher, but to the participants. Scholars must also welcome the crucial role that alternate methodologies can play in research, and they must redefine what counts as knowledge, acceding to participants the right to identify findings that are valid for their situations. Further, scholars must either decline to seek funding for research projects or turn to funding sources in agreement with the value critical interpretive research sets on empowerment. And finally, scholars must give up the legitimacy conferred by links to Lay's "patriarchal institutions of power" [36, p. 358], allying technical communication instead with grassroots initiatives for empowerment.

Clearly, such a vision for research and for our field represents a radical shift in perspective, challenging in fundamental ways assumptions and priorities that have long been a part of our research [see 10, p. 46]. Scholars, for example, may express the concern—commonly voiced in other fields—that critical interpretive research is "unscientific" [33, p. 152], raising the issue of its acceptability within academe—where the need for publication is a fact of life—and business and industry—where traditional research results may be favored. Scholars may also decline to undertake work where the researcher does not control the process, including the research questions asked and the choice of methods, or the uses of findings. Indeed, though our disciplinary discourse about the qualitative research process is changing to include some aspects of participation [see, for example, 10, 22], the radically participatory nature of critical interpretive research is still quite foreign to our field, thus posing distinct challenges. Scholars may also find the critical interpretive view of research funding untenable, believing that more and not less sponsored research—as well as sponsored research linked to traditional sources of power—best serve technical communication as a discipline.

I maintain, however, that we should regard critical interpretive research as a unique opportunity for scholars who desire to do so to rearticulate their research rather than as an unacceptable alternative to long-held and foundational assumptions. Granted, because of its radically participatory nature, critical interpretive research is not a perspective suited to all scholars. In addition, though critical interpretive research would expand our notion of the sites and methods acceptable for research, it is not suitable for all such sites, nor are alternative methods useful in every research situation. Critical interpretive research does, however, represent a choice for scholars who want to pursue an agenda that alters traditional concepts of power and legitimacy in fundamental ways. Through critical interpretive research, I claim, we can open up one more possibility for "mak[ing] good places to live" [48; qtd. in 49, p. 206]. Certainly this is a worthy goal for any field.

REFERENCES

1. N. R. Blyler, Research as Ideology in Technical Communication, *Technical Communication Quarterly, 4*:3, pp. 285-316, 1995.
2. C. G. Herndl, Tactics and the Quotidian: Resistance and Professional Discourse, *Journal of Advanced Composition, 16*:3, pp. 455-470, 1996.
3. C. G. Herndl, Teaching Discourse and Producing Culture: A Critique of Research and Pedagogy in Professional and Non-Academic Writing, *College Composition and Communication, 44*:3, pp. 349-363, 1993.
4. C. G. Herndl, Writing Ethnography: Representation, Rhetoric, and Institutional Practices, *College English, 53*:3, pp. 320-332, 1991.
5. B. Longo, An Approach for Applying Cultural Study Theory to Technical Writing Research, *Technical Communication Quarterly, 7*:1, pp. 53-74, 1998.
6. N. R. Blyler, Habermas, Empowerment, and Professional Discourse, *Technical Communication Quarterly, 3*:2, pp. 125-146, 1994.
7. B. A. Sauer, Sense and Sensibility in Technical Documentation: How Feminist Interpretation Strategies Can Save Lives in the Nation's Mines, *Journal of Business and Technical Communication, 7*:1, pp. 63-83, 1993.
8. B. F. Barton and M. S. Barton, Modes of Power in Technical and Professional Visuals, *Journal of Business and Technical Communication, 7*:1, pp. 138-162, 1993.
9. J. D. Slack, D. J. Miller, and J. Doak, The Technical Communicator as Author: Meaning, Power, and Authority, *Journal of Business and Technical Communication, 7*:1, pp. 12-36, 1993.
10. J. T. Grabill, Shaping Local HIV/AIDS Services Policy through Activist Research: The Problem of Client Involvement, *Technical Communication Quarterly, 9*:1, pp. 29-50, 2000.
11. P. Sullivan and J. E. Porter, *Opening Spaces: Writing Technologies and Critical Research Practices*, Ablex, Greenwich, Connecticut, 1997.
12. C. Thralls and N. Blyler, Cultural Studies: An Orientation for Research in Professional Communication, in *Research in Technical Communication*, L. Gurak and M. M. Lay (eds.), Praeger, Westport, Connecticut, pp. 185-209, 2002.
13. N. Blyler, Taking a Political Turn: The Critical Perspective and Research in Professional Communication, *Technical Communication Quarterly, 7*:1, pp. 33-52, 1998.
14. L. Grossberg, Critical Theory and the Politics of Empirical Research, in *Mass Communication Review Yearbook, Vol. 6*, M. Gurevitch and M. R. Levy (eds.), Sage, Newbury Park, California, pp. 86-106, 1987.
15. L. Grossberg (ed.), On Postmodernism and Articulation: An Interview with Stuart Hall, *Journal of Communication Inquiry, 10*:2, pp. 45-60, 1986.
16. N. R. Blyler, M. B. Graham, and C. Thralls, Scholarship, Tenure, and Promotion in Professional Communication, in *Academic Advancement in*

Composition Studies: Scholarship, Publication, Promotion, Tenure, R. C. Gebhardt and B. G. S. Gebhardt (eds.), Lawrence Erlbaum, Mahwah, New Jersey, pp. 71-86, 1997.

17. J. Perkins and N. Blyler, Introduction: Taking a Narrative Turn in Professional Communication, in *Narrative and Professional Communication*, J. M. Perkins and N. Blyler (eds.), Ablex, Stamford, Connecticut, pp. 1-36, 1999.

18. P. McLaren, Field Relations and the Discourse of the Other: Collaboration in Our Own Ruin, in *Experiencing Fieldwork: An Inside View of Qualitative Research*, W. B. Shaffir and R. A. Stebbins (eds.), Sage, Newbury Park, California, pp. 149-163, 1991.

19. D. K. Mumby, Critical Organizational Communication Studies: The Next 10 Years, *Communication Monographs, 60*:1, pp. 18-25, 1993.

20. O. Fals-Borda, Remaking Knowledge, in *Action and Knowledge: Breaking the Monopoly with Participatory-Action Research*, O. Fals-Borda and M. A. Rahman (eds.), Apex, New York, pp. 146-164, 1991.

21. J. Gaventa, Toward a Knowledge Democracy: Viewpoints on Participatory Research in North America, in *Action and Knowledge: Breaking the Monopoly with Participatory-Action Research*, O. Fals-Borda and M. A. Rahman (eds.), Apex, New York, pp. 121-131, 1991.

22. A. M. Blakeslee, C. M. Cole, and T. Conefrey, Evaluating Qualitative Inquiry in Technical and Scientific Communication: Toward a Practical and Dialogic Validity, *Technical Communication Quarterly, 5*:2, pp. 125-149, 1996.

23. A. J. Herrington, Reflections on Empirical Research: Examining Some Ties between Theory and Action, in *Theory and Practice in the Teaching of Writing: Rethinking the Discipline*, L. Odell (ed.), Southern Illinois University Press, Carbondale, pp. 40-70, 1993.

24. O. Fals-Borda, Some Basic Ingredients, in *Action and Knowledge: Breaking the Monopoly with Participatory-Action Research*, O. Fals-Borda and M. A. Rahman (eds.), Apex, New York, pp. 3-12, 1991.

25. P. Sullivan and J. E. Porter, On Theory, Practice, and Method: Toward a Heuristic Research Methodology for Professional Writing, in *Writing in the Workplace: New Research Perspectives*, R. Spilka (ed.), Southern Illinois University Press, Carbondale, pp. 220-237, 1993.

26. D. Charney, From Logocentrism to Ethnocentrism: Historicizing Critiques of Writing Research, *Technical Communication Quarterly, 7*:1, pp. 9-32, 1998.

27. R. Spilka, Influencing Workplace Practice: A Challenge for Professional Writing Specialists in Academia, in *Writing in the Workplace: New Research Perspectives*, R. Spilka (ed.), Southern Illinois University Press, Carbondale, pp. 201-219, 1993.

28. K. C. Rentz, What Can We Learn from a Sample of One?—The Role of Narrative in Case Study Research, in *Narrative and Professional Communication*, J. M. Perkins and N. Blyler (eds.), Ablex, Stamford, Connecticut, pp. 37-62, 1999.

29. S. E. Smith, Deepening Participatory Action-Research, in *Nurtured by Knowledge: Learning to Do Participatory Action-Research*, S. E. Smith and D. G. Willms (eds.), Apex, New York, pp. 173-263, 1997.

30. N. Blyler, Research in Professional Communication: A Post-Process Perspective, in *Post-Process Theory: Beyond the Writing-Process Paradigm*, Thomas Kent (ed.), Southern Illinois University Press, Carbondale, pp. 65-79, 1999.

31. S. Doheny-Farina, Research as Rhetoric: Confronting the Methodological and Ethical Problems of Research on Writing in Nonacademic Settings, in *Writing in the Workplace: New Research Perspectives*, R. Spilka (ed.), Southern Illinois University Press, Carbondale, pp. 253-267, 1993.

32. N. D. S. Lay, Promotion and Tenure Review of ESL and Basic Skills Faculty, in *Academic Advancement in Composition Studies: Scholarship, Publication, Promotion, Tenure*, R. C. Gebhardt and B. G. S. Gebhardt (eds.), Lawrence Erlbaum, Mahwah, New Jersey, pp. 103-116, 1997.

33. D. K. Mumby, *Communication and Power in Organizations: Discourse, Ideology, and Domination*, Ablex, Norwood, New Jersey, 1988.

34. J. S. Harris, Expanding the Definition of Technical Writing, *Journal of Technical Writing and Communication*, 8:2, pp. 133-138, 1978.

35. W. E. Britton, What Is Technical Writing? A Redefinition, in *The Teaching of Technical Writing*, D. H. Cunningham and H. A. Estrin (eds.), National Council of Teachers of English, Urbana, Illinois, pp. 9-14, 1975.

36. M. M. Lay, Feminist Theory and the Redefinition of Technical Communication, *Journal of Business and Technical Communication*, 5:4, pp. 348-370, 1991.

37. C. R. Miller, A Humanistic Rationale for Technical Writing, *College English*, 40:6, pp. 610-617, 1979.

38. T. P. Miller, Treating Professional Writing as Social Praxis, *Journal of Advanced Composition*, 11:1, pp. 57-72, 1991.

39. O. Fals-Borda and M. A. Rahman (eds.), *Action and Knowledge: Breaking the Monopoly with Participatory-Action Research*, Apex, New York, 1991.

40. W. F. Whyte, D. J. Greenwood, and P. Lazes, Participatory Action Research: Through Practice to Science in Social Research, in *Participatory Action Research*, W. F. Whyte (ed.), Sage, Newbury Park, California, pp. 19-55, 1991.

41. R. D. Klein, How to Do What We Do: Thoughts About Feminist Methodology, in *Theories of Women's Studies*, G. Bowles and R. D. Klein (eds.), Routledge & Kegan Paul, London, pp. 88-104, 1983.

42. F. E. Mascia-Lees, E. Francis, P. Sharpe, and C. B. Cohen, The Postmodern Turn in Anthropology: Cautions from a Feminist Perspective, *Signs: Journal of Women in Culture and Society*, 15:1, pp. 7-33, 1989.

43. D. J. Greenwood and M. Morton, *Introduction to Action Research: Social Research for Social Change*, Sage, Thousand Oaks, California, 1998.

44. M. Graham, The Business of Living: Letters from a Nineteenth-Century Landlady, in *Narrative and Professional Communication*, J. M. Perkins and N. Blyler (eds.), Ablex, Stamford, Connecticut, pp. 181-194, 1999.

45. M. M. Lay, Midwives' Birth Stories: Narratives that Expand the Boundaries of Professional Discourse, in *Narrative and Professional Communication*, J. M. Perkins and N. Blyler (eds.), Ablex, Stamford, Connecticut, pp. 137-151, 1999.

46. S. Gradwell, Interview, May 2, 1997.

47. S. Gradwell and J. Hall, History of the "Magic Beanstalk Farm," *Morning News*, 1:1, p. 4, 1995.
48. M. Strange, Transforming the Rot Belt, *Des Moines Register*, pp. 1-2C, February 25, 1996.
49. N. Blyler, Story Telling, Story Living: Sustainability, Habermas, and Narrative Models in the Rot Belt, in *Narrative and Professional Communication*, J. M. Perkins and N. Blyler (eds.), Ablex, Stamford, Connecticut, pp. 195-208, 1999.

CHAPTER 9

Tricksters, Fools, and Sophists: Technical Communication as Postmodern Rhetoric

Gerald J. Savage

MODERNITY AND TECHNICAL COMMUNICATION

Technical communication as generally practiced at the turn of the twenty-first century arose from the economic, technological, and political transformations in society that accompanied the Industrial Revolution with its highly rationalized principles of industrial organization; advanced technologies requiring increasing specialization for their development, production, and distribution; the consumerization and commodification of Western society [1-3]; and an educational system designed to meet the practical needs of business [4-6]. From such historical roots grew the modern professions, among them the promotion of engineering from the status of a shop trade to professional status [7, 8]. The professions as we know them today could not have emerged had not society abandoned the classical educational system that prevailed into the early American nineteenth century. The new educational structure was designed to meet the changing and expanding needs of a mechanized industrial economy. Engineers and businessmen needed practical skills, including communication skills, that bore little resemblance to the belletristic arts of the old system. By the end of the nineteenth century in the United States the demands for functional literacy for engineers had begun to motivate university engineering and English teachers to develop engineering writing courses as a pedagogical subdiscipline of English. Technical communication emerged as a discrete practice as a consequence of the advanced technologies that came out of World War II [9-19].

With the advent of a new millennium, however, arguments abound that the old (i.e., modern) order has passed/is passing/will soon pass away; that the industrial age has become the information age; and that we now live in a globalized/postindustrial/postcapitalist/postmodern world in which the models of conduct, business, the very practices of modernist everyday life, will no longer avail. The era of modernity is, of course, still a matter of considerable contention, not only as to what it is (or was), but as to whether or not we are still in it. One might well argue that many of the "truths" – about progress and expansion, labor and management, environmental resources, and even the "truths" about such social structures and relationships as race, class, and gender – upon which contemporary modernist institutions were founded are increasingly questioned by stakeholders who once had no voice. As truths have changed, so, inevitably, must institutions and the meanings and values that sustain them.

The contemporary field of technical communication emerged near the height of the modern era, a consequence, apparently, of a world war in which conflicting models of industrial organization, production, and delivery might be said to have been tested. It emerged, as well, from approaches to the teaching of composition that arose from the needs of late nineteenth century universities which were gearing up to prepare people for jobs in business and industry. Thus, writing teachers "began to teach writing particularly suited to current needs and, by extension, to teach thought forms that imitate modern consciousness – a form of consciousness largely molded by forms of production, or technology" [20, p. 375].

But now it begins to look like the hundred or so years of the modern industrial age were primarily a period of infrastructure building for what was to follow, the age of information and communication. Those of us with sufficient hubris might even argue that the technical communication field was instrumental in bringing the industrial age to a close and the information age to the fore. Surely there are few fields of practice which take more pride in assuming the mantle of postmodernism. But "ages" do not simply end. There is no clear, clean break with the old order. This, among other good reasons, may be why it is so difficult to say whether or not modernity is dead. Indeed, it isn't, and although postmodernists may rightly claim that modernity's relevance is fading away, in fact, without exception, many of the values, beliefs, truths, practices, and material structures of modernity still shape our understanding, behavior, and assumptions about ourselves individually, society, and the world. Thus, we live with contradictions, some, perhaps, more or less harmless, some burdensome, some dangerous. Among the contradictions we live with in technical communication is the notion of profession.

MODERNITY AND PROFESSIONALIZATION

As I have discussed at length elsewhere [see Savage, and also Faber and Johnson-Eilola, Volume I of this essay collection], the modern professions arose in concert with modern industrial practices, the modern university system, and the decline of aristocratic institutions of inherited wealth and social position. Sociological and historical studies reveal that a field must establish itself in a number of ways in order to attain the status of a profession.

- It must achieve market closure: as Pinelli and Barclay put it, it must achieve "A practitioner monopoly on the right to deliver a particular service" [21, p. 527].
- It must be autonomous in its practice, i.e., practitioners work for clients rather than employers, or at least practitioners are supervised by people who have credentials in the profession. Moreover, the practice is self-regulated; only professionals in the field can determine the competence of its members.
- It must have a formal body of knowledge, generally taught in formal educational settings, which must be learned in order for a person to practice in the field.
- It must have formal organizations which serve to establish standards for conduct, define the nature and conditions of practice, and represent the profession to the public.
- It must have a formal commitment to the welfare of the public and not simply to the interests of the profession and its members.
- It's members must be certified or hold some kind of formal credentials in order to practice or to claim membership in the profession.
- It must achieve broad public recognition and social status as a profession such that the public rejects non-professionals who might claim to be able to perform the profession's work.

Clearly, the technical communication field does not meet all of these criteria for professional status and may never achieve all of them, despite claims throughout the past several decades that we have become a "mature profession" and despite increasing efforts, particularly by the Society for Technical Communication, to move us toward full professional status. Although others have voiced the argument that we have not achieved professional maturity [21, 22], these arguments were based on the need for research specific to the field and the lack of a formal body of knowledge of our own. Nearly a decade later there is evidence that such a body of knowledge has begun to take shape. Nevertheless, some people continue to call for more aggressive and more carefully designed research. We continue to read of disagreements as to what constitutes legitimate and useful knowledge [23, 24]. My own argument, however, goes beyond this position.

The path of professionalization for technical communication is a path which I believe to be a blind maze—many branches but with no way out to the goal we envision. Instead, I want to propose an alternative. I believe that the goal of professionalization represents a modernist agenda which is no longer appropriate for a field of work for which modernist notions and practices are less and less relevant or useful. It represents a social model which will only frustrate and hamper us in the work we need to do today and in years to come.

MOORE'S INSTRUMENTALISM VS.
A FUNDAMENTALLY RHETORICAL PRACTICE

Central to my argument is the claim that technical communication is a rhetorical practice. That is, it is *fundamentally* rhetorical, not merely a field that employs rhetoric as one component of a larger array of competencies which are not commonly regarded as rhetorical. Certainly this is not a stunning suggestion; nevertheless, as Cezar Ornatowski has shown, the "acknowledgment did not come without resistance; many, especially among practitioners in business and industry, remain cautious as to the viability and usefulness of seeing technical communication in rhetorical terms" [25, p. 31]. The fact that various scholars in the past two decades have felt it necessary to argue for a fundamental relationship between technical communication and rhetoric suggests that it has been either a novel idea or a questionable one, or both [19, pp. 26-28].

Rachel Spilka has described technical communicators as "rhetoricians focusing their empirical, theoretical, or pedagogical inquiries on . . . workplace composing processes and products" [29, p. 219, n. 2] and as "agent[s] both of social accommodation and social change, or innovation" [p. 207]. But the term "rhetoric" has multiple meanings and associations, and despite its present acceptance among many academics in our field, it is not an idea in great favor with practitioners, nor even with all academics. Patrick Moore has been prominent in the past few years for his opposition to the emphasis on rhetoric in technical communication texts and courses [30-34]. Citing a report from a 1993 STC workshop in which "industry professionals" questioned the qualifications of college graduates entering technical communication jobs, Moore suggests that much of the blame for the alleged deficiencies of these graduates can be placed on "the dominance of rhetoric in the academy" [30, p. 105]. As recently as 1995, Saul Carliner wrote that some industry practitioners regard theories of rhetoric as "concerns that seem to have nothing to do with anything useful" [35, p. 52].

My own argument is that technical communicators should consider themselves as rhetoricians in the sophistic sense, that is, as politically and socially engaged communicators who recognize the inevitability of their texts as socially transformative [see Slack et al., and also Slack in Volume I of this essay collection]. But the sophist in ancient Greek society was a pariah (thanks, perhaps, to the influential defamations of Plato and Aristotle). Why, then, should technical communicators adopt such a label when their field is seeking recognition and acceptance?

The starting point for my argument corresponds with G. B. Kerferd's validation of the ancient Greek sophists. Although the sophists were condemned by Plato and others for accepting payment for "instruction in wisdom and virtue" [36, p. 25], ironically, they "are usually assumed to have aimed at nothing less than a wholesale modification and expansion of the repertory of poetic distortion and deception, taking it over and adapting it, in an argumentative context, to the very sort of inaccurate, immoral, or illogical discourse they had criticized in their [poet] predecessors" [37, p. 67]. They were accused of making the worse case the better, of artful lying, and of mere quibbling and wrangling. Thomas Cole points out that although Plato and Aristotle ridiculed the sophists, they also respected them. He suggests that "respect is linked to the feeling that they are influential enough to be dangerous" [p. 25]. Kerferd sheds further light on the subversive character of the sophists. "What is wrong is that the sophists sell wisdom to all comers without discrimination—by charging fees they have deprived themselves of the right to pick and choose among their pupils" [36, p. 25]. However, says Kerferd, there is evidence that the sophists were selective in taking on students.

> It is consequently likely that the real objection was . . . to all kinds of people being able to secure, simply by paying for it, what the sophists had to offer. What they had to offer, in the words attributed to Protagoras, included teaching a man about matters of state, so that he might become a real power in the affairs of the city both as a speaker and as a man of action . . . [36, p. 26].

The sophists were dangerous to the aristocratic establishment, making the skills and knowledge of the statesman accessible to any citizen (any who could afford their fee, at least) and making any citizen a politician.

Because of the centrality of the rhetorical perspective for my argument, it may be worthwhile to examine more closely Moore's position, as he has been one of the most outspoken advocates of an oppositional viewpoint. Moore argues that at best rhetoric constitutes only part of technical communication practice and that the field has been dominated by rhetorical scholars like Carolyn Miller, David Dobrin, and Russell Rutter who "want to make rhetoric mean everything and anything with some connection to discourse" [30, p. 104]. This argument, which appears to be influenced at least in part by practitioner resistance to "theory," makes use of the term "instrumental discourse" as a supposed opposite to "rhetorical discourse." Instrumental and rhetorical discourse are two of the four "aims of discourse" defined by Walter Beale to distinguish the various motives for discourse activity. Beale distributes them within quadrants formed by two intersecting axes "or lines of continuum for the placement of speech acts: the first . . . indicating the broad continuum between referentiality and non-referentiality; the second . . . between participation and non-participation" [38, p. 64]. James Kinneavy takes a similar perspective, identifying four categories of discourse: reference, persuasive, literary, and expressive. Kinneavy's reference discourse corresponds, approximately, to what Beale calls instrumental discourse. Kinneavy's persuasive discourse corresponds to what Beale calls rhetorical. Kinneavy, like Beale, defines these categories as separate forms of discourse, and both scholars argue that such distinctions help us avoid lumping all communicative acts under the term rhetoric. As Kinneavy insists, "persuasive discourse is generically different from reference discourse. . . . Otherwise everything is rhetoric" [39, p. 217]. Moore echoes this view, although he expresses it more eristically in portraying technical communication scholars like Dobrin, Miller, and Rutter as "totalizing rhetoricians" [33, p. 212].

Kinneavy's and Beale's projects carry forward the theoretical work of a number of other scholars in the fields of rhetoric, communication, linguistic theory, literary theory, and discourse analysis, which, by refining our descriptive and analytical terminologies, they believe should help us in the study and teaching of various discourse practices and texts.

Although Moore takes rhetorically-oriented technical communicators to task for what he portrays as their failure to recognize any other form of discourse but the rhetorical, he appears to commandeer one aspect of Beale's theory for his particular agenda. He does not acknowledge that Beale's work, as a whole, is a theory of rhetoric. Rhetoric, says Beale, "is in fact the central art of discourse, reflecting in its own subsystem of aims all the larger aims (rhetorical, scientific, instrumental, poetic). As such, rhetoric has a stake in all perspectives and all modes of discourse. . . . The other aims tend toward specializations both of language and of viewpoint, and their practitioners have a tendency to tend solely to their particular constructions of reality . . ." [38, p. 163]. Indeed, Moore appears to be unaware of the "character type" into which he is attempting to place the technical writer. The instrumental category of discourse, according to Beale, is characterized by the "technician." Beale contrasts the characters typical of the other three aims with that of the "statesman," or what we might more generally term the rhetorician. Focusing for the present argument on the differences between technician and statesman-rhetorician, here is Beale's comparison:

> Politically, these types reveal a tendency toward absolutism — toward utilitarian technocracy. . . . The statesman, by contrast . . . is a generalist, a "normal" personality, gregarious, and accustomed to hearing and negotiating a variety of points of view. Recognizing the social and intellectual value of a variety of specializations, as well as their separate tendencies toward absolutism, the statesman may be motivated simultaneously to create protective structures for the other three types and to place limits on their claims. His or her watchword is balance, often to the consternation of "deeper," more solitary, more committed thinkers. Historically, it is this type that reveals the greatest affinity for mixed, at least partially consensual forms of government and for pluralism in the social sphere [38, pp. 78-79].

What Moore has demanded is that technical communicators limit their practice to a narrow dimension of Beale's discourse model. Although he has denied that he would exclude rhetorical discourse from technical communication education and practice, he acknowledges its value only for "speeches, letters, and essays" [30, p. 107]. He would have technical communicators master a specialized discourse, to be sure, but not a specialization suited to professional status. At least in Beale's terms, the discourse Moore advocates for technical communicators is that of the technician, a position that is almost always strictly functional, precisely and narrowly applied, and subordinate. Both Carolyn Miller and Dale Sullivan call our attention to the common practice in ancient Athens of consigning workplace writing to slaves. Sullivan argues that the instrumentalist, industry-centered technical writing typically advocated in textbooks of the 1980s "is equivalent to . . . the rhetoric appropriate for slaves — those barred from making decisions about the ends, those whose decision-making authority is restricted to determining the most efficient means of obtaining predetermined ends" [20, p. 380]. Although Moore seems, on one hand, to equate instrumental discourse with people who work "at the loom, in the field, and at the forge" [33, p. 221], he nevertheless insists, in response to criticism from Robert Johnson, "In no way do I believe that technical communicators are mere scribes" [p. 213].

The issue for professional status, of course, is whether or not technical communicators should have sufficient authority in the workplace and society to be able to participate in making substantive decisions about the social meanings, purposes, and functions of their work. As technicians, they can have little authority. As rhetoricians the social nature and consequences of their texts should be paramount in their practice. Moore foregrounds the values of "economy, consistency, and efficiency" to justify the standardization of such meanings, purposes, and functions, pointing out that "technical people have gathered in company committees or in national or international professional associations to define and specify exactly their standards for nomenclatures, formats, programming languages, measurements, materials, procedures, and so on" [30, p. 110]. Thus, in his view, most of the economic, technological, and political terms of the contexts in which technical communicators work have already been defined; the rhetorical situation for technical communicators is beyond negotiation; the meanings, purposes, and functions of their texts and of the technologies and policies they represent are fixed.

Moore is correct in pointing out these realities of the environments in which technical communicators have to work. He usefully complicates the issues of meanings and values that other scholars have raised in discussions of technical communication ethics and responsibilities. In fact, he ultimately goes beyond his own initial effort to limit the definition of rhetoric to ancient classical terms: "2000-year-old rhetoric . . . was never intended to address the problems that technical communicators face in the marketplace today" [32, p. 172]. He made that claim in 1997; two years later he claimed that technical communicators must be "politicians and negotiators," and "creative thinkers and rhetoricians if they are to be effective in the workplace" [33, p. 213]. Thus, Moore attempts to retain the very qualities that constitute rhetorical competence while not quite being willing to acknowledge that technical communication might be a particular form of rhetorical practice.

Ultimately, Moore claims for instrumental discourse a wide array of "constituents, techniques, and complex social and technological environments" and provides some detail about "four main constituents . . .: managing resources, suitability, accessibility, and readability" [32, p. 167]. What Moore finally outlines under the category of instrumental discourse is a broadly interdisciplinary technical communication curriculum [34] much the same as we can find in most university technical communication programs today. Thus, in order to set his technical communicator apart from Beale's characterization of the technician, he is forced to subsume virtually everything that characterizes classical and contemporary rhetorical studies under the term instrumental discourse.

Ironically, although the technical communicator as technician lacks professional status, so does the generalist rhetorician, at least according to the criteria by which the modern professions are defined. The crucial difference between the two characters is that technicians, insofar as they adhere to their roles, apply a narrow set of skills and procedures that offer little latitude for independent judgment or interpretation. Rhetoricians, on the other hand, draw upon a range of discourses in which they have no specialization. "Not only is it the least specialized and differentiated of the aims of discourse in terms of its characteristic themes, forms, and conventions; . . . it is also the most assimilative, appropriating themes, forms, and conventions from the other aims of discourse," says Beale. In short, Beale sees rhetoric as "both a comprehensive language art and a despecializing force in human culture" [38, p. 80]. Thus, rhetoric actively works against the very social, organizational, and discursive forces that would set specialized practices apart from and above the broader society in which they operate. Rhetoric, then, is not so much nonprofessional as counterprofessional.

Modern professions, on the other hand, among other characteristics, separate themselves from the rest of society, or in Randall Collins' terms, "indigenous culture," and arrange themselves in "formal cultures" by virtue of their specialized knowledge and skills [40, p. 74]. Such separation appears to be necessary for several reasons. The public must believe that professionals have expert knowledge acquired through years of university study separated from plebian life. The rigorous life and the cost of such education are perceived to merit the exalted social status accorded to professionals who otherwise might have little motivation to earn their credentials.

The professions in general represent themselves as providing essential services to society, but because of the specialized nature of their practice and the inscrutability of their knowledge for laypersons, nobody outside of the profession is considered qualified to determine or apply the standards by which professional work should be evaluated. In short, says Geisler, "Because professionals were assumed to have expert knowledge that others could not understand, they were usually allowed to maintain direct control over their own affairs" [40, p. 72]. The self-discipline that is needed to acquire expert professional knowledge, the dedication to the good of society in professional practice, and the mystique of knowledge and skills beyond the ken of ordinary mortals all seem to warrant maintaining the separateness of high social prestige associated with professional status. "Because the professions needed to justify their professional privilege on grounds that would not offend democratic sensibilities, they found the apparent neutrality of formal culture appealing" [p. 74].

We should not forget the close relationship of the rise of modern professions with the rise of modern industry in this analysis. It appears unlikely, if we accept the arguments of sociologists and historians of the professions, that anything like the modern professions would have emerged without the support of industry and the uses to which industry put such professions. The production processes of modern industry, and the products themselves, required knowledge and skills well beyond the capabilities of traditional industrial trades. Some trades simply became obsolete because their skills became automated and mechanized, i.e., were embodied in increasingly sophisticated tools that required so much less advanced knowledge and skills to use that the trades were not needed any longer. Other trades bifurcated—along one path they became professionalized, i.e., expertise was theorized and academized, as was the case with civil and mechanical engineering; along the other path shop trade practices supported the professional branches of their fields—for example, automobile mechanics and electronic technicians.

Studies of the professions indicate that a necessary condition for the emergence of a profession is its ability to achieve market closure. It limits the ability to practice to those who have been formally admitted as members of the profession, thereby also bringing some measure of control over competition and standardization of prices. It also enables the profession to control access to the profession by limiting enrollments in professional education programs and governing certification of candidates as well as educational institutions. Thus, professionalization has the power to produce scarcity, thereby raising the value, and increasing the price of its services.

One of the arguments that Moore makes for emphasizing instrumental discourse in technical communication practice is a professionalization argument: instrumental discourse involves more advanced, more specialized, and more precise applications of language than does rhetoric, for which he recognizes primarily belletristic and public speaking applications. He seeks a technologized discourse that only experts would be qualified to apply, involving standardization of usage and meanings, "to execute physical tasks within narrow financial, temporal, and other constraints" [30, p. 115]. It is a rigidly centripetal, authoritative discourse, to use Bakhtin's terminology. He claims that such discourse is "as humanistic as rhetoric," although instead of emphasizing the kind of socially liberal principles generally associated with rhetorical humanism, Moore praises instrumental discourse as a "coercive" discourse of order, stability, control, and discipline, essential to the public good [30, pp. 112-113; 33, p. 217]. A humanistically applied instrumental discourse, he explains, is coercive in order "to save lives, minimize pain, minimize the socially destructive actions of dysfunctional people, provide the laws and procedures that keep social groups working more or less harmoniously together, apply material resources economically to solve problems, and improve the quality of our physical lives" [30, p. 115].

Moore recognizes the potential danger in the coerciveness of instrumental discourse, but insists that it can be properly used "to oppose the powers that try to destroy and dehumanize us" [33, p. 217]. This is an eloquent expression of a modernist industrial ideology, rooted equally, perhaps, in the American expansionist view of "untamed" nature as a threat to civilized human society, and equally as a resource to be managed and put to practical use [41].

The argument for approaching technical communication as an instrumentalist practice is by no means a new one. Indeed, it is a perspective that seems to have been widely held in the early years of the field. As Bernadette Longo points out in Volume I of this essay collection, the work of Rudolph Flesch in the 1940s and '50s represents an early effort to give writing a scientific basis and to reduce it to a technologized system, a move that was perceived to give workplace writers the status of specialists. David Dobrin points out that insofar as technical documentation such as user's manuals function within larger technological systems, they "might well be seen as part of the overall technology . . ." [42, p. 2]. He suggests that we may need to treat technical communication as instrumental in order for it to be managed within the complex, technologically determined systems of modern industry:

> Producing the product are specialists: the printer, the designer, and of course, the technical writer. They make up a production chain much like any other. Each link in the chain has specific skills and performs specific tasks; each falls into a separate job category. In large organizations, where manuals (reports, proposals) may require a team of forty or fifty people, the tasks involved in producing the manual are identified and enumerated. Performance is monitored and evaluated. When the manual is finished, its effectiveness is tested. So, treating writing as a technology also locates it within another network, the technology of production. And it legitimates the deployment of administrative strategies which are effective in that network.
>
> Within the technological apparatus, these strategies are normal and reasonable. But notice that they would rapidly become unreasonable if the manual itself were not thought of as instrumental. How, for instance, could effectiveness be tested if the effect were not well defined? How could we know whether the tasks enumerated were the proper ones if the job itself were not delimited? Would the separation of job categories really make sense? [p. 3].

Dobrin makes clear in this analysis the extent to which technical communication has emerged as an instrumentalist/rationalist practice bound up with the systemic logic of modernist industry. In order to function within such a model, technical communication had to replicate the logic of the model in its own practice. It is within the framework of this logic that Moore advances his argument for instrumental discourse.

Despite this apparent necessity, many teachers and scholars of technical communication have resisted it. As Sullivan points out, citing Robert Connors, there has been a "continuing battle over the issue of humanism versus vocationalism in technical communication, a battle that has apparently been part of the profession from its inception early in this century" [20, p. 376]. This struggle continues, with some evidence of increasing success for the rhetorical/humanistic direction in technical communication, perhaps because the field is now gaining its own academic niche and identity.

MOVING BEYOND INDUSTRIAL MODERNISM

Aiding the success of the rhetorical/humanistic direction for our field is a shift toward a postindustrial society that is itself resistant to modernist technological determinism. Andrew Feenberg describes this shift, with its inevitable social and economic struggles, as suggesting "the possibility of a change in the form of technical rationality. They prefigure a general reconstruction of modernity.... The goal would be to define a better way of life, a viable ideal of abundance, and a free and independent human type, not just to obtain more goods in the prevailing socioeconomic system" [2, pp. 224-225].

Developments in technical communication theory reflect this struggle and a shift toward a social-rhetorical postmodernism. Trends such as the practices of outsourcing and use of temp agencies to accomplish work that has in the past been done by in-house permanent employees, which in the short term threaten job security and financial security for technical communicators, in the long term offer opportunities to resituate their practice outside of the old technologically determined systems of modernist industry. We may need to embrace these trends and to construct our practice in a way that suits it more appropriately to a postindustrial world. Modernist notions of profession are increasingly inappropriate to the theory we are developing and, more significantly, inappropriate to the circumstances and needs of our practice.

Some scholars argue that many of the characteristic moves toward professionalization, although supposedly motivated by the public interest, are mainly self-serving, benefiting the members of the profession economically and socially more than they benefit society. As we are all aware, the public no longer regards any of the professions, even the so-called traditional or classical ones (the clergy, law, or medicine) with unqualified reverence. As Cheryl Geisler argues, "the cultural movement of professionalization has used the technology of literacy to sustain claims to professional privilege, creating a great divide between expert and layperson" [40, p. xiii]. Geisler blames the academy, in particular, for its role in this process, that is for structuring American education so that it transforms students into either producers (i.e., professionals) or consumers (the general public) of expert knowledge. (It is in the nature of expertise, as Svante Beckman suggests, that its value is in proportion to the incompetence of those who consume it. In Beckman's words, "the authority of the professional is not efficient unless it is trusted by those incompetent to judge it. . . . [T]he profession is entrusted with the interests of incompetent followers" [43, p. 128].) Geisler charges that "The academy has thus sidestepped the rhetorical burden of expertise, the burden to persuade others to believe and to act" [40, p. xiii].

Such arguments help us understand the contradiction involved in promoting the professionalization of technical writing, while equally insisting, as both Carolyn Miller and Dale Sullivan have done, that our students recognize the field as a rhetorical practice, or praxis. Sullivan, in particular, has tried to escape the dilemma of teaching "thought forms that imitate modern consciousness—a form of consciousness largely molded by forms of production, or technology" [20, p. 375]. When rhetorical principles are treated as techne they are for all practical purposes "forms of technology . . . and, as such, their products can be separated from the maker and marketed, relieving the writer of responsibility . . ." [p. 376]. Such a context-independent techne relying on technologized, management-oriented principles, is concerned mainly, as Martha Nusbaum argues, "with prediction and control concerning future contingencies . . ." [qtd. in 44, p. 66]. Techne leaves no place for the values that praxis demands—values oriented to democratic social change and not simply to economic efficiency and control.

In fact, as sociologist Elliot Freidson points out, generally it is not practitioners who promote socially responsible practice: "Historically, it has been the academics of the profession who have stressed professionalism and the need to serve the general public welfare . . ." [5, p. 222]. Practitioners have little interest in such ideals, regarding them to be, according to Freidson, "impractical or perfectionistic, unfitted for the real and complex world . . ." [p. 221].

Sam Dragga asserts that technical writers are not guided by principles of social responsibility taught to them in their formal education nor articulated by the STC. Instead "they look only to their employing organization for ethical insight" [45, p. 173]. It seems, then, that academics' efforts to prepare practitioners for socially responsible practice are overshadowed by the broader ideology of an industrial society which has produced and has been produced by the modern professions. This is a dilemma from which there appears to be no escape as long as we continue to pursue an agenda of professionalization. In the next section I will explore alternatives to the modernist profession as a model for technical communication practice.

IDIOTS, IMPOSTERS, ASIAN BEETLES: THE TECHNICAL COMMUNICATOR AS LIMINAL SUBJECT

Joseph Jeyaraj has argued recently that the technical communicator is a "liminal subject" occupying marginal zones between the subject matter expert and the lay audience, trading status both in the corporation and in larger society for relative freedom to travel across the boundaries of these socio-cultural domains [46]. This way of understanding the work of the technical communicator suggests some metaphors that diverge considerably from the way we usually think of professional practice.

Perhaps the most pervasive concern of technical communicators who wish to be recognized as professionals is the lack of respect for the field. This problem is manifested in a variety of ways. A major issue for Patrick Moore in his essays about instrumental discourse is the lack of respect for technical communication as an academic discipline among traditional scholars in English departments, a problem that many of us who teach technical communication continue to experience into the twenty-first century. In corporate settings, managers who know nothing about the field often believe that technology skills are the only important qualifications for technical communicators [47], or even that technical writers are not necessary at all because any competent native speaker of English should be able to do the kind of writing called for in the workplace [48, p. 28]. Prasad quotes consultant Will Kelly, who advises people thinking about entering the field that it is "a second class profession. It is up to you as a technical writer to distinguish yourself in a sometimes troubled and ill-appreciated profession. . . . You have to filter out the talk that 'the technical writer is supposed to be the idiot.' It's an urban myth in today's understaffed companies"[49]; see also [50].

Although many technical writers are treated with respect, misunderstanding and disrespect from managers and co-workers in other fields are not uncommon. Kendra Potts describes her experience as a new technical writer trying to interview a software developer. The developer was 40 minutes late for their meeting in his own cubicle. Even then, says Potts, "I stood there for at least twenty seconds before he even looked at me. I felt like one of those Asian beetles that found its way to the Midwest suburbs of America—unwanted and definitely where I didn't belong" [51, p. 31]. Another practitioner explains that she quit her first technical writing job because she was "tired of some programmers' attitudes, of being treated like a glorified secretary" [52, p. 53].

Technical communicators often feel like outsiders in the specialized technology cultures in which they work. Rahel Anne Bailie describes herself as an "imposter" in the telecommunications company where she worked as a consultant. The engineers she works with in documenting a product often fail to understand what she does, even when she tries to explain her job. One engineer asks, "Then what you do is more like rewriting what we write?" [53, p. 65]. Bailie and many other successful technical communicators maintain a sense of humor and work hard to gain credibility for themselves and their work, but often they are not able to achieve the status they desire and which they know would actually enable them to develop more effective documentation. Although Mark Bloom reports being well-respected in his job, he comments, "It's a rare situation in the technical communication field—a writer being an integral part of a development team—but I have fought throughout my entire career for the opportunity" [54, p. 81]. Saul Carliner has observed that "few of us feel 'strategic' to the organizations we work for" [55, p. 266]. Technical writers at DuPont became "discouraged and weary of what we perceived as lack of regard and respect on the part of our business partners for our work and our contributions to their business success" [56, p. 394]. Even David Dobrin, one of Moore's three "totalizing rhetorician" nemeses, has left the field after having worked for years both as an academic and a practitioner. He left because he felt that the best work it was possible for him to do was nevertheless not what really needed to be done. "I am clearly a misfit but don't dismiss my difficulties as purely those of a misfit. My successes and failures say something about the state of the profession. Other people also find it hard to give good weight or have stopped worrying about it" [57, pp. 105-106]. He says that "people in the field are too busy; they're overworked; they're underpaid; they don't have good training, and they don't get much respect" [p. 116].

Testimonials like these suggest the marginal status of technical communication. It appears that many who have been successful and enjoy their work have nevertheless had to deal with intentional or unintentional slights, disrespect, and misunderstanding. They seem to confirm what Dale Sullivan and Michael Martin [Volume I of this essay collection] argue: that prestige must be won by "cultivating an identity of belonging" and by understanding how to move from the periphery of organizational culture toward its center through social negotiation.

However, because technical communicators increasingly work as consultants and freelancers, or for other reasons do not remain for a long time in one organizational setting, marginality may need to be understood as a necessary dimension of practice in our field. Therefore, even at the risk of not being taken seriously, of seeming foolish, or of trying to make the worse case seem the better, I would like to explore the implications of characterizing technical communication as a border-line, marginalized practice. I wish to join a few other scholars in our field who have recently argued that we might usefully understand technical communication not simply as a rhetorical practice, but as a sophistic practice. Paul Dombrowski sees a sophistic approach as postmodern, pointing out that "Sophism both in the overthrow of absolutism and in the rhetorical shaping of meaning clearly resembles postmodernism in challenging received knowledge and authority" [58, p. 177]. I propose to extend Dombrowski's perspective by drawing upon two other sophist-like cultural figures: the native American trickster and the medieval fool. I will theorize these figures through the concept of *metis* from ancient Greek culture and John Poulakos' conception of the ancient Greek Sophists.

TRICKSTER, FOOL, SOPHIST:
THREE RHETORICAL ROLES FOR POSTMODERN PRACTICE

The trickster in native American cultures is usually an animal figure: coyote in southwestern cultures, raven in northwestern cultures. This figure is at once comic and deadly in the cosmological myths of native Southwestern cultures, possessed of a powerful vision, "a gaze that at once destroys and creates, inscribes and erases, kills and begets life," according to Scott Lyons.

> The trickster — the sustaining, contradictory union of human and animal, flesh and spirit, male and female, humor and sorrow, good and evil — can be either friend or foe to the individual but is always a boon to the collective community. Like Gloria Anzaldua's *mestiza*, the . . . trickster embodies a consciousness that "straddles cultures," develops "a tolerance for ambiguity," and works to break down subject-object duality in the development of a "new mythos" [59, p. 128].

Lyons describes the trickster as "at once ancient and postmodern," a figure who "plays discursively and refuses to be constrained by time" [p. 128]. Feminist rhetorical theorist Catherine Peaden adopts Dona Haraway's appropriation of Coyote-trickster in her development of a rhetorical theory " — one perhaps even having a sense of humor—" that resists "an ideology which sees the world as an object available for domination and mastery." Peaden compares the trickster perspective to Bakhtin's "view of language and the world as multiple, as constructed of many-stranded, conflicting cultural codes, as carnivalesque. These multiple, centrifugal, forces ensure that even a dominant discourse or cultural code will not have complete hegemony . . ." [60, p. 88]. The consequence of a trickster rhetoric, in Peaden's view, would be that it would "serve as a powerful force in rethinking and extending the Enlightenment project of democracy and liberty, helping us understand and write the world differently" [p. 89]. Similarly, Lyons portrays "a mixed-blood rhetoric that, trickster-fashion, both annoys individuals and benefits a community, that straddles both Indian and non-Indian cultures, that both laughs and cries" [56, p. 129].

The technical communicator-rhetorician, like the trickster, is an agent of social change. A widespread concern, not only among citizens and politicians but even among technical experts, is the increasing rate of technological change in our world and its impact upon society. Because the social nature of this process is often not understood, technology is often perceived as value-free and even as autonomous. But, as Andrew Feenberg argues, technologies "are human products, aspects of social life like any other, and . . . they inevitably vehiculate social meanings" [61, p. 225]. Feenberg says that one of the most important ways in which "technologies acquire broad cultural meaning and significance" is through "rhetorical procedures" [p. 227]. The rhetorical processes through which technologies often "annoy individuals and benefit communities" (or vice versa) are in part the work of technical communicators. They are processes that may make the worse case seem the better, that introduce the potentialities of technical objects and systems into the "dialogic imagination" of the culture in which they emerge. Because our practice is fundamentally rhetorical, and therefore social, says Ornatowski, "technical communicators not only adjudicate conflicting interests and goals, create representations of emerging technologies, and share the perception and reception of technologies" whether they fully understand their role and responsibility in these processes or not [62, p. 578]. But by understanding the change-agent, trickster nature of socially situated rhetoric and ourselves as rhetoricians, we are more likely, as well, to understand our responsibility in that role. As Stephen Bernhardt has argued,

> Rhetoric helps us recall our social obligations in the midst of change. The changes we see in social structures, in the academy, in technology, and in the workplace all create convergences that technical communicators are uniquely equipped to understand and take advantage of. We have only to think broadly of what kinds of expertise we might genuinely claim, what human and technological values we are interested in promoting, and what sort of society we are interested in creating. We can then claim a rightful place as an agent of change [63, p. 602].

Patricia Bizzell has examined the rhetorical position of the medieval fool, a figure similar in many ways to the trickster. She observes "that fools are typically liminal figures . . . , that they are or depict themselves as socially marginal" [64, p. 17]. Because the character of the fool imitates people with mental handicaps, among other marginalizing traits, they "typically cross over cultural boundaries that are supposed to be inviolable, or more precisely, fools wander over boundaries as if they didn't even know they were there. . . . The description recalls the wandering habits of the ancient Greek Sophists, which may have given them the necessary perspective for their cultural relativism to develop; Folly thus plays the Sophist in more ways than one" [p. 16].

The increasingly international nature of business and the recognition of even our domestic society as multicultural make the ability to mediate or translate across these real geographic and cultural boundaries more vital than ever. But, as James Paradis points out, the work of technical communicators has always required that they "mediate between the expert world of technologists and manufacturers and the lay operator world where the tools are employed" [65, p. 259]. Thus the metaphor of boundary-crossers is likely to seem familiar to most practitioners. For example, Rahel Bailie describes her boundary-crossing tactics for entering the culture of the engineers she has to work with in documenting the telecommunications technology they are developing. She "plays the fool" with them in multiple ways, using her gender, her non-engineer status, her age, and certainly her sense of humor at propitious moments.

On one occasion Bailie participated in a costume party at work by dressing up as a stereotypical engineer, a spur-of-the-moment decision in which one of the engineers participated. "They think I'm a bit of an oddity, but I think it increases my cachet," says Bailie.

> I've carefully let out my line, revealing my personal self bit by bit. It's hard enough being one of the few non-engineering staff. I don't want to scare them off by admitting to all of my differences. First, I let on that I was quite a bit older than them, then told them the car seats in my minivan are not really for my children but my grandchildren. Once they got comfortable with that idea, I revealed the next-safest detail.
>
> I imagine them talking together out of my earshot about what a strange duck I am. Maybe I'll dye a patch of my hair blue next week, just to keep them talking. . . . My boss, a motherhood-and-apple-pie kind of guy, has never quite figured out what to make of me; he probably thinks all tech writers come this way, but enjoys my company in an odd sort of way [53, pp. 66-67].

Michele Ballif advocates, not specifically for technical communication, but for what she calls a third sophistic rhetoric for the postmodern world. "The postmodern challenges to history, to politics, to communications, to political agency, along with our increasing digital and virtual experiences," Ballif argues, "have radically altered our conceptions of time, place, and rhetorical purpose, and have led us to question the form of a body politic that [traditional] rhetoric (a body of discourse) constructs" [44, p. 53]. Like Miller and Sullivan, Ballif critiques the traditional rhetoric of *techne*, proposing as an alternative, not praxis, but an older, Sophistic reliance upon *metis*, "a knowing, doing, making not in regards to Truth (either certain or probable), but in regards to a [continually changing, uncertain] situation such as our postmodern condition" [p. 53]. She associates *metis* with navigation: "Because the human condition is often characterized by change and the ungovernable forces of nature and fate, *metis* equips the possessor with the ways and means to negotiate the flux" [p. 65]. Similarly, Miller describes *metis* as "a quality frequently attributed to Odysseus, the polymetic, or many-skilled, the paragon of craftiness and cunning" [66, p. 138]. Including *metis* in her view of a postmodern form of rhetorical invention, Miller says,

> It has been called the . . . venatic paradigm, because it relies on "the epistemology of the hunt". . . . The venatic, or conjectural, worldview concerns the individual case rather than universal knowledge, probability rather than certainty, qualitative rather than cumulative or quantifiable information, and inferential rather than deductive thought, since it depends upon the reading of signs [p. 138].

Robert Johnson has applied *metis* specifically in the context of the user of technology. He argues that the conventional ways of representing technology to users in the technical communication field are based upon "a philosophy of knowledge that not only devalues the practices of the everyday, but also devalues the knowledge of those who function in that context" [67, p. 56]. He points out that in ancient Greek society, *metis* was a highly valued kind of knowledge, but for contemporary technical communicators (those modernist practitioners, I would argue, who seek professional status), "universal truth and certain knowledge . . . [have] subverted the situated and contingent knowledge of the practical arts, like *techne* and *metis*" [p. 56]. Users in such an epistemology are perceived primarily as "receptacles of information" [p. 57]. The notion of the user-as-receptacle seems consistent with Moore's conviction of the moral appropriateness of coercive instrumental discourse that rigidly constrains meaning for the purpose of controlling actions that could otherwise "significantly damage our society and diminish its power to cope with difficult problems in its many physical, social, and economic environments" [30, p. 115]. Johnson's portrayal of the user as marginalized in relation to the specialized knowledge underlying technology is similar to Jeyaraj's representation of users as subalterns in relation to the cultures of technology [46].

Although Johnson does not develop this idea, it seems inevitable that his notion of *metis* must be applied to the practice of the technical communicator, as well. As has already been discussed, technical communicators must be able to adapt to changing technical, organizational, and user environments, and to be able to imagine and advocate for the social contexts in which a technology may be applied. Such capabilities involve, as Johnson argues, "a complicated set of social, technological, and knowledge interactions that are difficult to decipher as reduced moments of mere interaction between a user and a technological artifact" [67, p. 57]. The technical communicator who possesses such art, like the ancient Sophists, is "cunning" and "wily" and thinks on her feet, rather than expert or masterful or relying upon predictive, generalizing models.

John Poulakos explores both the negative status of the sophists and their ability to work successfully in a society that did not give them the rewards they might have expected. He identifies three reasons for the sophists' negative status: First, they were officially resident aliens in Athens, meaning that they had no rights or status as citizens and were not seen as social or political equals with the citizens who made up their clientele.

Second, they were cosmopolitan in their political and cultural allegiances, and to teach their relativistic perspectives "was to shatter the belief in the universality of laws, to shake people's confidence in the propriety of Greek laws, and to leave the door open to practices regarded illegal and disgraceful in Hellas" [68, p. 17].

Third, their intellectualism, as represented in such notorious skills as being able to make the worse case the better, contradicted common sense and outraged many citizens who regarded the sophists as having a corrupting influence on Athenian society.

Nevertheless the sophists thrived in the pursuit of their practice. Poulakos characterizes them as follows:

> Faithful to no singular perspective, loyal to no specific political system, [the sophists] can be said to have lived and worked more according to the circumstances they encountered and less according to established custom or principle. The sociopolitical changes which they found themselves in the midst of, their extensive travels and their rhetorical lessons dictated that the sophists adapt to ever-changing situations, capitalize on opportunities, steer clear of risks,

adjust themselves to different laws and institutions, accommodate a variety of students, and tailor their messages to suit the sensibilities and tastes of their diverse audiences [68, p. 25].

Poulakos compares the ancient sophists with Gilles Deleuze's conception of the nomad, as well as Michel de Certeau's idea of *bricoleur*. Deleuze's nomads function, like the sophists, at the margins of the culture in which they work. They resist enculturation into the dominant formation while nevertheless having to understand the institutions they resist in order that their resistance can be successful. The life and work of the nomad depends upon this uneasy relationship; they cannot carry out their own project if they permit themselves to be co-opted into the structures of the dominant, nor can they succeed if they are utterly outcast.[1] Miller sees the sophistic function in *metis*, a quality she says is needed by sophists for reasons that parallel Poulakos' association of the sophist with Deleuze's nomad. *Metis*, she observes, "is the *aretê* of the banausic, not of the aristocrat" [66, p. 138].

De Certeau's bricoleur is characterized by a continually shifting use of language appropriated from discourses to which he/she is an outsider, a specifically tactical use, the efficacy of which is always dependent upon seizing the propitious moment. In contrast to the nomad, in Deleuze's perspective, is the philosopher. Philosophy, he says, tends to be "essentially related to law [and] institutions" [qtd. in 68, p. 26].

In contrast to the tactical discourse of the bricoleur, de Certeau identifies a discourse of strategy which derives its strength not from the ability to seize an opportune moment but from occupying a well-established position, a placement, a property. (Notice in this perspective the metaphors of space, specifically of location.)

As Poulakos suggests, "The connections between sophists and tactician on the one hand and between philosopher and strategist on the other are unmistakable" [68, p. 30].

> [T]he sophists depended on the resources of the cities they visited, worked as conditions permitted, and lived according to the circumstances they encountered. For them place represented not territory in which one settles, but a point through which one passes, only to go on. . . . [T]hey must be viewed not as settlers of clearly defined ideational territories, but as restless importers and exporters

---

[1] During the discussion period in the ATTW conference panel in which an earlier version of this chapter was presented, Steven Youra observed that this view of the sophist in some way resembles anthropologists who, as participant observers, are both inside and outside the cultures they observe. In that same discussion, Carolyn Miller pointed out that in *The Liberal Temper in Greek Politics*, Eric Havelock describes the Older Sophists as anthropologists.

of intellectual goods whose consumption by the local consumers unsettled communities of thought accustomed to the goods of the local economy [68, p. 31].

Poulakos' nomadic sophist/tactician has concrete parallels in the actual experience of many technical communicators. The particular ways this theoretical model might be applied have considerable promise, I believe, for understanding not only the nature of contemporary technical writing practice, but for theorizing ways of making that practice more effective. For example, as I mentioned above, technical writers are working for contracting and consulting agencies and moving from client to client, having to enter and learn a different organizational culture every few months to a year. Particularly when technical communicators work in consulting roles, they are often expected to help bring change into the organizational culture. As Glen Hotz, a manager of training for a major barge company, described the requirements of his company for communication and training consultants, "The technical communicator/ trainer needs to become part of the organization and to become a change agent" [69]. Revolutionary as this mandate may seem, coming from an industry executive, Spilka cites a 1989 claim that "training in social analysis is one of the fundamental competency areas New England employers are seeking in candidates for technical writing positions . . ." [29, p. 212]. Sullivan suggested in 1990 that teachers of technical communication "are really placed in a situation that allows us to be powerful agents for change" [20, p. 377]. Spilka was arguing as early as 1993 that "the technical communicator . . . has become known as an agent both of social accommodation and social change, or innovation" [29, p. 207]. These views may seem idealistic, even today, despite Hotz's insistence that managers with views consistent with his "aren't so few and far between." They surely indicate a promising direction for the field, and one which I believe offers a better prospect of successful, rewarding careers for the kind of practitioners many of us want to see coming out of our technical communication programs.

It is clear, I hope, that the sophistic model I am suggesting for technical communication precisely contradicts the agenda of modernist professionalization. The notion of the philosopher-strategist in Poulakos' characterization is co-extensive with codified systems, standards, and institutions. The goal of philosopher-strategists is to stabilize the knowledge on which their position is founded, to secure their position against competition from competing systems, to identify themselves and their position as much as possible with the state. Emphasizing stability of knowledge, secure positionality, and the state is consistent with emphasizing market closure, expertise, and social status. The parallels with the objectives of professionalization in this view are surely very clear.

Remembering Geisler's point, that the foundation of professional status is recognition for expertise in a domain of knowledge that is vital to the welfare of the community, we can see that expertise corresponds with the role of philosopher-strategist.[2] And yet, the work of technical writing seems to be consistent with a sophistic practice in which knowledge is always contingent, in which rhetorical purpose must be reconciled to the needs of a particular audience at a particular time and place. Technical writing as we find it today has emerged in relation to particular economic, political, and technological circumstances which combine in complex and contradictory ways that make the work our practitioners do both useful and disruptive, both materially rewarding and risky. Such circumstances tend to consign technical communicators' practice to the periphery of the corporate cultures in which they work.

As we so often lament, technology is changing at an ever faster pace, and changing in ways that destabilize knowledge, institutional structures, communities, and subjectivities. Yet these circumstances present us with the strongest argument for accepting the apparently weak role of the non-expert, unrecognized, incompletely professionalized, uncertified, hard to define sophist-technical communicator. Such a world is one in which no *position* can be counted on to last, in which change seems to rule and the ability to adapt to change is most valued [see Faber and Johnson-Eilola, Volume I of this essay collection]. Let us, rather than waging a tiresome and increasingly frustrating war of position for professional status, consider the possibility of teaching for a postmodern practice, a navigating practice, like the wily Odysseus, not mastering but negotiating continually shifting technologies, institutions, discourses, and cultures.

REFERENCES

1. M. Berman, *All That Is Solid Melts into Air: The Experience of Modernity*, Penguin Books, New York, 1988 and 1982.
2. A. Feenberg, *Questioning Technology*, Routledge, New York, 1999.
3. S. Toulmin, *Cosmopolis: The Hidden Agenda of Modernity*, University of Chicago Press, Chicago, 1990.

[2] Regarding my suggestion that our continuing efforts to achieve professional status are inconsistent with a sophistic model of technical communication practice, Dan Riordan suggested (again, during the conference discussion following presentation of this chapter) that a sophistic practice more resembles that of a movie star than of a traditional profession. I think what Riordan was implying is that the sophist's success depends upon celebrity more than upon status, as well as upon their ability to play a variety of roles in a variety of venues.

4. M. S. Larson, The Production of Expertise and the Constitution of Expert Power, in *The Authority of Experts: Studies in History and Theory*, T. L. Haskell (ed.), Indiana University Press, Bloomington, pp. 28-80, 1984.

5. E. Freidson, *Professional Powers: A Study of Institutionalization of Formal Knowledge*, University of Chicago Press, Chicago, 1986.

6. L. R. Veysey, *The Emergence of the American University*, University of Chicago Press, Chicago, 1965.

7. I. Inkster, *Science and Technology in History: An Approach to Industrial Development*, Rutgers University Press, New Brunswick, New Jersey, 1991.

8. E. T. Layton, Jr., *The Revolt of the Engineers: Social Responsibility and the American Engineering Profession*, Johns Hopkins University Press, Baltimore, 1986.

9. R. J. Connors, The Rise of Technical Writing Instruction in America, *Journal of Technical Writing and Communication, 12*:4, pp. 329-352, 1982.

10. T. Kynell, English as an Engineering Tool: Samuel Chandler Earle and the Tufts Experiment, *Journal of Technical Writing and Communication, 25*:1, pp. 85-92, 1995.

11. T. C. Kynell, *Writing in a Milieu of Utility: The Move to Technical Communication in American Engineering Programs 1850-1950*, Ablex, Norwood, New Jersey, 1996.

12. T. C. Kynell and M. G. Moran, *Three Keys to the Past: The History of Technical Communication*, Ablex, Stamford, Connecticut, 1999.

13. R. C. Grego, Science, Late Nineteenth-Century Rhetoric, and the Beginnings of Technical Writing Instruction in America, *Journal of Technical Writing and Communication, 17*:1, pp. 63-78, 1987.

14. J. W. Souther, Teaching Technical Writing: A Retrospective Appraisal, in *Technical Writing: Theory and Practice*, B. E. Fearing and W. K. Sparrow (eds.), Modern Language Association of America, New York, pp. 2-13, 1989.

15. C. R. Miller, Learning from History: World War II and the Culture of High Technology, *Journal of Business and Technical Communication, 12*:3, pp. 288-315, 1998.

16. K. T. Durack, Gender, Technology, and the History of Technical Communication, *Technical Communication Quarterly, 6*:3, pp. 249-260, 1997.

17. R. J. Brockmann, *From Millwrights to Shipwrights to the Twenty-First Century: Explorations in a History of Technical Communication in the United States*, Hampton Press, Cresskill, New Jersey, 1998.

18. B. Longo, *Spurious Coin: A History of Science, Management, and Technical Writing*, State University of New York Press, Albany, 2000.

19. M. D. Whitburn, *Rhetorical Scope and Performance: The Example of Technical Communication*, Ablex, Stamford, Connecticut, 2000.

20. D. Sullivan, Political-Ethical Implications of Defining Technical Communication as a Practice, *Journal of Advanced Composition, 10*:2, pp. 375-386, 1990.

21. T. E. Pinelli and R. O. Barclay, Research in Technical Communication: Perspectives and Thoughts on the Process, *Technical Communication, 39*:4, pp. 526-532, 1992.

22. R. Spilka, Preface, in *Writing in the Workplace: New Research Perspectives*, R. Spilka (ed.), Southern Illinois University Press, Carbondale and Edwardsville, Illinois, pp. vii-xi, 1993.

23. G. F. Hayhoe, What Research Do We Need, and Why Should Practitioners Care? *Technical Communication, 44*:1, pp. 19-21, 1997.
24. G. F. Hayhoe, Useful Research Is No Myth, *Technical Communication, 47*:3, pp. 289-290, 2000.
25. C. M. Ornatowski, Technical Communication and Rhetoric, in *Foundations for Teaching Technical Communication: Theory, Practice, and Program Design,* K. Staples and C. Ornatowski (eds.), Ablex, Greenwich, Connecticut, pp. 31-51, 1997.
26. C. R. Miller, A Humanistic Rationale for Technical Writing, *College English, 40*:6, pp. 610-617, 1979.
27. M. S. Samuels, Technical Writing and the Recreation of Reality, *Journal of Technical Writing and Communication, 15*:1, pp. 3-13, 1985.
28. R. VanDeWeghe, What is Technical Communication? A Rhetorical Analysis, *Technical Communication, 38*:3, pp. 295-299, 1991.
29. R. Spilka, Influencing Workplace Practice: A Challenge for Professional Writing Specialists in Academia, in *Writing in the Workplace: New Research Perspectives,* R. Spilka (ed.), Southern Illinois University Press, Carbondale and Edwardsville, Illinois, pp. 207-219, 1993.
30. P. Moore, Instrumental Discourse is as Humanistic as Rhetoric, *Journal of Business and Technical Communication, 10*:1, pp. 100-118, 1996.
31. J. Hagge, Ethics, Words, and the World in Moore's and Miller's Accounts of Scientific and Technical Discourse, *Journal of Business and Technical Communication, 10*:4, pp. 461-475, 1996.
32. P. Moore, Rhetorical vs. Instrumental Approaches to Teaching Technical Communication, *Technical Communication, 44*:2, pp. 163-173, 1997.
33. P. Moore, Myths about Instrumental Discourse: A Response to Robert R. Johnson, *Technical Communication Quarterly, 8*:2, pp. 210-223, 1999.
34. P. Moore, Pluralism, Instrumental Discourse, and the Limits of Social Construction: A Comment to Laurie Grobman, *Journal of Business and Technical Communication, 14*:1, pp. 74-83, 2000.
35. S. Carliner, Finding a Common Ground: What STC Is, and Should Be, Doing to Advance Education in Information Design and Development, *Technical Communication, 42*:4, pp. 546-554, 1995.
36. G. B. Kerferd, *The Sophistic Movement,* Cambridge University Press, New York, 1981.
37. T. Cole, *The Origins of Rhetoric in Ancient Greece,* Johns Hopkins University Press, Baltimore, 1991.
38. W. H. Beale, *A Pragmatic Theory of Rhetoric,* Southern Illinois University Press, Carbondale and Edwardsville, Illinois, 1987.
39. J. L. Kinneavy, *A Theory of Discourse,* Norton, New York, 1980.
40. C. Geisler, *Academic Literacy and the Nature of Expertise: Reading, Writing, and Knowing in Academic Philosophy,* Lawrence Erlbaum Associates, Hillsdale, New Jersey, 1994.
41. T. B. Farrell and G. T. Goodnight, Accidental Rhetoric: The Root Metaphors of Three Mile Island, *Communication Monographs, 48,* pp. 271-300, 1981.

42. D. N. Dobrin, *Writing and Technique,* National Council of Teachers of English, Urbana, Illinois, 1989.

43. S. Beckman, Professionalization: Borderline Authority and Autonomy in Work, in *Professions in Theory and History: Rethinking the Study of the Professions,* M. Burrage and R. Torstendahl (eds.), Sage, Newbury Park, California, pp. 115-138, 1990.

44. M. Ballif, Writing the Third-Sophistic Cyborg: Periphrasis on an Intense Rhetoric, *Rhetoric Society Quarterly, 28:4,* pp. 51-72, 1998.

45. S. Dragga, A Question of Ethics: Lessons from Technical Communicators on the Job, *Technical Communication Quarterly, 6:2,* pp. 161-178, 1997.

46. J. L. Jeyaraj, *Situatedness, Othering, and Rhetorical Authority in Technical and Professional Writing,* Ph.D. dissertation, Illinois State University, Normal, Illinois, 2001.

47. S. W. Spanier, How Can Technical Writers Further Their Professional Development? in *Solving Problems in Technical Writing,* L. Beene and P. White (eds.), Oxford University Press, New York, pp. 206-234, 1988.

48. P. Daniels, Job Competencies Committee: Defining Who We Are, *Intercom,* 43:8, p. 28, 1996.

49. C. Prasad, *Careers in Technical Writing,* Vol. 2001: Vault.com, 2000.

50. D. Jones, A Question of Identity, *Technical Communication, 42:4,* pp. 567-569, 1995.

51. K. Potts, My Entry-Level Life, in *Writing a Professional Life: Stories of Technical Communicators On and Off the Job,* G. J. Savage and D. L. Sullivan (eds.), Allyn & Bacon, Needham Heights, Massachusetts, pp. 23-33, 2001.

52. C. Hoeniges, It's Not Mark Twain's River Anymore, in *Writing a Professional Life: Stories of Technical Communicators On and Off the Job,* G. J. Savage and D. L. Sullivan (eds.), Allyn & Bacon, Needham Heights, Massachusetts, pp. 50-59, 2001.

53. R. A. Bailie, Three Months, Three Pages, in *Writing a Professional Life: Stories of Technical Communicators On and Off the Job,* G. J. Savage and D. L. Sullivan (eds.), Allyn & Bacon, Needham Heights, Massachusetts, pp. 63-68, 2001.

54. M. Bloom, Try and Try Again: The Story of a Software Project, in *Writing a Professional Life: Stories of Technical Communicators On and Off the Job,* G. J. Savage and D. L. Sullivan (eds.), Allyn & Bacon, Needham Heights, Massachusetts, pp. 74-89, 2001.

55. S. Carliner, Evolution-Revolution: Toward a Strategic Perception of Technical Communication, *Technical Communication, 43:3,* pp. 266-276, 1996.

56. C. L. Breuninger, The DuPont Experience: Strategic Planning for Information Design and Development Organizations, *Technical Communication, 44:4,* pp. 394-400, 1997.

57. D. N. Dobrin, Guest Editorial: Why I Don't, *Journal of Technical Writing and Communication, 27:2,* pp. 105-117, 1997.

58. P. M. Dombrowski, Post-Modernism as the Resurgence of Humanism in Technical Communication Studies, *Technical Communication Quarterly, 4:2,* pp. 165-185, 1995.

59. S. Lyons, Crying for Revision: Postmodern Indians and Rhetorics of Tradition, in *Making and Unmaking the Prospects for Rhetoric*, T. Enos (ed.), Lawrence Erlbaum Associates, Mahwah, New Jersey, pp. 123-131, 1997.
60. C. H. Peaden, Understanding Differently: Re-Reading Locke's Essay Concerning Human Understanding, *Rhetoric Society Quarterly*, 22:1, pp. 75-90, 1992.
61. A. Feenberg, *Alternative Modernity: The Technical Turn in Philosophy and Social Theory*, University of California Press, Berkeley, California, 1995.
62. C. M. Ornatowski, Educating Technical Communicators to Make Better Decisions, *Technical Communication*, 42:4, pp. 576-580, 1995.
63. S. A. Bernhardt, Teaching for Change, Vision, and Responsibility, *Technical Communication*, 42:4, pp. 600-602, 1995.
64. P. Bizzell, The Praise of Folly, The Woman Rhetor, and Post-Modern Skepticism, *Rhetoric Society Quarterly*, 22:1, pp. 7-17, 1992.
65. J. Paradis, Text and Action: The Operator's Manual in Context and in Court, in *Textual Dynamics of the Professions: Historical and Contemporary Studies of Writing in Professional Communities*, C. Bazerman and J. Paradis (eds.), University of Wisconsin Press, Madison, pp. 256-278, 1991.
66. C. R. Miller, The Aristotelian Topos: Hunting for Novelty, in *Rereading Aristotle's Rhetoric*, A. G. Gross and A. E. Walzer (eds.), Southern Illinois University Press, Carbondale and Edwardsville, Illinois, pp. 130-146, 2000.
67. R. R. Johnson, *User-Centered Technology: A Rhetorical Theory for Computers and Other Mundane Objects*, State University of New York Press, Albany, New York, 1998.
68. J. Poulakos, *Sophistical Rhetoric in Classical Greece*, University of South Carolina Press, Columbia, 1995.
69. G. N. Hotz, *Technical Writers and Trainers as Facilitators of Change*, presented at Council on Programs in Technical and Scientific Communication, Menomonee, Wisconsin, 2000.

CHAPTER 10

Technical Communication in the 21st[1] Century: Where Are We Going?

M. Jimmie Killingsworth

NOT EXTRAPOLATION BUT DESCRIPTION: OUR MYTHS AND THE FUTURE

Of course it's impossible to write the history of the future, but that doesn't keep people from trying. Futurists, prophets, and utopians crowd the shelves of our bookstores with their speculative products. References to the most technically sophisticated of these prophetic works — the books of Alvin Toffler and Paul Ehrlich [1-4], for example — occasionally find their way into writings about technical communication. Their method is to extrapolate from recent trends toward a plausible story about the future and then moralize about how to prepare for it.

I could do this kind of extrapolation for technical communication. No doubt, many of us have already performed extrapolation in the manner of Toffler and Ehrlich, particularly when we are asking for money. We go to the latest Department of Labor reports, grab up statistics about projected growth in the high tech and service sectors, link ourselves to those sectors, and ask for expanded and better-funded programs in technical communication.

---

[1] This essay was originally published under the same title in *Technical Communication Quarterly*, 8:2, pp. 165-174, 1999.

This practice has its uses, for sure. But I must beg forgiveness if my title suggests that I am about to engage in useful extrapolation. I have come not to make proposals but to criticize the act of proposing in the extrapolative fashion. When we do it, we are not projecting history into the future, which is what we seem to be claiming in extending the prophetic lines of graphs, even when we hedge by using dotted lines. We can get in trouble this way. Think of all the people who believed the Modern Language Association's prediction 10 years ago that, based on projected population increases among people of college age by the late 1990s, we would experience great growth in English faculties to accommodate increased enrollments; the job crisis would be over. Now instead, the job crisis grows worse. Sure enough, the enrollments grew as predicted, but no one anticipated the systematic depletion, or "reengineering," of faculties by administrators who find ever better ways to exploit an overcrowded labor market and who, in their latest vision, see palliatives like distance education as a way of saving further expensive faculty positions.

The old predictions now appear as wishful thinking. Wishful thinking, as Freud taught us, is the stuff of dream and fantasy. When fantasy assumes a cultural significance and a standard narrative form, it becomes a myth. In embodying our understanding of the past and our hopes for the future, myths bear a strong resemblance to those dotted lines on graphs depicting trends. Will an understanding of the concept of myth and our own favored myths help us to understand where we are going? My claim in this essay is that it will—in a limited way. It will help us to understand our *attitudes* toward the future, and it will help us to guard against excessive hubris about our predictions. We cannot know the future, but we can know ourselves (to some extent) and in this knowledge face the future with reasonable expectations—and no shortage of wariness.

Of all the possible myths that touch upon the business of technical communication, I will focus on only one because I think that it will be foremost in the near future and because it stands to do great damage to the spirit of our profession. I call it the myth of immediate communication. It is an old dream, supporting such concepts as empathetic insight and telepathy. The idea is that the medium of communication disappears so that communication partners know one another's minds without troubling over trifles like language, media technology, and social contexts. In technical communication, the myth usually appears in claims for particular styles (the "clearest" diction and syntax) and particular technologies (the fastest and easiest to use). Ironically, our ideal language and the best technologies for us seem to be the ones that somehow fade away in use. The great goal is to develop an immediate medium.

I remember myself saying once to a colleague, "My goal in designing my textbook is to write a book that the students don't have to read in order to get the information." I intended, of course, a paradox, one that turns on the idea of reading. I had hoped that even students who merely scanned the headings and graphics would get my main ideas. Generally we use the myth of immediacy in just such a figural fashion. We know in our hearts that whatever access we have to one another's minds comes through moderately successful acts of representation and interpretation via media of communication (*media* being the key word, that which disappears in the concepts of im*media*cy). Figurative language and wishful myth-making can be dangerous, though. My dream of a textbook that students do not have to read could support a form of uncritical learning and slipshod study that I abhor.

Partly because I find too much of this kind of self-analysis painful, my method in the remainder of this essay is to confront the problem of the immediacy myth in technical communication only indirectly, looking at another field of practice that puts great stock in narratives about the future—science fiction. Science fiction is way ahead of us in many ways. Long familiar with the myth of immediate communication, practitioners in that field have for 30 years or more been developing a counter narrative, a critical tradition that holds the myth up to scrutiny and foregrounds communication media so that we might learn more about their strengths and their limits. Let us follow so that we might see where we might be going.

TECHNOLOGIES OF IMMEDIACY:
THE ANSIBLE

Any seasoned reader of science fiction knows that extrapolation is not really what it pretends to be. In the introduction to her novel *The Left Hand of Darkness*, Ursula K. LeGuin speaks to the topic: "Science fiction," she says, "is often described, and even defined, as extrapolative. The science fiction writer is supposed to take a trend or phenomenon of the here-and-now, purify and intensify it for dramatic effect, and extend it into the future" [5]. LeGuin rejects the extrapolative definition as "far too rationalist and simplistic to satisfy the imaginative mind, whether the writer's or the reader's." She thinks of science fiction not as *predictive* but as *descriptive*, not as future-oriented but as reflecting the present, thematically and psychologically, if not literally.

The kind of description that science fiction writers give of the present world is quite obviously fabulous or mythological. Their myths about communication media, the same myths we find in textbooks and articles on technical communication, tend to go in two directions, which I call progressivism and Luddism. The progressivist version of the myth of immediacy sees media not as an inevitable intervention, the things that come between communication partners, but simply as technologies and techniques that improve, speed up, or facilitate communication. Over and against the progressivist view stands the Luddite version of immediacy, which holds that immediate communication only happens under primitive conditions, and that in every departure from the situation of face-to-face, one-on-one communication, preferably in a village of indigenous peoples, something is inevitably lost. The great modern prophet of communicative Luddism was the American poet Walt Whitman, who tried desperately to recover the intimacy of oral communication in his writing. He said (or rather he wrote),

> I was chilled with the cold types and cylinder and wet paper between us. I pass poorly with papers and types. . . . I must pass with the contact of bodies and souls [6, p. 89].

Holding both progressivism and Luddism at bay, we may recall the semiotic or skeptical critique of the immediacy principle. It says that *all* communication is mediated. When I speak to you, I have only your language and your gestures to work with; I don't have your soul. Even touching your body, feeling hot or cold beneath my fingers, taking your temperature, listening to your beating heart, I have only my interpretations of the signs and symptoms I perceive. Am I a lover or a doctor? My role mediates my response. The cold I feel in your touch may represent an absence of warmth toward me or a need of warmth from me. Even talking about your body like this makes me uncomfortable. What is coming between us? It could be the distance of experience, of manners, of social prohibitions, the fear of overstepping the limits, of removing one layer of mediation too many. These social phenomena are media of communication as surely as writing is—or television, computer programs, and answering machines.

Media represent a major concern in science fiction, the master narrative of which, according to writer and critic Brian Aldiss, is *"Hubris clobbered by nemesis"* [7, p. 26] (emphasis in original). When communication appears as a theme in science fiction, the characteristic hubris arises almost always from the myth of immediacy as applied to technologies or techniques. The overly enthusiastic claim for some new way or means of communication is that it will save us from the distance we feel from each other, our isolation and alienation. The countervailing nemesis is the final recognition of a layer of mediation that has gone unnoticed or the social need for some mediation initially perceived as an obstruction.

The lone ambassador from an interplanetary federation in LeGuin's *Left Hand of Darkness,* for example, whose mission is to bring a new planet into a trade relation, has recourse to a communication device that LeGuin invented for this novel. Called the "ansible," it allows the user to communicate instantaneously with people scattered across galaxies. Our protagonist, the ambassador, can call a starship from orbit to complete his mission at any time he chooses. The ansible closes the distance of space and time in a way that transportation cannot. In a later novel, *The Dispossessed* [8], LeGuin introduces the physicist who provided the basis for the discovery of the ansible by developing the Principle of Simultaneity as an adjunct to Relativity. That character compares the ansible to the telephone, the promoters of which have always presented their device as a substitute for physical presence ("Reach Out and Touch Someone"). In both novels, however, the characters are forced to admit the importance of bodily presence, much as the advocates of telecommuting must explain why the great majority of high-tech offices still require the bodies of their employees to be present at work. In *The Left Hand of Darkness,* the humanoid aliens the protagonist encounters distinguish themselves from earthlings by cultivating what may be missing in our theories of work—a philosophy of *presence* to match the Terran obsession with *progress,* a philosophy of *being here* rather than a philosophy of *getting there.* The ambassador at first denies himself the use of the ansible to go deeper into relationships with the people he longs to know. Ultimately he loses the ansible in a confrontation with authorities and must develop a network of friendship among the aliens to regain communication with his own kind. The ansible saves him no trouble at all and certainly fails to be the powerful extension of his own voice that it had proved to be before. He learns the limits of the technology, which may breed distrust and is always liable to loss or mechanical failure.

The ansible with its claim to shrink the universe by overcoming the limits of space and time has proved attractive to other science fiction writers as well and has appeared in a number of stories, including the widely read Ender trilogy by Orson Scott Card [9-11]. Card hints that the ansible is an intrusive medium that nearly always brings unwelcome news, interplanetary demands upon people adjusting to new cultural media and new ecologies on faraway planets. Any writer or reader interrupted by the telephone can sympathize. And while lonely people no doubt welcome the blinking light of the answering machine, the busy writer or reader, seeking a world of solitude to pursue satisfaction and completion, may fear it as foretelling another demand for time forced upon an already overbooked schedule. Even for the lonely, neither the telephone nor the many kinds of new and improved cyber-encounters can fully live up to the claim to create a space "marked by the feeling that the person you're talking to is 'in the same room,'" as a recent *Time* magazine story on computer-mediated discourse puts it [12, p. 6]. The instantaneous voice of the loved one on the other end of the phone line, or even the digitized face on the computer screen, may bring either comfort or unbearable longing. What it assuredly does not bring is the fearful certainty or the blissful satisfaction that comes with bodily encounters in which we really do "reach out and touch someone."

TECHNIQUES OF IMMEDIACY: MIND SPEAK

Using technology or arcane techniques to touch another person's mind—or for that matter, another person's body, as in the fantasy of "sim-stim," or simulated stimulation, in cyberpunk fiction (see Gibson [13])—has long been a subject for science fiction writers. In LeGuin's *Left Hand of Darkness*, our Terran ambassador is armed not only with the ansible, but also with the technique of "mind speak," a form of telepathy that allows an ostensibly unmediated communion between two minds and that by law can only be taught to citizens of planets linked into the trade network the protagonist represents. Denied the use of his ansible, he ultimately teaches mind speak to his one sympathizer on the planet, a renegade minister from one of the two major nation-states. The communion of the two minds completes the development of an unconditional friendship and trust between the two characters and thereby embodies the great hope contained in the myth of immediacy: If only we could see into one another's minds, we could dispel our worries that we are being manipulated or deceived. It is the communication medium that makes lying possible; indeed, the *sign* (another word for "communication medium") has been defined by Umberto Eco as anything that can be used to lie [14].

But even mind speak, as LeGuin imagines it, cannot escape mediation. When the ambassador finally manages to break through to his friend, his words strike the mind of the alien in the voice of a beloved but long-dead brother. He thinks he is hearing his brother in a dream until the ambassador confirms his own authorship. The communication still requires representation and interpretation. The listener is deeply moved by the form of the representation but does not enjoy an immediate and total oneness with his interlocutor, only a communion made palatable by an association of the listener with the lost presence of his loved one. Here we come to an ancient definition of the sign—a presence that stands for an absence (see Killingsworth and Gilbertson [15, p. 15])—and we return to the main theme of *The Left Hand of Darkness*, the need to cultivate a theory of presence to complement the theory of progress. The ambassador represents himself as the voice of brotherhood, though how much of this *ulation Bomb*, Ballantine, New York, 1976.

ulation Explosion, Simon and Schuster, New York, 1990.

ft Hand of Darkness, Ace, New York, 1969.

lete Poetry and Collected Prose, Library of America, New

Wingrove, *Trillion Year Spree: The History of Science Fiction*, 986.

Dispossessed, Harper, New York, 1974.

Game, Tor, New York, 1985.

for the Dead, Tor, New York, 1986.

de, Tor, New York, 1991.

Welcome to Cyberspace, in *Literacy, Technology, and Society: sues*, G. E. Hawisher and C. L. Selfe (eds.), Prentice-Hall, *ver*, New Jersey, pp. 4-9, 1997.

mancer, Ace, New York, 1984.

of Semiotics, Indiana University Press, Bloomington, Indiana,

rth and M. K. Gilbertson, *Signs, Genres, and Communities in nication*, Baywood, Amityville, New York, 1992.

E. King, *The Online Student*, Harcourt Brace, Ft. Worth, Texas,

r and C. L. Selfe, *Literacy, Technology, and Society: Confronting tice-Hall*, Upper Saddle River, New Jersey, 1997.

representation is under his control and how much is effected by the interpretive mind of the receiver remains ambiguous. The point is that, even when a mind speaks directly to another mind, the communication remains mediated; the mind is already full of language, experiences, associations through which the message must travel, must be *mediated*. This view is consistent with the semiotic theory that thought itself requires signs, and the presence of signs presupposes representation and interpretation.

HUBRIS CLOBBERED BY NEMESIS: TECHNICAL COMMUNICATION'S FUTURE

In composition and in technical communication, we too often promote technologies and techniques in the spirit of LeGuin's ambassador in his naive state, with hubris unchastened by nemesis. I do not mean to say that we are totally uncritical. We have become better, for example, at recognizing the impact of culture, gender, and geographical region, more aware of social and political filters that function as communication media. Even in our social criticism, though, the perceived need to offer alternatives for communicative action often falls into the promotion of half-way measures like genderless language or utopian schemes like "international English" and "world-ready communication" that, to my mind, sound too much like *Newspeak* on the one hand and mind speak on the other.

That's why we need the conservative element suggested in theories of discourse like that of Eco [14]. The development of new technologies and techniques follows the sad but ever-binding law of compensation. In every new communication initiative, something is lost along with what is gained. Compensation requires that we stop talking about the new and improved and start seeing change as the inevitable onset of new challenges. Compensation applies to both techniques and technologies. When we ask an author to give up jargon or convert paragraphs into bulleted lists, we may be asking that person to sacrifice some precious, hard-earned portion of an identity — and for whom? Some abstract being we call "the reader"? How can we make this being seem more real, more alive, without slipping over to the other extreme and suggesting that the author might write so clearly as to give the reader everything that person might need or desire?

While technique certainly has its costs, I am worried more these days about our faith in technology. In a new textbook on how to use the Internet for research and writing, I saw a claim about "Empowerment" — "Empowerment of students to learn, to be independent, and to slip the constraints imposed by the conditions at their particular college or university" [16, p. 2]. I wasn't really in the mood to read this after a disk crash at my university kept me from getting my e-mail all week and a server failure kept my students from getting the writing prompt from our class Web site. Independent is not what I felt, and for that matter, how independent are students who have to buy a textbook to achieve this vaunted empowerment?

But if computers do not empower us, why use them in the classroom? Some have suggested that computers help people to learn. We hear, for example, that the kind of playfulness inspired in chat rooms and interactive classroom MOO-MUDs tends to remove inhibitions. For students who are shy in face-to-face situations, this change may be a good thing. But what happens to the extroverts? Do they stay the same, shift to introversion, or gear up to a new level of extroversion bordering on aggression? It probably depends upon how well they type and what new kinds of inhibitions the medium will ultimately have to present.

The best answer I've seen to the question of why we want computers in the classroom is that they prepare our students for the workplace. In other words, we admit our dependence on the workplace to set the standards for academic life. An empowerment based on such dependence is thoroughly mediated, of course, by the values of corporate culture. It may be good for us to follow corporate culture, but if that is what we are doing, then let's be honest and skip the line about personal empowerment.

We hear a great deal about the democracy and openness of the net and of course we approve—up to a point. In a distance class in engineering at my university, the professor and students from across the country were gleefully holding class like the Jetsons, using software that allowed them to present digitized pictures of each other in little windows on the screen, something like the old TV show Hollywood Squares. They were suddenly greeted by a new window opening on the bare backside of a class-crasher from the no-man's land of the Internet. Such actions, not to mention the desire to profit from online textbooks and course offerings, inexorably lead to limitations on free access. The costs of access keep going up right along with textbooks and college tuition. New layers of mediation appear every day.

It clearly takes more than electricity and increasing RAM to bring personal power, in communication or any other human endeavor, but our perception of power takes on great size through the magnifying potency of myth. The myth of immediate communication stands ready to glorify the next technological advance in communication, but it will never tell us what is not advanced by such improvements. Only the critic who names the myth and reveals it for what it is can say what it is not. What are the other myths of technical communication? Can we stand to name them and see ourselves from the critical vantage that such naming allows?

Myths may b[...]
the future, and the[...]
aspirations than abc[...]
prove it, I would lik[...]
prepare us better for[...]
Motors that we can[...]
themselves guided by[...]
tions about what will[...]
myths, our master na[...]
what we will carry wit[...]
coming events.

A NOTE O[...]

In this essay and in[...]
using science fiction as[...]
technical communication[...]
theory among students, pra[...]
advantage is that fiction pr[...]
ways that undermine resista[...]
do the same by assigning[...]
overlap—even the formal cor[...]
technical communication have[...]
and provocative.

I am pleased to acknowled[...]
collection of essays—Gail Hawi[...]
this direction of thought and crit[...]
in their book Literacy, Technology[...]
If we can get over the idea that sc[...]
literature (a criticism often levele[...]
by the same people), we may disco[...]
in the sociocultural study of tech[...]
characteristic readerships overlap.[...]
are among the most avid readers[...]
assignments in science fiction be a w[...]
majors closer to the cast of mind chara[...]
people? If so, such readings could[...]
pedagogies in programs that "conve[...]
writers and editors.

REFEREN[...]

1. A. Toffler, *Future Shock*, Random House, [...]
2. A. Toffler, *The Third Wave*, Morrow, New [...]

3. P. R. Ehrlich, *The Pop[...]
4. P. R. Ehrlich, *The Pop[...]
5. U. K. LeGuin, *The L[...]
6. W. Whitman, *Comp[...] York, 1982.
7. B. W. Aldiss and D[...] Avon, New York, [...]
8. U. K. LeGuin, *The[...]
9. O. S. Card, *Ender's[...]
10. O. S. Card, *Speaker[...]
11. O. S. Card, *Xenoci[...]
12. P. Elmer-DeWitt,[...] Confronting the Is[...] Upper Saddle Ri[...]
13. W. Gibson, *Neur[...]
14. U. Eco, *A Theory[...] 1976.
15. M. J. Killingsw[...] *Technical Comm[...]
16. R. Reddick and[...] 1996.
17. G. E. Hawishe[...] the Issues, Pren[...]

Contributors

NANCY ROUNDY BLYLER is a professor emeritus at Iowa State University, where she taught graduate and undergraduate courses in the rhetoric and professional communication program. She has published in such journals as *Technical Communication Quarterly* and *Journal of Business and Technical Communication*, and is the editor of two collections in technical communication. She has received three NCTE awards for her work.

MARJORIE T. DAVIS is professor and founding chair of the Technical Communication Department at Mercer University, Macon and Atlanta, Georgia, where she teaches in both the BS and the MS degree programs. She is a senior member of STC and has held several elected and appointed positions; an IEEE senior member, serving as membership chair on the AdCom for the Professional Communication Society; and member of ATTW, CPTSC, and ASEE. She received a Frank R. Smith Outstanding Article Award (Distinguished) for this article and is a 2002 recipient of the Jay R. Gould Award for Excellence in Teaching Technical Communication.

ROBERT R. JOHNSON is Professor of Rhetoric and Technical Communication in the Department of Humanities at Michigan Technological University where he also serves as Chair of the department. His scholarship and teaching have focused on technical communication pedagogy, curriculum development, rhetorical theory, and the history of the profession. His book, *Usercentered Technology: A Rhetorical Theory for Computers and Other Mundane Artifacts* (SUNY Press), was chosen as the "Best Book of 1998 in Technical and Scientific Communication" by the National Council of Teachers of English.

M. JIMMIE KILLINGSWORTH, Professor of English at Texas A&M University, is the author or co-author of over 50 articles and 5 books on technical communication, rhetoric and composition, and American literature, including *Ecospeak: Rhetoric and Environmental Politics in America* (with Jacqueline Palmer) and *Signs, Genres, and Communities in Technical Communication* (with Michael Gilbertson). He is currently exploring new avenues of study in creative nonfiction, science fiction, and the literature of ecology.

TERESA KYNELL-HUNT is a professor of English at Northern Michigan University and holds the Ph.D. in Rhetoric and Technical Communication from Michigan Technological University. She is currently Chair of the NCTE Committee on Technical and Scientific Communication and a member of the ATTW Executive Committee. Her articles have appeared in a variety of journals, including the *Journal of Technical Writing and Communication, Reader, The Writing Instructor,* and *Technical Communication Quarterly.* She is the author of *Writing in a Milieu of Utility: The Move to Technical Communication in American Engineering Programs, 1850-1950* and (with Wendy Stone) *Scenarios for Technical Communication: Critical Thinking and Writing.* She edited, with Michael Moran, *Three Keys to the Past: The History of Technical Communication.*

LOUISE REHLING has over 10 years of technical writing teaching experience and currently is Director of the Technical & Professional Writing Program at San Francisco State University. Dr. Rehling also has over 15 years of industry experience, including a recent two-year leave from academia spent as Manager of the Technical Publications Department at a Bay Area software company, AvantGo, Inc. Dr. Rehling has published in academic journals, including *Technical Communication Quarterly* and the *Journal of Technical Writing and Communication.* She also has published in the Society for Technical Communication's journal and magazine and served as President of the San Francisco Chapter of STC. Her A.B., A.M., and Ph.D. degrees are in English Language and Literature, from The University of Michigan, Ann Arbor.

CAROLYN D. RUDE is professor of English and director of the programs in technical communication at Texas Tech University, which offers degrees in technical communication at the bachelor's, master's, and doctoral levels. She edited the special issue of *Technical Communication Quarterly* on the discourse of public policy (winter 2000), and she has written as well on environmental discourse and on reports for decision making. She is author of the textbook *Technical Editing* (Allyn & Bacon) and is president of the Association of Teachers of Technical Writing (2001–2003).

GERALD J. SAVAGE holds a Ph.D. in Rhetoric and Technical Communication from Michigan Technological University and is an associate professor in the English Department at Illinois State University where he teaches technical communication and technical editing. He is co-editor with Dale L. Sullivan of *Writing a Professional Life: Stories of Technical Communicators On and Off the Job.* He has published articles on technical communication in *Journal of Technical Writing and Communication,*

Technical Communication Quarterly, and *Journal of Business and Technical Communication.*

ELIZABETH OVERMAN SMITH is associate professor in the Department of English at Auburn University. Her research interests include the recent history of technical communication and access to bibliographic information for technical communication sources. She is editor of the ATTW annual bibliography and manager of the Society for Technical Communication honor societies Sigma Tau Chi and Alpha Sigma.

ELIZABETH TEBEAUX is Professor of English and Director of Distance Education at Texas A&M University. With nearly 30 years experience in teaching composition and technical writing at several universities, she has served as Chair of the CCCC Committee on Technical and Scientific Communication and President of the Association of Teachers of Technical Writing. She has authored/coauthored five text books on business as technical writing, numerous articles on the history, pedagogy, and curriculum in technical communication, and *Emergence of a Tradition: Technical Writing in the English Renaissance, 1475-1640.* She established Texas A&M's Office of Distance Education, was the first TAMU faculty member to teach on the World Wide Web, and has begun research into cost/pricing strategies for distance education programs. She continues her historical research in technical writing and plans a second book, *The Flowering of a Tradition: Technical Writing in England in the Seventeenth Century.*

Index

representation is under his control and how much is effected by the interpretive mind of the receiver remains ambiguous. The point is that, even when a mind speaks directly to another mind, the communication remains mediated; the mind is already full of language, experiences, associations through which the message must travel, must be *mediated*. This view is consistent with the semiotic theory that thought itself requires signs, and the presence of signs presupposes representation and interpretation.

HUBRIS CLOBBERED BY NEMESIS: TECHNICAL COMMUNICATION'S FUTURE

In composition and in technical communication, we too often promote technologies and techniques in the spirit of LeGuin's ambassador in his naive state, with hubris unchastened by nemesis. I do not mean to say that we are totally uncritical. We have become better, for example, at recognizing the impact of culture, gender, and geographical region, more aware of social and political filters that function as communication media. Even in our social criticism, though, the perceived need to offer alternatives for communicative action often falls into the promotion of half-way measures like genderless language or utopian schemes like "international English" and "world-ready communication" that, to my mind, sound too much like *Newspeak* on the one hand and mind speak on the other.

That's why we need the conservative element suggested in theories of discourse like that of Eco [14]. The development of new technologies and techniques follows the sad but ever-binding law of compensation. In every new communication initiative, something is lost along with what is gained. Compensation requires that we stop talking about the new and improved and start seeing change as the inevitable onset of new challenges. Compensation applies to both techniques and technologies. When we ask an author to give up jargon or convert paragraphs into bulleted lists, we may be asking that person to sacrifice some precious, hard-earned portion of an identity—and for whom? Some abstract being we call "the reader"? How can we make this being seem more real, more alive, without slipping over to the other extreme and suggesting that the author might write so clearly as to give the reader everything that person might need or desire?

While technique certainly has its costs, I am worried more these days about our faith in technology. In a new textbook on how to use the Internet for research and writing, I saw a claim about "Empowerment" — "Empowerment of students to learn, to be independent, and to slip the constraints imposed by the conditions at their particular college or university" [16, p. 2]. I wasn't really in the mood to read this after a disk crash at my university kept me from getting my e-mail all week and a server failure kept my students from getting the writing prompt from our class Web site. Independent is not what I felt, and for that matter, how independent are students who have to buy a textbook to achieve this vaunted empowerment?

But if computers do not empower us, why use them in the classroom? Some have suggested that computers help people to learn. We hear, for example, that the kind of playfulness inspired in chat rooms and interactive classroom MOO-MUDs tends to remove inhibitions. For students who are shy in face-to-face situations, this change may be a good thing. But what happens to the extroverts? Do they stay the same, shift to introversion, or gear up to a new level of extroversion bordering on aggression? It probably depends upon how well they type and what new kinds of inhibitions the medium will ultimately have to present.

The best answer I've seen to the question of why we want computers in the classroom is that they prepare our students for the workplace. In other words, we admit our dependence on the workplace to set the standards for academic life. An empowerment based on such dependence is thoroughly mediated, of course, by the values of corporate culture. It may be good for us to follow corporate culture, but if that is what we are doing, then let's be honest and skip the line about personal empowerment.

We hear a great deal about the democracy and openness of the net and of course we approve—up to a point. In a distance class in engineering at my university, the professor and students from across the country were gleefully holding class like the Jetsons, using software that allowed them to present digitized pictures of each other in little windows on the screen, something like the old TV show Hollywood Squares. They were suddenly greeted by a new window opening on the bare backside of a class-crasher from the no-man's land of the Internet. Such actions, not to mention the desire to profit from online textbooks and course offerings, inexorably lead to limitations on free access. The costs of access keep going up right along with textbooks and college tuition. New layers of mediation appear every day.

It clearly takes more than electricity and increasing RAM to bring personal power, in communication or any other human endeavor, but our perception of power takes on great size through the magnifying potency of myth. The myth of immediate communication stands ready to glorify the next technological advance in communication, but it will never tell us what is not advanced by such improvements. Only the critic who names the myth and reveals it for what it is can say what it is not. What are the other myths of technical communication? Can we stand to name them and see ourselves from the critical vantage that such naming allows?

Myths may be no better than trend analysis as moral guides to the future, and they are similar in revealing more about our hopes and aspirations than about the future as it will really exist. But though I cannot prove it, I would like to suggest that knowing what our myths are may prepare us better for the future than all the analysis of IBM and General Motors that we can stomach. I am convinced that those analyses are themselves guided by mythology. Myths may not make reliable predictions about what will happen, but if we become aware of our dominant myths, our master narratives, then we can say with some reliability what we will carry with us into the future and how we may respond to coming events.

A NOTE ON METHOD AND PEDAGOGY

In this essay and in my classes, I have been experimenting with using science fiction as a way of getting around a big problem in technical communication criticism and pedagogy: The resistance to theory among students, practitioners, and even scholars in the field. The advantage is that fiction provides an "environment" to "test" ideas in ways that undermine resistance. Teachers in history and sociology often do the same by assigning socially realistic novels. The mythological overlap — even the formal correspondences — between science fiction and technical communication have struck my students and me as remarkable and provocative.

I am pleased to acknowledge that the editors of at least one superb collection of essays — Gail Hawisher and Cynthia Selfe — have anticipated this direction of thought and criticism by including science fiction stories in their book *Literacy, Technology, and Society: Confronting the Issues* [17]. If we can get over the idea that science fiction comprises a trivial "pulp" literature (a criticism often leveled at technical writing, too, sometimes by the same people), we may discover in science fiction a useful resource in the sociocultural study of technical communication. Certainly the characteristic readerships overlap. Students of science and technology are among the most avid readers of science fiction. Could reading assignments in science fiction be a way to bring technical communication majors closer to the cast of mind characteristic of technologically oriented people? If so, such readings could make a valuable contribution to pedagogies in programs that "convert" literature majors to technical writers and editors.

REFERENCES

1. A. Toffler, *Future Shock,* Random House, New York, 1970.
2. A. Toffler, *The Third Wave,* Morrow, New York, 1980.

3. P. R. Ehrlich, *The Population Bomb*, Ballantine, New York, 1976.
4. P. R. Ehrlich, *The Population Explosion*, Simon and Schuster, New York, 1990.
5. U. K. LeGuin, *The Left Hand of Darkness*, Ace, New York, 1969.
6. W. Whitman, *Complete Poetry and Collected Prose*, Library of America, New York, 1982.
7. B. W. Aldiss and D. Wingrove, *Trillion Year Spree: The History of Science Fiction*, Avon, New York, 1986.
8. U. K. LeGuin, *The Dispossessed*, Harper, New York, 1974.
9. O. S. Card, *Ender's Game*, Tor, New York, 1985.
10. O. S. Card, *Speaker for the Dead*, Tor, New York, 1986.
11. O. S. Card, *Xenocide*, Tor, New York, 1991.
12. P. Elmer-DeWitt, Welcome to Cyberspace, in *Literacy, Technology, and Society: Confronting the Issues*, G. E. Hawisher and C. L. Selfe (eds.), Prentice-Hall, Upper Saddle River, New Jersey, pp. 4-9, 1997.
13. W. Gibson, *Neuromancer*, Ace, New York, 1984.
14. U. Eco, *A Theory of Semiotics*, Indiana University Press, Bloomington, Indiana, 1976.
15. M. J. Killingsworth and M. K. Gilbertson, *Signs, Genres, and Communities in Technical Communication*, Baywood, Amityville, New York, 1992.
16. R. Reddick and E. King, *The Online Student*, Harcourt Brace, Ft. Worth, Texas, 1996.
17. G. E. Hawisher and C. L. Selfe, *Literacy, Technology, and Society: Confronting the Issues*, Prentice-Hall, Upper Saddle River, New Jersey, 1997.